US

KNOWLEDGE DEVELOPMENT
IN EARLY CHILDHOOD

Knowledge Development in Early Childhood

SOURCES OF LEARNING AND CLASSROOM IMPLICATIONS

edited by

**Ashley M. Pinkham
Tanya Kaefer
Susan B. Neuman**

THE GUILFORD PRESS
New York   London

Knowledge development in
 early childhood

© 2012 The Guilford Press
A Division of Guilford Publications, Inc.
72 Spring Street, New York, NY 10012
www.guilford.com

Printed in the United States of America

This book is printed on acid-free paper.

Last digit is print number: 9   8   7   6   5   4   3   2   1

Library of Congress Cataloging-in-Publication Data is available
from the Publisher

ISBN 978-1-4625-0499-2

About the Editors

Ashley M. Pinkham, PhD, is a Research Fellow at the University of Michigan. Dr. Pinkham earned her doctoral degree in cognitive-developmental psychology from the University of Virginia. Her research focuses on sources of children's knowledge acquisition and conceptual development, including observational learning, adult–child conversations, and book-reading experiences.

Tanya Kaefer, PhD, is a Research Fellow at the University of Michigan. Dr. Kaefer earned her doctoral degree in developmental psychology from Duke University. She studies reading development and the influence of content knowledge on early literacy skills.

Susan B. Neuman, EdD, is a Professor in Educational Studies at the University of Michigan. A former U.S. Assistant Secretary for Elementary and Secondary Education, Dr. Neuman established the Early Childhood Educator Professional Development Program and was responsible for all activities in Title I of the Elementary and Secondary Education Act. Her research and teaching interests include early literacy development, early childhood policy, curriculum, and early reading instruction. Her publications include 12 books and over 100 journal articles.

Contributors

Daniel R. Anderson, PhD, Department of Psychology, University of Massachusetts Amherst, Amherst, Massachusetts

Erica M. Barnes, MA, Peabody College of Education and Human Development, Vanderbilt University, Nashville, Tennessee

Maureen Callanan, PhD, Psychology Department, University of California, Santa Cruz, Santa Cruz, California

James Christie, PhD, School of Social and Family Dynamics, Arizona State University, Tempe, Arizona

Carol McDonald Connor, PhD, Department of Psychology, Florida State University, Tallahassee, Florida

Sherryse L. Corrow, MA, Institute of Child Development, University of Minnesota, Minneapolis, Minnesota

Jason Cowell, MA, Institute of Child Development, University of Minnesota, Minneapolis, Minnesota

David K. Dickinson, EdD, Peabody College of Education and Human Development, Vanderbilt University, Nashville, Tennessee

Sabine Doebel, MA, Institute of Child Development, University of Minnesota, Minneapolis, Minnesota

Nell K. Duke, EdD, College of Education, Michigan State University, East Lansing, Michigan

Roberta Michnick Golinkoff, PhD, Departments of Psychology and Linguistics, School of Education, University of Delaware, Newark, Delaware

Anne-Lise Halvorsen, PhD, College of Education, Michigan State University, East Lansing, Michigan

Annemarie H. Hindman, PhD, College of Education, Temple University, Philadelphia, Pennsylvania

Sara Hines, PhD, School of Education, Hunter College, The City University of New York, New York, New York

Kathy Hirsh-Pasek, PhD, Department of Psychology, Temple University, Philadelphia, Pennsylvania

Tanya Kaefer, PhD, School of Education, University of Michigan, Ann Arbor, Michigan

Jennifer A. Knight, MEd, College of Education, Michigan State University, East Lansing, Michigan

Melissa A. Koenig, PhD, Institute of Child Development, University of Minnesota, Minneapolis, Minnesota

Heather J. Lavigne, MEd, Department of Psychology, University of Massachusetts Amherst, Amherst, Massachusetts

Jin-Sil Mock, EdM, Peabody College of Education and Human Development, Vanderbilt University, Nashville, Tennessee

Frederick J. Morrison, PhD, Department of Psychology and School of Education, University of Michigan, Ann Arbor, Michigan

Charlotte Nolan-Reyes, MS, Psychology Department, University of California, Santa Cruz, Santa Cruz, California

Ashley M. Pinkham, PhD, School of Education, University of Michigan, Ann Arbor, Michigan

Jessa Reed, BA, Department of Psychology, Temple University, Philadelphia, Pennsylvania

Jennifer Rigney, MS, Psychology Department, University of California, Santa Cruz, Santa Cruz, California

Kathleen Roskos, PhD, Department of Education and Allied Studies, John Carroll University, University Heights, Ohio

Rebecca Silverman, EdD, College of Education, University of Maryland, College Park, Maryland

Graciela Solis, BA, Psychology Department, University of California, Santa Cruz, Santa Cruz, California

Jennifer Van Reet, PhD, Department of Psychology, Providence College, Providence, Rhode Island

Barbara A. Wasik, PhD, College of Education, Temple University, Philadelphia, Pennsylvania

Tanya S. Wright, PhD, College of Education, Michigan State University, East Lansing, Michigan

Preface

Children's knowledge is undeniably important. We know, for example, that knowledge is essential for young children's conceptual development, academic achievement, and lifelong success. Those with greater content knowledge will exhibit stronger oral language and reading comprehension and greater proficiency in critical reasoning. Content knowledge is also positively linked to learning and achievement across academic content domains, including mathematics, science, and social sciences, as well as overall academic success.

Why is it so crucial to provide children with a strong foundation of content knowledge during the early childhood years? First, knowledge begets knowledge. Everything that children read or hear is automatically interpreted relative to what they already know about similar subjects. How children understand a storybook about a beagle is related to what they already know about dogs; whether they understand a lesson on cloud formation depends, at least in part, on their knowledge of weather. Knowledge is both cumulative *and* exponential: children with rich knowledge bases are more successful at learning new information. The breadth and depth of knowledge also enhances cognitive processes, including comprehension, problem solving, and working memory. When it comes to children's knowledge, the rich get richer.

Second, prior knowledge can help children remember new information. It is easier for children to encode (and later retrieve) new information when they already possess knowledge about a topic. For example, children who already know a lot about dinosaurs tend to remember more dinosaur-related information than children with less prior knowledge. Having a rich network of associations strengthens children's memory. New knowledge is more likely to be remembered if it is related to what is already known.

Third, children's knowledge can help facilitate their critical thinking skills. Knowledge assists working memory, freeing up space that can be devoted to other important tasks, such as comprehension and analysis. Knowledge can also facilitate thinking by providing children with things they have previously thought about. If a child has already thought about why wearing a helmet is important when riding a bicycle, for example, she will be able to quickly infer the meaning of "Don't forget your helmet!" as she rushes out the front door. If children do not possess sufficient background knowledge, however, simply understanding a conversation (or book or lesson) may consume most of their working memory resources, leaving little space for solutions. Critical thinking is not content independent; rather, it depends on factual content. This, in part, is why interventions designed to improve children's knowledge base tend to be more successful than those that do not.

Clearly, then, children's knowledge base is a critical component of their cognitive development and academic success. But while a significant amount of research has focused on the importance of domain-specific skills (e.g., phonemic awareness, decoding) in early childhood, there has been relatively little discussion of children's content knowledge and its relationship to their long-term achievement. As Pianta, Belsky, Houts, and Morrison (2007) reported, many teachers spend too much time on basic reading and math skills and not enough time on content areas, such as science and social studies. In fact, recent surveys (e.g., Center on Education Policy, 2007; Teale, Paciga, & Hoffman, 2007) have reported a striking lack of instruction focused on developing children's general world knowledge, as well as their knowledge of core concepts in content domains. This is a critical oversight because limited content knowledge in the early years may ultimately account for what appears to be reading comprehension difficulties or higher-order thinking difficulties in older children.

Researchers from a variety of disciplines now acknowledge that knowledge acquisition must be a primary goal of early childhood education (e.g., Hirsch, 2006; Kamhi, 2007; Neuman, 2006). However, a serious disconnect from theory to practice continues to persist. As a result, children—particularly those from socioeconomically disadvantaged backgrounds—continue to be shortchanged when it comes to building background knowledge.

This book is designed to fill this gap: to highlight the importance of knowledge and to build bridges between theory and practice. Our goals are twofold. First, we consider how children acquire knowledge in the "real world." Second, we highlight strategies that can help practitioners build children's knowledge bases in classrooms and beyond.

There are many ways that children may acquire new knowledge. Reading, for example, is just one way that children may learn new information. Firsthand experience and direct instruction are others. Some resources may be more reliable than others depending on the context and what information needs to be learned. When learning about the dietary habits of lions or chimpanzees, for example, children are probably more likely to seek out books or nature documentaries than travel to Africa. But when learning about the dietary habits of cats or humans, children's firsthand observations may be just as important as such third-person information. It is thus crucial that we understand all of the potential resources for children's knowledge development, as well as the circumstances under which these resources can be utilized to teach content knowledge.

Sources of children's knowledge can be conceptualized as three nested levels (see Figure 1). In the center are children's firsthand observations and direct experiences. Third-person information, such as the observations and teachings of other people, are embedded in the next

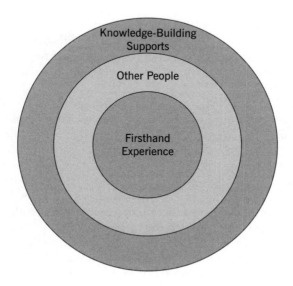

FIGURE 1. Sources of children's knowledge development.

level, while knowledge-building supports, such as books and media, make up the third level. Importantly, from an early age, children can use third-person information to create first-person knowledge, which in turn accelerates their overall knowledge development. For a particular domain, children may be able to access and utilize one or multiple different levels to contribute to their learning. Because knowledge is most flexible when it is understood in deeper, more abstract terms and can be applied in new contexts, children's learning may in fact be most effectively supported when new content converges across multiple sources.

This book addresses both how young children acquire knowledge and how practitioners can help further facilitate children's knowledge development. In Part I, chapters consider the variety of learning resources available to young children. In Chapter 1, Kaefer argues that children's observations of their environment can serve as powerful sources of new information. In Chapter 2, Van Reet extends this point by highlighting the role of play in the development of procedural and declarative knowledge. In Chapters 3 and 4, authors focus on how other people can influence children's knowledge acquisition. Corrow, Cowell, Doebel, and Koenig (Chapter 3) and Callanan, Rigney, Nolan-Reyes, and Solis (Chapter 4) examine how children actively seek new information through their interactions with more knowledgeable partners. In Chapters 5 through 7, authors consider the role of knowledge-building supports for children's learning. Reed, Hirsh-Pasek, and Golinkoff (Chapter 5) argue that the arts are a relatively untapped but potentially powerful source of knowledge development. Pinkham (Chapter 6) and Lavigne and Anderson (Chapter 7) then examine how children gain knowledge from books and screen media, respectively, highlighting how children's learning can be influenced by the quality of the knowledge-building supports themselves.

In Part II, authors focus on how we can apply the resources discussed in Part I as a means of improving children's knowledge development (and, by extension, their long-term academic success) in early childhood classrooms. In Chapter 8, Roskos and Christie demonstrate how educators can utilize children's natural desire to play as a means of simultaneously building their knowledge. In Chapters 9 through 11, authors focus on how teachers can directly scaffold their students' learning. In Chapter 9, Wright argues that direct instruction can help provide children with the foundational knowledge needed for future learning. Dickinson, Barnes, and Mock (Chapter 10), and Wasik and Hindman (Chapter 11) examine the influence of teacher language on children's knowledge acquisition and discuss how high-quality teacher–student interactions can be facilitated in early childhood classrooms. Practical applications of knowledge-building supports are then addressed in Chapters 12 through

14. Duke, Halvorsen, and Knight (Chapter 12) argue for a greater role of informational books and text in early childhood, while Connor and Morrison (Chapter 13) describe facilitating children's learning through individualized instruction and instructional supports based on preexisting skills and knowledge. In Chapter 14, Silverman and Hines focus on how teachers can use high-quality multimedia programs to foster children's literacy skills and build a strong foundation of knowledge.

This book argues that the important role of knowledge has been woefully underestimated in early childhood development. Children are natural knowledge seekers. This book emphasizes how we can best support their desire for knowledge and encourage a lifetime of learning.

REFERENCES

Adams, M. J. (2005). Hopeful signs of change in reading education. Commentary on "Evidence-based reading policy in the United States: How scientific research informs instructional practices" by G. Reid Lyon, Sally E. Shaywitz, Bennett A. Shaywitz, & Venita Chhabra. In D. Ravitch (Ed.), *Brookings papers on education policy: 2005*. Washington, DC: Brookings Institution.

Center for Educational Policy. (2007). *Choices, changes, and challenges: Curriculum and instruction in the NCLB era*. Washington, DC: Author.

Hirsch, E. D. (2006). *The knowledge deficit: Closing the shocking education gap for American children*. New York: Houghton Mifflin.

Kamhi, A. G. (2007). Knowledge deficits: The true crisis in education. *The ASHA Leader, 12*(7), 28–29.

National Research Council. (2007). *Taking science to school*. Washington, DC: National Academies Press.

Neuman, S. B. (2006). How we neglect knowledge—and why. *American Educator, 30*, 24–27.

Pianta, R. C., Belsky, J., Houts, R., & Morrison, F. (2007). Opportunities to learn in America's elementary classrooms. *Science, 315*(5820), 1795–1796.

Teale, W. H., Paciga, K. A., & Hoffman, J. L. (2007). Beginning reading instruction in urban schools: The curriculum gap ensures a continuing achievement gap. *The Reading Teacher, 61*(4), 344–348.

Contents

Part II.
Promoting Knowledge Development in the Classroom

KNOWLEDGE DEVELOPMENT IN EARLY CHILDHOOD

PART I

SOURCES OF CHILDREN'S KNOWLEDGE

CHAPTER 1

■　■　■　■　■

What You See Is What You Get

LEARNING FROM THE AMBIENT ENVIRONMENT

Tanya Kaefer

Many things can only be learned from direct instruction, but the knowledge children gain from merely attending to their surroundings is also invaluable. Although William James once characterized young children's world as "one great blooming, buzzing confusion" (James, 1890/1999, p. 462), a wealth of research has since demonstrated that infants and children are able to make sense of their surroundings and learn a great deal from observing the world around them. Children's observations and experiences may considerably inform their understanding of the world. Because this understanding may, in turn, inform the reciprocal relationship between knowledge development and future educational success, children's indirect learning experiences can be as crucial as those encountered in more pedagogical contexts.

The goal of this chapter is to address the nature of children's indirect experiences as an important source of knowledge development. First, I examine the extent to which exposure to ambient language influences children's language development. Next, I investigate whether indirect exposure to written language may scaffold children's developing orthographic knowledge. I then conclude by discussing possible implications for the role of indirect learning experiences for children from socioeconomically disadvantaged backgrounds and suggest new directions for future research on knowledge development in nonpedagogical contexts.

Learning from Ambient Language

Adult–child conversations can be an invaluable resource for children knowledge development (see Callanan, Rigney, Nolan-Reyes, & Solis, Chapter 4, this volume; Dickinson, Barnes, & Mock, Chapter 10, this volume). Before children can learn from such conversations, however, they must first comprehend what is being said. And before children can begin to comprehend oral language, they must have some knowledge of the properties of speech.

Research has long established that child-directed language is instrumental for children's language development (e.g., Pinkham, Kaefer, & Neuman, 2011; Snow, 1972). However, the majority of what children know about language may, in fact, be acquired through their *indirect* exposure to speech. Rather than being confused by seemingly meaningless sounds, even newborn infants appear to make some sense of the language that they hear. In particular, children may learn about the phonological and distributional properties, lexical categories, and vocabulary of their native language simply through listening to ambient language.

Phonetic Perception

Before children learn to speak, they have already acquired a great deal of knowledge about their native language. Language is perceived categorically, as phonemes: a spectrum of sounds is heard as variations on different categorical prototypes rather than as fully distinct sounds (Kuhl, 1991). Languages are distinguished by their different phonemic categories. The sounds of Japanese or !Kung, for example, are distinct (although not mutually exclusive) from the sounds of English.

At birth, infants can perceive all the sounds of every human language—about 600 consonants and 200 vowels (Tsao, Liu, & Kuhl, 2004). By 1 month of age, infants are able to make sharp distinctions between speech sounds (Aslin, Jusczyk, & Pisoni, 1998; Eimas, Siqueland, Jusczyk, & Vigorito, 1971), suggesting they are already somewhat adult-like in their phonological perception. With experience to a single (i.e., native) language, however, infants experience perceptual narrowing; by the end of the first year, they only distinguish the sounds of their language (Werker, 1989). Speech perception is not a skill that is taught; rather, children's speech perception is governed by their ambient language. Importantly, young children need relatively little indirect exposure to influence their language development. After listening to a foreign language (e.g., American infants interacting with a Mandarin Chinese speaker), 9-month-old infants retained their ability to perceive the sounds of that language—an effect that emerged after as few as 12 exposures (Kuhl, Tsao, & Liu, 2003).

Children's early phonetic perception may influence their later language development. Infants who are better at discriminating among sounds from their native language at 6 months of age also tend to score higher on vocabulary and grammar assessments during the second year of life (Rivera-Glaxiola, Silva-Pereyra, & Kuhl, 2005; Tsao et al., 2004). In fact, young children may be able to use their early perceptual discrimination abilities to help build their vocabularies (Swingley & Aslin, 2002). Furthermore, adults learning a second language are able to speak with more native-like accents if they had overheard (but never spoken) the language as a child (Au, Knightly, Jun, & Oh, 2002).

Distributional Probabilities

To a native speaker, continuous speech is heard as a sequence of individual words—even though there may be no explicit cues indicating where one word ends and the next word begins. Before they can comprehend oral language, young children must first solve the problem of extracting individual words from continuous speech before they can associate them with individual meanings. When overhearing the statement "It is raining outside," a child must figure out that her mother is saying "It-is-raining-outside" and not, for example, "Itis-rainingoutside" or "Itisrainingout-side."

Remarkably, even infants as young as 7.5 months of age are capable of extracting individual words from continuous speech (Jusczyk & Aslin, 1995). They may rely on a variety of cues in order to make these determinations. Children may attend to prosody and intonational changes, such as initial stress and pitch movements marking the ends of clauses (Cutler & Butterfield, 1992), to help isolate individual words. They may listen for familiar carrier phrases, such as "Look at the _____!" or "Where is the _____?" to help identify unfamiliar words (Fernald & Hurtado, 2006). And by 11 months, infants appear to understand that pauses may occur between individual words, but not between syllables within words (Myers et al., 1996).

Children may also learn about the distributional properties of speech through statistical learning. After as little as 2 minutes of exposure to an unfamiliar language, infants in the first year of life are able to group together syllables that frequently co-occur (Aslin, Saffran, & Newport, 1998; Saffran, Aslin, & Newport, 1996). Given even limited experience listening to English, for example, young children can establish that in the four-syllable sequence *happybirthday,* the syllables *ha + ppy* and *birth + day* are each more likely to co-occur than *ppy + birth.*

Through statistical learning, children may be able to correctly identify individual words and word boundaries. Interestingly, this type of learning is not limited to children's ability to segment speech. They may also learn the patterns of animal sounds (Marcus, Fernandes, & Johnson, 2007), musical tones (Saffran, Johnson, Aslin, & Newport, 1999) and visual patterns (Fiser & Aslin, 2002; Kirkham, Slemmer, & Johnson, 2002) through brief, indirect exposure.

Children's facility segmenting continuous speech may positively influence their later knowledge acquisition. For example, Estes, Evans, Alibali, and Saffran (2007) gave 17-month-olds limited experience with fluent (novel) speech. In a subsequent task, children were better able to learn new object labels if the labels were consistent with the distributional properties of the novel speech stream. When presented with object–label pairings that used statistically improbable words, children failed to learn the new words. As children gain more experience listening to a language, they begin to construct a lexicon of phonological forms that exemplifies the typical phonological properties of words in that language. Children may then use these properties to segment speech in a usefully biased manner, thereby helping them identify even more new words and facilitating subsequent word learning (Thiessen, Hill, & Saffran, 2005).

Lexical Categories

Despite being necessary, simply identifying the boundaries of words is insufficient for children to comprehend the speech they are hearing. Children must also learn that there are different categories of words (e.g., nouns, verbs) and that they serve distinct functions (e.g., to label objects, to describe actions). Although children may not explicitly learn about lexical categories until elementary school grammar lessons, they nonetheless appear to derive an intuitive understanding through mere exposure to language.

By as early as 6 months of age, infants appear sensitive to some of the differences between grammatical and nongrammatical speech in their native language (Shi & Werker, 2001). By the second year, children are sensitive to the proper inflection and word order of nouns and verbs (Soderstrom, White, Conwell, & Morgan, 2007) and can use distributional cues to segregate words and phrases into different syntactic categories (Gerken, Wilson, & Lewis, 2005; Nazzi, Dilley, Jusczyk, Shattuck-Hufnagel, & Jusczyk, 2005). Furthermore, 2-year-old children's understanding of lexical categories is sufficiently precise to allow the mapping of unfamiliar verbs to event categories and unfamiliar nouns to object categories (Waxman, Lidz, Braun, & Lavin, 2009).

Collectively, these results suggest that young children may develop sensitivity to the lexical and grammatical properties of their native language simply by listening to speech.

Vocabulary

When discussing vocabulary development, researchers tend to focus on children's ability to learn new words in ostensive contexts, such as from language directed to them or during pedagogical book-reading contexts. Recent research, however, suggests that young children may monitor others' conversations and learn new words through these indirect experiences. For example, Akhtar, Jipson, and Callanan (2001) had 2.5-year-olds either engage in an explicit word-learning task themselves or observe a word-learning task between two adults. Children were able to learn new words equally well in both contexts, suggesting that ambient language may be a valuable source of new vocabulary knowledge. In subsequent studies, Akhtar and colleagues demonstrated that children may learn from overheard conversations even when distracting activities were going on (Akhtar, 2005) and, under certain conditions, even 18-month-olds may be able to learn from third-party conversations (Floor & Akhtar, 2006). Taken together, these studies suggest that word learning can occur outside of typical ostensive contexts. Indeed, children may actively seek information from interactions occurring in the world around them.

Although children may be able to learn new words equally well through direct and indirect experiences (Jaswal & Markman, 2003), some words may only be learned indirectly. As compared to object labels, for example, there are fewer natural pedagogical situations in which verbs can be directly taught to children. Verbs tend to be used to refer to impending or completed actions rather than ongoing actions (Tomasello & Kruger, 1992). Therefore, learning new verbs may at least partially be a function of children's ability to observe and interpret contingencies in the real world. One possibility is that children use the syntactic framing of a sentence in order to narrow down or deduce the meaning of a verb (Gleitman, 1990; but see Pinker, 1994, for an alternative interpretation). In this way, children may use the language they hear—particularly the syntactic structure of that language—as a means of bootstrapping their understanding of new words. Blind children may use a similar process to learn action verbs, even though their sensory limitation prevents the use of visual cues to word meaning (Landau & Gleitman, 1985). Taken together, this research suggests that children are able to use the structure of language to determine the meaning of words and gain new vocabulary.

When encountering an unfamiliar word, children must determine the correct referent for the new label. When hearing his mother discussing a glass of juice, baby Gene must figure out that *glass* refers to the glass and not the plate or fork or family pet. In direct word-learning contexts, children may be able to rely on ostensive cues, such as joint attention or child-directed speech (e.g., Csibra & Gergely, 2009; Tomasello & Farrar, 1986). When overhearing ambient language, however, a great deal of ambiguity may exist concerning word–world mappings. In such cases, children's sensitivity to statistical probabilities may again be important. Smith and Yu (2008), for example, repeatedly exposed children to six unfamiliar word–object pairings. Two words at a time were said aloud while the corresponding illustrations were displayed on a screen. There were no clues as to which word corresponded to which object. Over 4 minutes each of the six word–object pairings was shown repeatedly in random combination with the other word–object pairings. They found that children were able to extract the contingencies and successfully form new word–object mappings. This suggests that young children may determine the referent of overheard words by tracking co-occurances across situations. When baby Gene hears "the glass of juice" and later "the glass on the shelf" and later still "the glass on the counter," he may begin to notice that *glass* co-occurs with the clear drinking container, despite temporal and contextual changes. Thus not only is it possible for children to learn vocabulary from nondirect contexts, but a great deal of vocabulary learning may occur this way.

Summary

Ambient language may be a rich source of meaningful information and a significant contributor to children's language development, but only if children can first find ways to make sense of it. Research suggests that infants, toddlers, and young children are eager learners and may actively seek out ways gain knowledge from the world around them.

Ambient Experience and Literacy Learning

In addition to language, children may also gain a great deal of literacy-related knowledge from observing their surroundings. The knowledge acquired through these indirect learning experiences may, in turn, influence children's educational outcomes. In this section, I examine one specific area in which children's everyday experiences may facilitate their educational outcomes: orthographic knowledge. Although most children require direct instruction in the processes of decoding and reading comprehension, they may nonetheless acquire some of the foundational knowledge through their naturally occurring experiences with and explorations of print.

Children's knowledge about written words before they enter school is a significant predictor of their long-term academic success (for review, see La Paro & Pianta, 2000). How young children acquire knowledge about words is therefore a crucial focus of developmental research. Thus far, however, researchers have primarily focused on how children learn to identify individual written words on sight (e.g., Ehri, 1991, 2005). Yet learning to read (at least in English) also requires an understanding of the more general rules of how letters combine to form words. Although this kind of knowledge is rarely taught directly, children's understanding of how words work is nonetheless a key milestone for reading development.

Orthographic knowledge includes "both knowledge of the actual spelling of particular words and higher level conceptual skills, such as the recognition of the properties of words and sequences and typical positions of letters in English" (Siegel, Share, & Geva, 1995, p. 250). There are thus two important elements to orthographic knowledge: lexicalized knowledge of individual word representations (e.g., knowing that *llama* is the written code for the spoken word /lama/) and generalized knowledge of patterns across words (e.g., that English words generally do not start with a double consonant). In this section, I particularly focus on children's generalized orthographic knowledge, including the rules governing what constitutes orthographic symbols ("symbolic knowledge") and how these orthographic symbols are combined ("pattern knowledge").

Symbolic Knowledge

Although it was once thought children must have an understanding of letter-to-sound correspondences before they can develop orthographic knowledge (e.g., Frith, 1986), more recent evidence suggests that pre-reading children do in fact demonstrate some orthographic knowledge. For example, when presented with different types of printed stimuli, 5-year-old children label printed words and pseudo-words as writing but refuse to label non-letter symbol strings, Chinese characters, and shapes as writing (Lavine, 1977). Similarly, when shown printed stimuli along with pictures, squiggles, and shapes, 4- and 5-year-olds are able to identify print and cursive writing as words, but label squiggles and pictures as non-words (Bialystok, 1995). These findings suggest that even young children may possess early orthographic understanding of what kinds of symbols belong in words.

Importantly, children's knowledge may begin to develop even before they have experienced any reading instruction. In recent work (Kaefer, 2009), 3- and 5-year-old nonreaders viewed a series of pseudo-words, strings of letter–number combinations, and strings of letter–symbol combinations. They were asked to identify whether each combination was or was not a "word." Consistent with previous studies, 5-year-olds were able to explicitly identify pseudo-words as "words" but letter–symbol combinations and letter–number combinations as non-words. Three-year-olds, by contrast, did not explicitly distinguish between number–letter combinations and pseudo-words. However, eye-tracker data revealed that they *looked* significantly longer at numbers in the number–letter combinations than letters in the same position of pseudo-words, suggesting early implicit orthographic knowledge in 3-year-olds.

Overall, 3-year-olds could explicitly detect some symbolic ortho-graphic violations (symbol–letter) and implicitly detect others (letter–number), while 5-year-olds could explicitly detect all presented symbolic violations. These findings suggest a possible progression in children's orthographic knowledge from the implicit to explicit. Before children learn to read—or even have explicit knowledge of what a word is—they may have acquired some implicit sense of what constitutes an ortho-graphic representation.

Pattern Knowledge

In addition identifying which symbols can go into words, evidence sug-gests that children may also possess some generalized orthographic knowledge of the patterns of letters within words. Zivian and Samuels (1986), for example, found that 9-year-old children were more likely to identify orthographically correct letter patterns as "good" words than orthographically incorrect letter patterns. It should be noted, however, that the illegal orthographic combinations used in this study were also unpronounceable. If children were sensitive to the phonological makeup of the non-words, they could have used their phonological, rather than orthographic, knowledge to make decisions about which words were "best."

To address this limitation, subsequent studies used illegal ortho-graphic combinations that were also pronounceable. In particular, Cas-sar and Treiman (1997) used words with initial consonant doublings as an example of a generalized orthographic rule. Kindergarteners were presented with pairs of letter strings, one of which had a doubled letter at the end (e.g., BAFF) and one that had a double letter at the beginning (e.g., BBAF). They recognized that doubled letters were more acceptable at the end of words than at the beginning. However, when presented with a pair of words in which one had a legal double at the end (e.g., YILL) and one had an illegal double at the end (e.g., YIHH), kindergartners' performance did not differ from chance. First graders, by comparison, were able to identify which doublings are considered more appropriate at the end of words (e.g., FF versus KK).

Importantly, children's generalized orthographic knowledge may also be inferred from tasks that do not require explicit judgments. Wright and Ehri (2007), for example, taught kindergarteners and first graders to read and recognize real, meaningful words with modified spellings. Both age groups required fewer trials to learn orthographically legal spellings (e.g., PADD) than orthographically illegal ones (e.g., RRAG). More impressively, children who were relatively advanced readers often spontaneously regularized the orthography when writing previously learned illegal non-words during a spelling test (e.g., spelling RRAG as RAGG).

The Role of Environmental Print on Generalized Orthographic Knowledge

An important factor that may contribute to children's orthographic knowledge is their experience with environmental print. There are multiple (although not necessarily mutually exclusive) ways that print exposure may influence children's developing orthographic knowledge. First, the experience of decoding text may contribute to children's knowledge. Share and colleagues (e.g., Jorm & Share, 1983; Share, 1995) developed a "self-teaching" hypothesis, which suggests that children gain orthographic knowledge through the process of decoding. According to self-teaching, the process of decoding gives children the opportunity to attend to and process the orthographic patterns in words. In fact, a single encounter with an unfamiliar word is often sufficient for children to encode orthographic detail (Share, 2004). In this way, differences in decoding ability may influence children's orthographic knowledge, such that children who are skilled decoders may have more of an opportunity to process and learn the orthographic patterns encountered in their environment.

Second, recent work suggests that children may be able to extract the statistical probabilities of the print they see in their environment, and this, in turn, influences their orthographic knowledge. If children are sensitive to the relative frequency of letter combinations occurring in environmental print, they may thus begin to recognize frequently co-occurring combinations as legal and infrequently co-occurring combinations as illegal. In fact, research has shown that children are able to recognize and generalize probabilistic orthographic patterns in their environment and use this information when producing written language. Treiman and Kessler (2006) showed that children use consonant context to spell vowels. For example, /ɑ/ is typically spelled as "a" when it follows /w/ (as in wand) but as "o" when it follows other consonants (as in pond). Even kindergartners appear sensitive to this kind of contextual information and may utilize it when spelling words (i.e., selecting the correct vowel in a particular context). Similarly, children can also use vowel context when spelling vowels (Hayes, Treiman, & Kessler, 2006). In fact, the consistency with which vowel spellings occur in context significantly influences children's success in spelling vowel patterns over and above the complexity or frequency of the pattern (Caravolas, Kessler, Hulme, & Snowling, 2005). In this way, children may use contextual orthographic cues to help them determine the appropriate spelling of a word.

Through their experiences with environmental print, children may become sensitive to the context of individual letters and begin to acquire knowledge of the patterns and combinations in which letters operate. They may then use their knowledge of these patterns when learning to produce written language. This is consistent with Lété, Peereman, and Fayol (2008), who found that not only do children use context when learning how to spell, but their reliance on contextual information increases as their orthographic knowledge increases. Thus, as children gain more experience with patterns in written language, they appear to increasingly rely on these patterns to produce written language.

Overall, research suggests that children's indirect experiences with printed language may directly affect their acquisition of orthographic knowledge. As children are given more opportunities to experience written language, they accumulate more input from which to determine statistical probabilities, and the greater their ability to detect probabilities, the greater their understanding of orthographic patterns. And when children possess greater orthographic knowledge, their ability to anticipate and expect written words to behave in certain ways may free cognitive resources to focus on more important aspects of literacy, such as comprehension. In this way, exposure to written language may be foundational to children's orthographic knowledge in the short term and their overall literacy development in the long term.

Implications for the Achievement Gap

Given that exposure to oral and written language is critical for children's language and literacy development, it is possible that socioeconomic-related variability in children's indirect learning experiences may contribute to the well-established knowledge gaps. Differences in children's orthographic knowledge, for example, may be linked to their access to print. Children from socioeconomically disadvantaged backgrounds tend to have less access to print in their homes (Purcell-Gates, 1996), schools (Duke, 2000), and neighborhoods (Neuman & Celano, 2001). Perhaps relative deficits in print exposure may lead to weaker skills in extracting patterns from print and, correspondingly, less orthographic knowledge. The relative lack of this knowledge may then contribute to impoverished overall literacy skills.

Indeed, children from lower socioeconomic backgrounds often demonstrate striking deficits in reading achievement as compared to children from more socioeconomically advantaged homes (e.g., Chall, Jacobs, & Baldwin, 1990; Hart & Risley, 1995). These differences typically persist throughout the school years (Alexander, Entwisle, & Horsey, 1997) and may perpetuate the ever-widening achievement gap (Stanovich, 1986). Increases in print exposure and access to print have been cited as one way to help close this gap. As discussed in this chapter, orthographic knowledge may be yet another reason why print exposure is vital to children's knowledge development.

Future Directions and Conclusions

As this chapter has shown, children's indirect experience with oral and printed language may be crucial for their knowledge development and future academic success. However, much more research is needed. How children build content knowledge through observing their environment is vital for our understanding of how children's direct experiences contribute to their learning. In addition, as technology continues to advance, more sensitive measures of children's implicit knowledge are needed to chart the progression of knowledge development from implicit to explicit awareness.

In conclusion, children are able to learn a great deal of important information simply by observing the world around them. From infancy, children acquire and process information in their environment and begin to convert it into a knowledge base. This knowledge may then be used as a framework to build additional knowledge (for discussion, see also Kaefer, Pinkham, & Neuman, 2011; Neuman, Pinkham, & Kaefer, in press). Oral language knowledge and generalized orthographic knowledge are only two examples of the kind of knowledge that children may acquire through their informal learning experiences and then directly apply to formal educational tasks, such as literacy. Nonetheless, children's ability to process the world around them into a coherent knowledge base appears to be an important and key developmental process.

REFERENCES

Akhtar, N. (2005). The robustness of learning through overhearing. *Developmental Science, 8*(2), 199–209.

Akhtar, N., Jipson, J., & Callanan, M. A. (2001). Learning words through overhearing. *Child Development, 72*(2), 416–430.

Alexander, K. L., Entwisle, D. R., & Horsey, C. S. (1997). From first grade forward: Early foundations of high school dropout. *Sociology of Education,* 87–107.

Aslin, R. N., Jusczyk, P. W., & Pisoni, D. B. (1998). Speech and auditory processing during infancy: Constraints on and precursors to language. In W. Damon (Ed.), *Handbook of child psychology: Vol. 2: Cognition, perception, and language* (pp. 147–198). Hoboken, NJ: Wiley.

Aslin, R. N., Saffran, J. R., & Newport, E. L. (1998). Computation of conditional probability statistics by 8-month-old infants. *Psychological Science, 9*(4), 321–324.

Au, T. K., Knightly, L. M., Jun, S. A., & Oh, J. S. (2002). Overhearing a language during childhood. *Psychological Science, 13*(3), 238–243.

Bialystok, E. (1995). Making concepts of print symbolic: Understanding how writing represents language. *First Language, 15*(45), 317.

Caravolas, M., Kessler, B., Hulme, C., & Snowling, M. (2005). Effects of orthographic consistency, frequency, and letter knowledge on children's vowel spelling development. *Journal of Experimental Child Psychology, 92*(4), 307–321.

Cassar, M., & Treiman, R. (1997). The beginnings of orthographic knowledge: Children's knowledge of double letters in words. *Journal of Educational Psychology, 89*(4), 631.

Chall, J. S., Jacobs, V. A., & Baldwin, L. E. (1990). *The reading crisis: Why poor children fall behind.* Cambridge, MA: Harvard University Press.

Csibra, G., & Gergely, G. (2009). Natural pedagogy. *Trends in Cognitive Sciences, 13*(4), 148–153.

Cutler, A., & Butterfield, S. (1992). Rhythmic cues to speech segmentation: Evidence from juncture misperception. *Journal of Memory and Language, 31*(2), 218–236.

Duke, N. (2000). 3.6 minutes per day: The scarcity of informational texts in first grade. *Reading Research Quarterly, 35*(2), 202–224.

Ehri, L. C. (1991). Development of the ability to read words. In R. Barr, M. L. Kamil, P. B. Mosenthal, & P. D. Pearson (Eds.), *Handbook of reading research Vol. 2* (pp. 383–417). Hillsdale, NJ: Erlbaum.

Ehri, L. C. (2005). Learning to read words: Theory, findings, and issues. *Scientific Studies of Reading, 9*(2), 167–188.

Eimas, P. D., Siqueland, E. R., Jusczyk, P., & Vigorito, J. (1971). Speech perception in infants. *Science, 171*(3968), 303–306.

Estes, K. G., Evans, J. L., Alibali, M. W., & Saffran, J. R. (2007). Can infants map meaning to newly segmented words? *Psychological Science, 18*(3), 254.

Fernald, A., & Hurtado, N. (2006). Names in frames: Infants interpret words in sentence frames faster than words in isolation. *Developmental Science, 9*(3), 33–40.

Fiser, J., & Aslin, R. N. (2002). Statistical learning of higher-order temporal structure from visual shape sequences. *Journal of Experimental Psychology: Learning, Memory, and Cognition, 28*(3), 458–467.

Floor, P., & Akhtar, N. (2006). Can 18-month-old infants learn words by listening in on conversations? *Infancy, 9*(3), 327–339.

Frith, U. (1986). A developmental framework for developmental dyslexia. *Annals of Dyslexia, 36*(1), 67–81.

Gerken, L., Wilson, R., & Lewis, W. (2005). Infants can use distributional cues to form syntactic categories. *Journal of Child Language, 32*(2), 249–268.

Gleitman, L. (1990). The structural sources of verb meanings. *Language Acquisition, 1*(1), 3–55.

Hart, B., & Risley, T. R. (1995). *Meaningful differences in the everyday experience of young American children.* Baltimore: Brookes.

Hayes, H., Treiman, R., & Kessler, B. (2006). Children use vowels to help them spell consonants. *Journal of Experimental Child Psychology, 94*(1), 27–42.

James, W. (1999). *The principles of psychology* (Vol I). New York: Holt. (Original work published 1890)

Jaswal, V. K., & Markman, E. M. (2003). The relative strengths of indirect and direct word learning. *Developmental Psychology, 39*(4), 745–760.

Jorm, A. F., & Share, D. L. (1983). Phonological recoding and reading acquisition. *Applied Psycholinguistics, 4*(2), 103–147.

Jusczyk, P. W., & Aslin, R. N. (1995). Infants' detection of the sound patterns of words in fluent speech. *Cognitive Psychology, 29*(1), 1–23.

Kaefer, T. (2009). *Implicit, eclipsed, but functional: The development of orthographic knowledge in early readers* (doctoral dissertation). Available from the ProQuest Dissertations & Theses database (AAT 3366786).

Kaefer, T., Pinkham, A. M., & Neuman, S. B. (2011, March). *Taxonomic organization scaffolds young children's learning from storybooks: A design experiment.* Paper presented at the semiannual meeting of the Society for Research on Educational Effectiveness, Washington, DC.

Kirkham, N. Z., Slemmer, J. A., & Johnson, S. P. (2002). Visual statistical learning in infancy: Evidence for a domain general learning mechanism. *Cognition, 83*(2), 35–42.

Kuhl, P. K. (1991). Human adults and human infants show a "perceptual magnet effect" for the prototypes of speech categories, monkeys do not. *Perception and Psychophysics, 50*(2), 93–107.

Kuhl, P. K., Tsao, F.-M., & Liu, H.-M. (2003). Foreign-language experience in infancy: Effects of short-term exposure and social interaction on phonetic learning. *PNAS, 100*(15), 9096–9101.

La Paro, K. M., & Pianta, R. C. (2000). Predicting children's competence in the early school years: A meta-analytic review. *Review of Educational Research, 70*(4), 443.

Landau, B., & Gleitman, L. R. (1985). *Language and experience.* Cambridge, MA: Harvard University Press.

Lavine, L. O. (1977). Differentiation of letterlike forms in prereading children. *Developmental Psychology, 13*(2), 89.

Lété, B., Peereman, R., & Fayol, M. (2008). Consistency and word-frequency effects on spelling among first- to fifth-grade French children: A regression-based study. *Journal of Memory and Language, 58*(4), 952–977.

Marcus, G. F., Fernandes, K. J., & Johnson, S. P. (2007). Infant rule learning facilitated by speech. *Psychological Science, 18*(5), 387–391.

Myers, J., Jusczyk, P. W., Kemler Nelson, D. G., Charles-Luce, J., Woodward, A. L., & Hirsh-Pasek, K. (1996). Infants' sensitivity to word boundaries in fluent speech. *Journal of Child Language, 23*, 1–30.

Nazzi, T., Dilley, L. C., Jusczyk, A. M., Shattuck-Hufnagel, & Jusczyk, P. W. (2005). English-learning infants' segmentation of verbs from fluent speech. *Language and Speech, 48*(3), 279–298.

Neuman, S., & Celano, D. (2001). Access to print in low-income and middle-income communities: An ecological study of four neighborhoods. *Reading Research Quarterly, 36*(1), 8–26.

Neuman, S. B., Pinkham, A. M., & Kaefer, T. (in press). Building word and world knowledge in the early years. In K. Hall, T. Cremin, B. Comber, & L. Moll (Eds.), *International handbook of research on children's literacy, learning and culture.* Malden, MA: Wiley-Blackwell.

Pinker, S. (1994). How could a child use verb syntax to learn verb semantics? *Lingua, 92*, 377–410.

Pinkham, A. M., Kaefer, T., & Neuman, S. B. (2011). Representational demand positively influences kindergartners' language development. In N. Danis, K. Mesh, & H. Sung (Eds.), *BUCLD 35: Proceedings of the 35th annual Boston University Conference on Language Development* (Vol. 2, pp. 488–499). Somerville, MA: Cascadilla Press.

Purcell-Gates, V. (1996). Stories, coupons, and the *TV Guide*: Relationships between home literacy experiences and emergent literacy knowledge. *Reading Research Quarterly, 31*(4), 406–428.

Rivera-Gaxiola, M., Silva-Pereyra, J., & Kuhl, P. K. (2005). Brain potentials to native and non-native speech contrasts in 7- and 11-month-old American infants. *Developmental Science, 8*(2), 162–172.

Saffran, J. R., Aslin, R. N., & Newport, E. L. (1996). Statistical learning by 8-month-old infants. *Science, 274*(5294), 1926.

Saffran, J. R., Johnson, E. K., Aslin, R. N., & Newport, E. L. (1999). Statistical learning of tone sequences by human infants and adults. *Cognition, 70*(1), 27–52.

Share, D. L. (1995). Phonological recoding and self-teaching: Sine qua non of reading acquisition. *Cognition, 55*(2), 151–218.

Share, D. L. (2004). Orthographic learning at a glance: On the time course and developmental onset of self-teaching. *Journal of Experimental Child Psychology, 87*(4), 267–298.

Shi, R., & Werker, J. F. (2001). Six-month-old infants' preference for lexical words. *Psychological Science, 12*(1), 70–75.

Siegel, L. S., Share, D., & Geva, E. (1995). Evidence for superior orthographic skills in dyslexics. *Psychological Science, 6*(4), 250.

Smith, L., & Yu, C. (2008). Infants rapidly learn word-referent mappings via cross-situational statistics. *Cognition, 106*(3), 1558–1568.

Snow, C. E. (1972). Mothers' speech to children learning language. *Child Development, 43*(2), 549–565.

Soderstrom, M., White, K. S., Conwell, E., & Morgan, J. L. (2007). Receptive grammatical knowledge of familiar content words and inflection in 16 month olds. *Infancy, 12*(1), 1–29.

Stanovich, K. E. (1986). Matthew effects in reading: Some consequences of individual differences in the acquisition of literacy. *Reading Research Quarterly, 21*(4), 360–407.

Swingley, D., & Aslin, R. N. (2002). Lexical neighborhoods and the word-form representations of 14-month-olds. *Psychological Science, 13*(5), 480–484.

Thiessen, E. D., Hill, E. A., & Saffran, J. R. (2005). Infant-directed speech facilitates word segmentation. *Infancy, 7*(1), 53–71.

Tomasello, M., & Farrar, M. J. (1986). Joint attention and early language. *Child Development, 57*(6), 1454–1463.

Tomasello, M., & Kruger, A. C. (1992). Joint attention on actions: Acquiring verbs in ostensive and non-ostensive contexts. *Journal of Child Language, 19,* 311–333.

Treiman, R., & Kessler, B. (2006). Spelling as statistical learning: Using consonantal context to spell vowels. *Journal of educational psychology, 98*(3), 642.

Tsao, F.-M., Liu, H.-M., & Kuhl, P. K. (2004). Speech perception in infancy predicts language development in the second year of life: A longitudinal study. *Child Development, 75*(4), 1067–1084.

Waxman, S. R., Lidz, J. L., Braun, I. E., & Lavin, T. (2009). Twenty-four-month-old infants' interpretations of novel verbs and nouns in dynamic scenes. *Cognitive Psychology, 59*(1), 67–95.

Werker, J. (1989). Becoming a native speaker. *American Scientist, 77,* 54–59.

Wright, D., & Ehri, L. C. (2007). Beginners remember orthography when they learn to read words: The case of doubled letters. *Applied Psycholinguistics, 28*(1), 115.

Zivian, M. T., & Samuels, M. T. (1986). Performance on a word-likeness task by normal readers and reading-disabled children. *Reading Research Quarterly,* 150–160.

CHAPTER 2

■ ■ ■ ■ ■

Learning through Play

PROCEDURAL VERSUS DECLARATIVE KNOWLEDGE

Jennifer Van Reet

Children learn through play. This idea is widely accepted by experts in both psychology (e.g., Singer, Golinkoff, & Hirsh-Pasek, 2006) and education (e.g., National Association for the Education of Young Children [NAEYC], 2009), and it has been broadly incorporated into our society's general conception of childhood. Advertisements for "educational" toys imply that particular objects can afford lessons about the world by structuring play in a certain way. Articles in parenting magazines tell their readers play is crucial for their children's future success. Preschools and children's museums design and promote programs based on the tenet that play will teach children something. But what exactly do children learn in play? And is all play equally informative? The idea of "play to learn" is pervasive and compelling, but it can be somewhat misleading. It is undoubtedly true that children gain a variety of different skills through play, like literacy (Saracho & Spodek, 2006), self-regulation (Elias & Berk, 2002) and social understanding (Taylor & Carlson, 1997), to name just a few. But the relationship between play and the acquisition of explicit knowledge is more tenuous.

The many contributions play makes to children's procedural knowledge, defined as their motor, social, and cognitive skills, have been thoroughly and well reviewed many times (e.g., Hirsh-Pasek, Golinkoff, Berk, & Singer, 2009; Pearson, Russ, & Cain Spannagel, 2008; Pellegrini,

2009), so they will be only briefly reviewed here. Instead, the focus of this chapter is to examine an equally important, but less frequently studied, issue: what play can and cannot add to children's declarative knowledge. Declarative knowledge includes information from both episodic and semantic memory: specifically, all our autobiographical information, like who we are and what happens to us, as well as all of the facts we know. Procedural and declarative knowledge are distinct memory systems, governed by different areas of the brain (Squire, 2004). They also have different developmental timetables; the ability to acquire and retain procedural information matures early and does not change dramatically with age, whereas declarative memory capacities increase substantially throughout childhood (Lum, Kidd, Davis, & Conti-Ramsden, 2010).

Notably, learning happens differently in each system. Declarative knowledge is obtained consciously and relatively quickly, while procedural learning happens incrementally outside one's awareness (Sherry & Schacter, 1987). This distinction highlights why it is dangerous to assume that children can learn declarative information like words or facts through play simply based on evidence that they acquire skills in play. Instead, it may be that play is especially suited to procedural learning, but is not appropriate for declarative learning. To explore this possibility, I first review three domains in which play and procedural knowledge are positively correlated. Next, drawing on research about both reality-oriented play and pretend play, I explore whether a similar relationship exists between play and declarative knowledge.

Play and Procedural Knowledge Acquisition

Over the past several decades, researchers have shown time and time again that play is correlated with a wide variety of positive outcomes. This body of research has led many to the general conclusion that play is beneficial for all learning. There are two problems with this deduction. One, as already described, many of the reported gains are in procedural knowledge, not declarative knowledge, making the conclusion too broad. And two, the correlational design used in much of this research makes it impossible to know with any certainty to what degree play is responsible for these advantages. In other words, we do not know whether play is causing the positive effects. To illustrate, I consider three domains: language and literacy, executive functioning, and social competence.

First, play and language ability are positively correlated, a relationship that can be detected as early as the toddler years (Tamis-LeMonda & Bornstein, 1994). And play strongly predicts children's emerging literacy skills like phonological and print awareness in preschool, which can foster later literacy skills like storytelling and writing ability in the elementary years (Nicolopoulou, McDowell, & Brockmeyer, 2006). Thus play is strongly linked to the procedural knowledge of how to use language appropriately, like knowing to add "-ed" to indicate the past tense or being able to discriminate between the sounds /ə/ and /æ/. This knowledge is procedural because it is acquired over time through observation and trial-and-error learning, not immediately as a result of direct instruction. Yet because this research is correlational, it is not clear whether children gain this knowledge as a result of play.

It could simply be that play affords children the time and gives them the opportunity to practice language. After all, when children are playing, they are usually talking—either to themselves in solitary play or to their playmates. This time spent using language also likely allows them to try out sounds, words, or grammatical structures that they have heard but may not yet have had a chance to use. Children's natural experimentation with language is known to be an important mechanism for language development. For example, babbling allows infants to practice with the phonemes of their native language (Petitto & Marentette, 1991), and private speech and crib talk have long been thought to help children practice conversational and grammatical rules. Thus it stands to reason that language use during play similarly adds to language development.

Providing children with time to practice language is unlikely to be the whole story, however, considering that children also get experience and opportunity to practice language outside of play. Another possible explanation for the correlation between play and language is that they share a common root ability. Researchers point specifically to pretend play as a way that children can strengthen their understanding of symbols. This symbolic competence could carry over to and boost language, which is also a symbolic ability. In other words, understanding that a real object can arbitrarily stand for something else in the pretend world (e.g., that a cup can be a hat) might help children understand that a word (or sign) is a symbol for an object. Of course, it is entirely possible that language ability bootstraps pretend-play ability, not the reverse. Or, as is the most probable case, that the relationship is bidirectional and practice with each ability facilitates the other. The exact nature and direction of this relationship is an area ripe for further research.

Both of these hypotheses, practice and symbolic competence, are also cited as explanations for the relationship between play and literacy skills. When children are given access to literacy objects (e.g., calendars, writing utensils, newspapers, labels), they incorporate them into their play, which, in turn, facilitates their literacy development (Neuman & Roskos, 1992; Roskos & Christie, Chapter 8, this volume). In addition being able to practice and experiment with what they already know and have available, play gives children the chance to create their own novel materials. In enacting a restaurant scenario, for example, children can create menus, order forms, bills, and receipts. Furthermore, sociodramatic play requires children to develop characters and narratives, which may translate into creative writing and storytelling ability. Thus, through practice, experimentation, and construction of new objects, children become even more familiar with language in both its spoken and written forms. Children can then use their increased language proficiency in non-play interactions at home and at school in order to gain knowledge from other people and print materials.

Second, play has long been thought to increase executive function and self-regulation abilities, like attention and inhibitory control (Whitebread, Coltman, Jameson, & Lander, 2009). The executive functions are mental processes can be consciously controlled and strengthened with practice. We can, for example, gradually learn to focus our atention or to ignore distractions. Because this knowledge of how to control our minds and bodies is acquired through experience, it is governed by the procedural system, not the declarative one (Lum et al., 2010). Although there is not yet enough empirical evidence to state with certainty that play increases self-regulation, initial research suggests it does. One observational study that found sociodramatic play with peers predicted increases in self-regulation behavior in preschoolers (Elias & Berk, 2002). And a preschool curriculum called *Tools of the Mind,* which utilizes a large amount of dramatic play, was shown to increase executive function ability (Diamond, Barnett, Thomas, & Munro, 2007). In this program, teachers encourage and show children how to collaboratively develop a plan for their play scenarios before acting them out. This is hypothesized to teach children not only how to plan, but how to focus on a task, attend to their play partners, inhibit impulses, and remember their goals. However, it is not known whether dramatic play actually teaches these skills or whether the dramatic play component of the curriculum contributed to children's increased executive function ability independent of the program's other elements.

My own research over the past several years has also centered on this question of whether play contributes to children's self-regulatory abilities. I have concentrated specifically on pretend play and inhibitory control and have found that these abilities are positively correlated in 3- and 4-year-old children. Specifically, the quality of children's pretend play is associated with two different components of procedural knowledge: knowing how to manage conflicting information and knowing how to wait for a reward (Van Reet & Boguszewski, 2011). In an effort to determine the directionality of this relationship, one study varied the order of the pretending and inhibitory control tasks. The relationship between pretend play ability and inhibitory control disappeared when children engaged in the conflict management tasks before the pretending tasks (Van Reet, 2011). In other words, "warming up" children's conflict inhibitory control ability helped them subsequently to pretend at a qualitatively higher level, hinting that this mental ability is foundational to the ability to pretend. Thus my research suggests that play does not teach children how to self-regulate; rather, it seems that knowing how to control one's thoughts helps children pretend.

As is the case with language, the relationship between play and self-regulation may be bidirectional. Children need to know how to control themselves in order to play, and then every time they play, they practice regulating their thoughts, actions, and emotions. Good executive function ability then leads to knowledge acquisition: executive function is a better predictor of early school success than children's IQ scores (Blair & Razza, 2007). In other words, when children know how to pay attention, ignore distractions, delay gratification, remember instructions, and control their impulses, they are able to learn. The true value of play is not that it directly gives children knowledge, but that it provides children with the skills they need in order to gain knowledge in other contexts.

Last, social competence is related to play. Like language ability, social competence has both procedural and declarative components. Social skills, or the implicit understanding of how to interact with others, are procedural knowledge. Explicit knowledge of social rules (e.g., being able to explain that one is supposed to share), by contrast, is declarative knowledge. The association between play and social competence is hardly surprising, given that much of children's play occurs with other people. Even solitary play is sometimes social, as when children create imaginary companions, impersonate characters, or engage in hypothetical conversations. Once again, play is practice. Through play, children gain more experience in being a social partner and engaging in social behavior. But again it is important to ask: What exactly are children learning about being a social partner through these play experiences?

Research shows that play is correlated with children's theory of mind, or the ability to see the world from someone else's point of view and to understand another person's mental states and behaviors. This relationship holds in the preschool period (Taylor & Carlson, 1997), as well as in middle childhood (Goldstein & Winner, 2010). The bulk of the research investigating the relationship between play and theory of mind has focused specifically on pretend play. Pretend play is considered by many to be an important precursor to, or even an early manifestation of, theory of mind ability (Leslie, 1987; Lillard, 1993). This is because, in pretend play, children can take on another's point of view by becoming someone other than themselves or they can create scenarios that allow them to explore emotions or situations they cannot in the real world. It is thought that through these experiences, rather than through direct instruction, children gradually realize that not everyone sees the world as they do, and they come to understand the connections between people's emotions, desires, beliefs, and actions.

Despite lingering questions about exactly how play contributes to better language, executive function, and social abilities, the fact that play is associated with all of these positive outcomes suggests that play is an important mechanism for procedural learning. Indeed, this link between play and procedural learning makes considerable sense given what we know about the procedural system. Specifically, learning in this system occurs subconsciously and as the result of multiple experiences, not all at once. Furthermore, it is performance based, not recollection based (Squire, 2004). Play would seem to be the perfect context for this type of learning, considering both how frequently children play and that play is a largely repetitive and action-based activity.

Can Children Acquire Declarative Knowledge in Play?

In contrast to procedural knowledge, declarative knowledge is concrete and is acquired consciously and rapidly (Squire, 2004). We know that children can obtain declarative knowledge from a variety of sources, including their own direct experiences and others' testimony. But can they learn this type of information while in a playful state? In order to acquire declarative knowledge in play, children would first have to encounter novel information while playing. In certain situations this would be possible, such as when children play with a more knowledgeable partner or use an object in a novel way. However, the child also must accept the novel information as true. Considering that play is, by definition, a non-serious activity that is often divorced from reality, it may not seem like a context that would afford easy learning of declarative information. Surprisingly little empirical research addresses this exact issue, but what we do know suggests that only appropriately structured reality play is a reliable source of declarative knowledge.

Reality Play: Objects and Games

Piaget proposed that young children are "little scientists," and that play is actually children performing mini-experiments with the objects and people in their environments (Piaget & Inhelder, 1969/2000). He argued that these playful experiences allow children to construct knowledge about real-world principles. In a recent line of studies, Schulz and her colleagues tested Piaget's hypothesis by investigating whether preschoolers' exploratory play can reveal information about cause and effect. In one study, children were given experience with a toy during a structured play session with an adult. When the experience did not reveal exactly how the toy worked, children continued to play with it more during a free play period, compared to children who were initially given unambiguous experience with the toy (Schulz & Bonawitz, 2007). Furthermore, the children given ambiguous experience tended to play with the toy in such a way that allowed them to learn on their own how the toy worked, suggesting that children are motivated to fill gaps in their existing knowledge through experimentation.

But sometimes children fail to discover the properties of objects in play. Cook, Goodman, and Schulz (2011) showed preschoolers a novel machine that activated when it came in contact with certain beads. Children saw it activate for all or some individual beads, paired beads that were separable, and nonseparable paired beads. Then children were left alone to play with the machine and paired beads. The authors observed whether children behaved in a way that would accurately test which bead(s) caused the machine to activate. They found that the demonstration largely affected how the children played. Children who initially saw 100% of the individual beads activate the machine did not structure their play to determine how the machine worked (e.g., separate the beads and test each one). But approximately half of the children who initially saw only 50% of the individual beads activate the machine experimented during their play in a way that revealed the causal relation between the beads and the machine. Furthermore, the authors note that some of these children's behaviors were creative, novel actions, not simply imitations of the experimenter. This study suggests that although play can provide opportunities for learning about real-world principles like causality, play materials must have the right affordances and be presented appropriately in order to do so.

The structure of play materials may also be important. Just as an adult can influence the focus of a child's attention, an object's affordances can also highlight specific properties or relationships. Ramani and Siegler (2008) designed and tested whether a simple board game could increase preschoolers' numerical understanding. Children played a board game with an adult experimenter where the goal was to be the first to move a token forward ten squares. The squares were presented in a straight line. For half of the children the squares contained the numbers 1–10; for the other half, the squares had alternating colors but no numbers. After playing the game four times over the course of 2 weeks, children in the numbers condition showed significant improvement on a variety of measures of numerical understanding, like number identification and counting, but children in the color condition did not. Furthermore, the numeracy gains made by children in the number condition were still apparent 2 months later. In a subsequent study, the game board was modified so that the numbers were arranged in a circle instead of a straight line. This modest change was enough to affect children's learning: children who played this version scored no better than children who played the color version (Siegler & Ramani, 2009). This example illustrates just how influential the configuration of children's play materials can be. In order to learn, play must be set up in a way that facilitates knowledge acquisition.

However, structure can also be limiting. In pedagogical contexts, adults may actually inhibit children's exploration and learning. In a recent experiment (Bonawitz et al., 2011), preschoolers were allowed to freely play with a novel object. Prior to the play, some preschoolers were taught about one of the object's four novel causal properties, some watched the adult "accidentally" discover the property, and others did not see an adult interact with the object. Children who were in the teaching condition ended up learning significantly *less* about the object overall than children in the other two conditions, likely due to the fact that they spent significantly more time performing the specific action demonstrated by the adult.

Children clearly can acquire knowledge about real-world concepts through object play and games. However, there are two important lessons we can take from the research on children's object play and their declarative knowledge: (1) just because children *can* learn from play, does not mean they *will* learn; and (2) adult influence may have both positive and negative effects on children's acquisition of declarative knowledge. Thus the implications for parents and teachers are complex. On one hand, a more knowledgeable adult can highlight something that a child might not have discovered on his or her own during free play (Klahr & Nigam, 2004). In addition, the inferences preschoolers make as a result of their free play may not always be completely accurate (Schulz, Gopnik, & Glymour, 2007), so they might benefit from adult oversight to avoid drawing incorrect conclusions. On the other hand, adults may focus children's attention too narrowly, curbing their exploration and learning. To help children learn about the real world, play time should be balanced between direct instruction and allowing children to uncover knowledge on their own, in an environment structured to afford self-discovery.

Pretend and Fantasy Play

Children spend a remarkable amount of their free time engaged in pretense and fantasy play. Pretend play, sometimes called symbolic play, occurs when an individual intentionally mentally represents both reality and a modified version of reality at the same time (Lillard, 1993). Fantasy play is simply a subset of pretend play that involves the pretender representing some object, place, event, action, or property that could not exist in the real world. Take, for example, a child pretending a stick is a magic wand. By using the stick as a stand-in for a magic wand, the child is using the stick symbolically (hence, the term "symbolic play"). Mentally, the child is thought to be representing both the stick and a magic wand in a "layered" fashion (Perner, 1991). That is, one representation is layered over the other so that they remain separate—both the stick and the wand are mentally active at the same time, yet the two representations do not merge. In the child's mind, the stick does not actually become a wand. Last, and most crucially, the child is fully aware of this dual representation. If the child performed the exact same actions but had a different intention (e.g., if he or she *believed* the stick was a magic wand), this would not be a pretend action.

Pretend and fantasy play present a considerable challenge for declarative knowledge acquisition. Children are interacting with both the real world and an alternative version of the world when they are engaged in pretense. In this situation, if children encounter something new, how can they know whether this novel information belongs to the real world or the pretend one? Imagine two children pretending to cook. One child says, "I'll mix the glicks into the batter to make it sweet." The second child has never heard the word *glick* before, but she or he has experienced the action of mixing batter many times in the real world. What is this child to think? Glicks could be a real ingredient that she or he has not happened to encounter yet. Or glicks could simply be a made-up, fantastical addition to the play scenario. If the former is true, this child has an opportunity to learn a new word and a new type of food. But if the latter is true, it would be best if the child left any information they encounter about glicks, like the fact that they are sweet, in the pretend world. This would prevent the child from trying to use this new fact in the real world, such as asking for "glick cookies" at a bakery.

Leslie (1987) termed this problem—the potential to acquire incorrect knowledge in pretense—*representational abuse*. He proposed that children solve this problem by cognitively "quarantining" representations of pretense in order to protect and maintain accurate representations of the real world. This would effectively prevent declarative knowledge acquisition in pretense. Subsequent theories of pretense also acknowledge that pretend and real representations must remain mentally separate (e.g., Amsel & Smalley, 2000; Harris, 2000; Lillard, 2001; Nichols & Stich, 2000; Van Reet & Lillard, 2007).

Despite widespread agreement that pretense must be cognitively quarantined, no empirical evidence yet exists to support these theories. However, there is considerable evidence that young children keep their declarative knowledge about the real world distinct from their knowledge about pretend worlds (Woolley, 1997). Children as young as 4 years know the reality status of most entities, for instance correctly categorizing dragons as "not real" but dinosaurs as "real" (Samuels & Taylor, 1994; Wellman & Estes, 1986). Furthermore, they attribute different biological, social, and physical properties to real and fantastical entities (Sharon & Woolley, 2004). Even children with imaginary companions appear to have little doubt about the difference(s) between real friends and pretend ones (Taylor, 1999).

Establishing boundaries between reality and pretense is an impressive cognitive feat, especially considering this ability is present in preschoolers. Children's next challenge is to determine the rigidity or flexibility of these boundaries. For instance, if I am pretending to have a tea party, many of the rules and conventions that are true in the real world are probably also true in the pretend world I create. If I drop my teacup, it will fall because the laws of gravity still apply. If I pretend to eat all of the cake, my playmates will likely protest because they recognize this as a violation of real-world social etiquette. Considering how often children bring their real-world knowledge into their pretend worlds, the boundary between pretense and reality must not be impermeable. But does information flow both ways? Do children take information from pretense back into the real world?

In order to do this, children would first have to determine whether a piece of knowledge belongs in the real world or in the pretend one. They may use a variety of evidence to make these ontological judgments. For one, they may be sensitive to social cues given by playmates. For instance, mothers interacting with their young children engage in a particular sequence of behaviors—acting, eye contact, smiling—when pretending (Nishida & Lillard, 2007). The combination of eye contact and smiling directly after a pretend action might serve as a signal to a child that what she or he is seeing is not real. Once children identify a pretend action, they typically respond in kind. After watching an adult pretend to draw, children as young as 2 years old will also pretend. When the adult does the same exact physical behavior without pretending (e.g., tries but fails to draw), children do not pretend; rather, they imitate the adult's intention (i.e., drawing; Rakoczy, Tomasello, & Striano, 2004). In another study, children who were shown how to use a novel object during pretense subsequently used it less and were less creative when given the opportunity to play with the object than children who saw a real-world demonstration (Rakoczy, Tomasello, & Striano, 2005). If children adopt the mental state of an adult model, it follows that young children should be taught new information in a real-world context, not a pretend one.

Children may also take supporting evidence into account when deciding what is real and what is not. For example, direct experience is often privileged over others' testimony. Children who experienced a novel fantasy figure called the Candy Witch were more likely to believe in her than children who only heard about her (Woolley, Boerger, & Markman, 2004). In fact, children may believe in some fantasy figures, like Santa Claus and the Easter Bunny, for much longer than other fantastical entities, like fairies and witches, due to the large, consistent amount of "evidence" they experience (Woolley, 1997). Another clue children may use to determine reality status is the context surrounding the information. When children are told about a novel entity in relation to a known fantastical entity (e.g., ghosts collect surnits), they are more likely to judge it as pretend than when the same entity is presented in relation to a known real entity (Woolley & Van Reet, 2006). If children assume that new information encountered in a pretend context belongs to the pretend world and not the real one, they may not bring knowledge from pretense or fantasy play back into the real world. This again suggests that the potential to learn declarative information about reality in pretense may be low.

In addition to differentiating between the pretend world and the real world, children also draw clear distinctions between different pretend worlds. When asked whether one fantastical character could talk to or see a character from a different story (e.g., would Batman know SpongeBob SquarePants?), both preschoolers and adults claimed that the characters could have no contact with each other. Furthermore, they claimed that characters from one fantastical world would think that the characters in the other fantastical world were make-believe (Skolnick & Bloom, 2006). The construction of boundaries between worlds is also seen in children's pretend play with objects. When preschoolers engage in multiple simple pretend situations with an experimenter, they appear reluctant to use an object from one scenario in a subsequent scenario, even when it is appropriate. After using a block as a pillow when pretending to put one doll to bed, for example, children are more likely to pick a new block when a character in a different story needs a pillow rather than use the original pillow block (Weisberg & Bloom, 2009).

One way to assess the question of whether children take information from pretense back into reality is to see what children remember about a pretense scenario after it is over. Studies testing whether children can recall the real and pretend identities of objects used in pretense have reported mixed results. Gopnik and Slaughter (1991) reported that 3- and 4-year-olds had no trouble remembering an object's previous pretend identity, but Amsel, Bobadilla, Coch, and Remy (1996) found that children sometimes failed to remember an object's pretend identity, although they could reproduce the pretend action (see also Wyman, Rackoczy, & Tomasello, 2009). This indicates that children had an implicit, procedural memory of the scenario but an incomplete explicit, declarative one. Complicating this story further, sometimes children fail to remember the object's *real* identity (Foley, Harris, & Hermann, 1994). After pretending a block is a car, they sometimes claim that they actually used a toy car, not a block. These discrepant findings suggest that young children's explicit memories of their previous pretense may be tenuous. Although they are sometimes able to correctly report on their actions, they often confuse the real and pretend identities of the objects they used. In other words, pretense does not appear to readily support the creation of autobiographical declarative knowledge, at least not for young children.

Richert and her colleagues have also explored these issues, asking whether children can transfer knowledge to and from fantasy in the domain of analogical problem solving. In one set of studies (Richert, Shawber, Hoffman, & Taylor, 2009), 3- through 6-year-old children heard several vignettes, each describing a problem with its solution. In some vignettes, the main characters were real, while in others, they were fantastical. Next, children were asked to solve novel, yet structurally similar, problems. Again, these problems sometimes featured a fantastical character and sometimes a real character. By and large, children were less likely to transfer the solution from the original vignette to solve the novel problem when the characters were fantastical. This effect was especially pronounced in younger children and children with low interest in fantasy.

Young children's difficulty in transferring solutions from fantasy to reality also occurs outside of the laboratory environment. Richert and Smith (2011) read stories describing how characters solved two different problems to 3- to 5-year-old children. For half of the children, the story occurred in a fantasy world; for the other half, it was set in the real world. Later, after ensuring that the children remembered the solutions presented in book, children were presented with novel problems similar to the ones from the story. As in the previous study, children who were read the story set in the real-world were more likely to successfully use the solution from the story to solve the novel problems than when the story was set in a fantasy world.

Taken together, this research showing children's understanding of the pretend–reality distinction and their unwillingness to take information from the pretend world back to the real world suggests that pretend contexts and fantastical content should be used cautiously and sparingly in lessons for young children. Furthermore, adults should be modest in their expectations of what children may learn about the real world from pretend and fantastical play, as well as from books, television, and movies featuring fantastical settings and characters.

Summary and Conclusion

When considering whether children can acquire new knowledge through play, we must remember that knowledge is not a single construct. The declarative memory system governs our concrete knowledge of the world and our lives, like who George Washington was and what we ate for breakfast this morning. Our other knowledge, like knowing to wait to take a turn or how to communicate a thought appropriately, is implicit and is processed by separate cognitive and neural systems. Research strongly suggests that play contributes in some way to procedural knowledge acquisition, namely in the domains of language and literacy, self-regulation, and social competence. However, plenty of questions remain, such as the causal direction of these relationships and precisely what components of play are responsible for positive outcomes.

Whether play can foster declarative knowledge acquisition is an interesting and important question. It is also one in need of much more empirical research. The various studies reviewed in this chapter all touch on this issue in some way, yet most of this research was not intended to directly assess whether children can learn about reality in pretense (studies by Richert and her colleagues are the notable exceptions). Nonetheless, the reviewed research hints that play, especially pretend and fantasy play, may not be a reliable source of declarative knowledge. Although children are quite good at keeping reality and pretense/fantasy distinct, and this ability helps them preserve their real-world knowledge, they may also judge new information learned in pretend contexts (e.g., how to use novel objects, novel entities, solutions to novel problems) as less reliable than information encountered in real-world contexts.

Reality-oriented play, in contrast, appears to have much greater potential to support declarative knowledge acquisition. Children can learn real-world principles, like causality and numeracy, through play with objects and games. However, play must happen under certain conditions in order for learning to occur. Specifically, both the environment and adults' behavior can either facilitate or impede children's learning.

To make declarative knowledge acquisition in play more likely, adults are recommended to avoid providing too much direct instruction while structuring children's environment in a way that makes it easy for children to discover information on their own.

Play is both an integral part of childhood and a powerful mechanism for both cognitive and social development. In this chapter, I have argued that the true value of play is not that it can teach children facts, but that it can help them acquire important procedural knowledge. This procedural knowledge may be especially useful for acquiring subsequent declarative knowledge. Before children can learn vocabulary words and multiplication tables, they must first possess certain skills, like how to formulate a question and how to pay attention to a teacher. Play can provide the opportunity to develop, practice, and strengthen this fundamental procedural knowledge in the early years, building the foundation for later social and academic success.

ACKNOWLEDGMENTS

This chapter was supported in part by a Committee on Aid to Faculty Research award from Providence College and by RI-INBRE Award No. P20RR016457-10 from the National Center for Research Resources (NCRR), National Institutes of Health (NIH). The content is solely the responsibility of the author and does not necessarily represent the official views of the NCRR or the NIH.

REFERENCES

Amsel, E., Bobadilla, W., Coch, D., & Remy, R. (1996). Young children's memory for the true and pretend identities of objects. *Developmental Psychology, 32,* 479–491.

Amsel, E., & Smalley, D. (2000). Beyond really and truly: Children's counterfactual thinking about pretend and possible worlds. In P. Mitchell & K. J. Riggs (Eds.), *Children's reasoning and the mind* (pp. 121–148). East Sussex, UK: Psychology Press.

Blair, C., & Razza, R. P. (2007). Relating effortful control, executive function, and false belief understanding to emerging math and literacy ability in kindergarten. *Child Development, 78,* 647–663.

Bonawitz, E., Shafto, P., Gweon, H., Goodman, N. D., Spelke, E., & Schulz, L. (2011). The double-edged sword of pedagogy: Teaching limits children's spontaneous exploration and discovery. *Cognition, 120,* 322–330.

Cook, C., Goodman, N. D., & Schulz, L. E. (2011). Where science starts: Spontaneous experiments in preschoolers' exploratory play. *Cognition, 120,* 341–349.

Diamond, A., Barnett, W. S., Thomas, J., & Munro, S. (2007). Preschool program improves cognitive control. *Science, 317,* 1387–1388.

Elias, C. L., & Berk, L. E. (2002). Self-regulation in young children: Is there a role for sociodramatic play? *Early Childhood Research Quarterly, 17,* 216–238.

Foley, M. A., Harris, J., & Hermann, S. (1994). Developmental comparisons of the ability to discriminate between memories for symbolic play enactments. *Developmental Psychology, 30,* 206–217.

Goldstein, T. R., & Winner, E. (2010). Engagement in role play, pretense, and acting classes predict advanced theory of mind skill in middle childhood. *Imagination, Cognition and Personality, 30,* 249–258.

Gopnik, A., & Slaughter, V. (1991). Young children's understanding of changes in their mental states. *Child Development, 62,* 89–109.

Harris, P. L. (2000). *The work of the imagination.* Oxford, UK: Blackwell.

Hirsh-Pasek, K., Golinkoff, R. M., Berk, L. E., & Singer, D. G. (2009). *A mandate for playful learning in preschool: Presenting the evidence.* New York: Oxford University Press.

Klahr, D., & Nigam, M. (2004).The equivalence of learning paths in early science instruction: Effects of direct instruction and discovery learning. *Psychological Science, 61,* 661–667.

Leslie, A. M. (1987). Pretense and representation: The origins of "theory of mind." *Psychological Review, 94,* 412–422.

Lillard, A. S. (1993). Pretend play skills and the child's theory of mind. *Child Development, 64,* 348–371.

Lillard, A. S. (2001). Pretend play as Twin Earth: A social-cognitive analysis. *Developmental Review, 21,* 495–531.

Lum, J., Kidd, E., Davis, S., & Conti-Ramsden, G. (2010). Longitudinal study of declarative and procedural memory in primary school-aged children. *Australian Journal of Psychology, 62,* 139–148.

National Association for the Education of Young Children. (2009). *Developmentally appropriate practice in early childhood programs serving children from birth through age 8.* Retrieved June 2011 from *www.naeyc.org/positionstatements/dap.*

Neuman, S. B., & Roskos, K. (1992). Literacy objects as cultural tools: Effects on children's literacy behaviors in play. *Reading Research Quarterly, 27,* 202–225.

Nichols, S., & Stich, S. P. (2000). A cognitive theory of pretense. *Cognition, 74,* 115–147.

Nicolopoulou, A., McDowell, J., & Brockmeyer, C. (2006). Narrative play and emergent literacy: Storytelling and story-acting meet journal writing. In D. G. Singer, R. M. Golinkoff, & K. Hirsh-Pasek, (Eds.), *Play = learning: How play motivates and enhances children's cognitive and social-emotional growth* (pp. 124–144). New York: Oxford University Press.

Nishida, T. K., & Lillard, A. S. (2007). The informative value of emotional expressions: "Social referencing" in mother–child pretense. *Developmental Science, 10,* 205–212.

Pearson, B. L., Russ, S. W., & Cain Spannagel, S. A. (2008). Pretend play and positive psychology: Natural companions. *The Journal of Positive Psychology, 3,* 110–119.

Pellegrini, A. D. (2009). *The role of play in human development.* New York: Oxford University Press.

Perner, J. (1991). *Understanding the representational mind.* Cambridge, MA: MIT Press.

Petitto, L. A., & Marentette, P. F. (1991). Babbling in the manual mode: Evidence for the ontogeny of language. *Science, 251,* 1493–1496.

Piaget, J., & Inhelder, B. (2000). *The psychology of the child.* New York: Basic Books. (Original work published 1969)

Rakoczy, H., Tomasello, M., & Striano, T. (2004).Young children know that trying is not pretending: A test of the "behaving-as-if" construal of children's early concept of pretense. *Developmental Psychology, 40,* 388–399.

Rakoczy, H., Tomasello, M., & Striano, T. (2005). On tools and toys: How children learn to act on and pretend with "virgin objects." *Developmental Science, 8,* 57–73.

Ramani, G. B., & Siegler, R. S. (2008). Promoting broad and stable improvements in low-income children's numerical knowledge through playing number board games. *Child Development, 79,* 375–394.

Richert, R. A., Shawber, A. B., Hoffman, R. E., & Taylor, M. (2009). Learning from fantasy and real characters in preschool and kindergarten. *Journal of Cognition and Development, 10,* 41–66.

Richert, R. A., & Smith, E. I. (2011). Preschoolers' quarantining of fantasy stories. *Child Development, 82,* 1106–1119.

Samuels, A., & Taylor, M. (1994). Children's ability to distinguish fantasy events from real-life events. *British Journal of Developmental Psychology, 12,* 417–427.

Saracho, O. N., & Spodek, B. (2006). Young children's literacy-related play. *Early Child Development and Care, 176,* 707–721.

Schulz, L. E., & Bonawitz, E. B. (2007). Serious fun: Preschoolers engage in more exploratory play when evidence is confounded. *Developmental Psychology, 43,* 1045–1050.

Schulz, L. E., Gopnik, A., & Glymour, C. (2007). Preschool children learn about causal structure from conditional interventions. *Developmental Science, 10,* 322–332.

Sharon, T. L., & Woolley, J. D. (2004). Do monsters dream? Children's understanding of the fantasy-reality distinction. *British Journal of Developmental Psychology, 22,* 293–310.

Sherry, D. F., & Schacter, D. L. (1987). The evolution of multiple memory systems. *Psychological Review, 94,* 439–454.

Siegler, R. S., & Ramani, G. B. (2009). Playing linear number board games—but not circular ones—improves low-income preschoolers' numerical understanding. *Journal of Educational Psychology, 101,* 545–560.

Singer, D. G., Golinkoff, R. M., Hirsh-Pasek, K. (Eds.). (2006). *Play = learning: How play motivates and enhances children's cognitive and social-emotional growth.* New York: Oxford University Press.

Skolnick, D., & Bloom, P. (2006).What does Batman think about SpongeBob? Children's understanding of the fantasy/fantasy distinction. *Cognition, 101,* B9–B18.

Squire, L. R. (2004). Memory systems of the brain: A brief history and current perspective. *Neurobiology of Learning and Memory, 82,* 171–177.

Tamis-LeMonda, C. S., & Bornstein, M. H. (1994). Specificity in mother-toddler language-play relations across the second year. *Developmental Psychology, 30,* 283–292.

Taylor, M. (1999). *Imaginary companions and the children who create them.* New York: Oxford University Press.

Taylor, M., & Carlson, S. M. (1997). The relation between individual differences in fantasy and theory of mind. *Child Development, 68,* 436–455.

Van Reet, J. (2011, May). *Inhibitory control facilitates pretense quality in young preschoolers.* Poster presented at the meeting of the American Psychological Society, Washington D.C.

Van Reet, J., & Boguszewski, K. (2011, October). *Specifying the relationship between pretense and inhibitory control in preschoolers.* Poster presented at the biennial meeting of the Cognitive Development Society, Philadelphia, PA.

Van Reet, J. & Lillard, A. S. (2007, March). *Preliminary evidence for the inhibition/activation theory of pretense representation.* Paper presented at the biennial meeting of the Society for Research in Child Development, Boston, MA.

Weisberg, D. S., & Bloom, P. (2009). Young children separate multiple pretend worlds. *Developmental Science, 12,* 699–705.

Wellman, H. M., & Estes, D. (1986). Early understanding of mental entities: A reexamination of childhood realism. *Child Development, 57,* 910–923.

Whitebread, D., Coltman, P., Jameson, H., & Lander, R. (2009). Play, cognition and self-regulation: What exactly are children learning when they learn through play? *Educational and Child Psychology, 26,* 40–52.

Woolley, J. D. (1997). Thinking about fantasy: Are children fundamentally different thinkers and believers from adults? *Child Development, 68,* 991–1011.

Woolley, J. D., Boerger, E. A., & Markman, A. B. (2004). A visit from the Candy Witch: Factors influencing young children's belief in a novel fantastical being. *Developmental Science, 7,* 456–468.

Woolley, J. D., & Van Reet, J. (2006). Effects of context on judgments concerning the reality status of novel entities. *Child Development, 77,* 1778–1793.

Wyman, E., Rakoczy, H., & Tomasello, M. (2009).Young children understand multiple pretend identities in their object play. *British Journal of Developmental Psychology, 27,* 385–404.

CHAPTER 3

■ ■ ■ ■ ■

How Children Understand and Use Other People as Sources of Knowledge

CHILDREN'S SELECTIVE USE OF TESTIMONY

Sherryse L. Corrow
Jason Cowell
Sabine Doebel
Melissa A. Koenig

Throughout our lives, we are frequently faced with the task of gaining new knowledge. Although we may learn a lot through direct observation, some knowledge can only be acquired through the assistance of others. Our knowledge of language, history, and geography, for example, depends on what other people tell us. In the present chapter, we address how children learn from other people. Specifically, we review research on children's evaluation of others' testimony; that is, how children determine whether the assertions that speakers make and share are credible and should be treated as reliable evidence (Harris & Koenig, 2006). Testimony research focuses on the set of cues children use to distinguish knowledgeable from less knowledgeable speakers, the assumptions children bring to their everyday interactions, whether these assumptions vary by culture and age, and the shared mechanisms that might underlie social learning in human ontogeny. Because a great deal of important cultural and world knowledge cannot be derived solely from direct experiences with the environment, children's ability to learn from others' testimony is thus crucial to both the breadth and depth of their knowledge.

Although a relatively new area of research, the issues addressed by testimony researchers build upon classic theories. Piaget (1970) stressed that children are active agents in their own knowledge acquisition. He proposed that children construct their knowledge through interactions between their progressively developing intelligence, experiences with concrete objects, and experiences of phenomena in the real world. But while children may be active agents in their own knowledge, they are far from independent. According to Vygotsky (1978), children are embedded within particular sociocultural contexts; to understand children's acquisition of knowledge, one must understand the culture and context in which they develop. From a Vygotskian perspective, the motivation for knowledge acquisition resides within the relation between children and significant adults. Demonstration and assistance from more knowledgeable members of the surrounding culture, for example, are considered crucial for advancing children's cognitive development.

Drawing from these historical perspectives, the study of testimony may be viewed as an integration of the active child pursuing his or her own epistemic aims and the influence of outside sources scaffolding and providing new knowledge. In the pursuit of knowledge that is not directly observable, children must rely on others (Koenig, Clément, & Harris, 2004; Pasquini, Corriveau, Koenig, & Harris, 2007). As Vygotsky emphasized, social input plays a primary role in children's learning. The goal of testimony researchers is to understand the nature of children's active participation and evaluation of this social input.

In this chapter, we examine how children utilize others' testimony to advance their own knowledge acquisition. First, we review evidence of young children's selective trust when acquiring knowledge from others, highlighting the many ways in which children use testimony to guide their learning. We next discuss why past inaccuracy may be a particularly salient cue in guiding children's decisions about whom to trust, and then consider possible mechanisms underlying their selective trust. Finally, we address possible implications of the recent findings on how children use testimony to their guide learning and provide future directions for this growing area of research.

Children's Selective Trust in Testimony

Within the last 10 years, an impressive amount of literature has demonstrated that from a young age, children are sensitive to the fact that people may be more or less reliable in their ability to convey accurate information about the world. Children rely on an impressive range of cues to critically judge speakers and assess the reliability of their testimony. Their use of these cues demonstrates how children are active in constructing their own knowledge while also relying on outside sources (e.g., parents and teachers) to scaffold their knowledge acquisition.

In one of the first studies of its kind, Koenig et al. (2004) asked whether young children are uncritical, indiscriminate recipients of testimony or whether they critically evaluate sources of new information. In the basic paradigm, children first observe two adults labeling familiar objects. One adult labels the objects accurately (e.g., "That is a ball"); the other adult labels the objects inaccurately (e.g., labeling a ball a *shoe*). Children are then asked to make an explicit judgment about the reliability of each informant (e.g., "Did one of these people say something right? Did one of these people say something wrong?"). In the next phase, children are shown an unfamiliar object. The accurate and inaccurate speakers each provide a different label for that object, and children are asked to endorse one of the two labels.

If children are simply credulous and uncritical of new testimony, it is likely that they would be equally willing to accept either label as the name of the unfamiliar object. However, Koenig et al. (2004) found that 3- and 4-year-old children were more likely to endorse the label provided by the accurate than the inaccurate informant. These results provide evidence that children use a speaker's past reliability to extend selective trust when learning new information. Subsequent research has shown that 3- and 4-year-old children also (1) distinguish between inaccurate and accurate speakers, (2) predict speakers' future assertions, and (3) preferentially seek and accept information from speakers who were accurate in the past (e.g., Birch, Vauthier, & Bloom, 2008; Clément, Koenig, & Harris, 2004; Koenig & Harris, 2005; Pasquini et al., 2007; Scofield & Behrend, 2008). Furthermore, using modified procedures, selective learning has been documented in children as young as 24 months (Ganea, Koenig, & Millet, 2011; Koenig & Woodward, 2010). Collectively, this research demonstrates that when young children lack prior knowledge about a given topic, they have recourse to an important protective strategy: extending their trust to previously accurate informants.

Encountering consistently accurate (or inaccurate) speakers in everyday life, however, is rare. People occasionally make mistakes in their testimony; they may also intentionally provide erroneous information in an effort to deceive. When evaluating whether someone is a reliable informant, it is important to be able to evaluate whether the speaker is accurate or inaccurate *most* of the time. To investigate whether children differentiate speakers based on relative (in)accuracy, 3- and 4-year-old children encountered informants who correctly labeled familiar objects either all of the time (100%) or most of the time (75%) and informants who were correct either some of the time (25%) or none of the time (0%) (Pasquini et al., 2007). When later asked to endorse a novel label, 3-year-olds significantly preferred the speaker who provided correct labels for 100% of the familiar objects; however, their performance did not differ from chance when the speaker was only relatively accurate. In contrast, 4-year-olds differentiated between the two speakers across all contrasts. Even when one speaker was correct 75% of the time and the other only 25% of the time, 4-year-olds demonstrated selective trust in favor of the more accurate speaker. Therefore, it appears that older preschoolers attended to the relative frequency of errors and used this information to determine whose testimony to trust, whereas younger children required a sharper contrast in accuracy. While 3-year-olds may expect adults to be consistently correct, 4-year-olds may have less rigid expectations and show greater flexibility when extending selective trust on the basis of past accuracy. This age-related variability is consistent with recent research showing that 4- but not 3-year-olds are sensitive to the different reasons why people may provide incorrect information (e.g., benevolent mistake versus intentional deception; Mascaro & Sperber, 2009).

These findings suggest a possible developmental sequence in how children learn to rely on other people as sources of knowledge. If young children are reluctant to learn from speakers who show even rare instances of inaccuracy, this could have implications for their ability to learn new information, particularly when that information is unobservable or nonobvious. By 4 years of age, children appear to make more adult-like global assessments of informants' reliability, forgiving occasional inaccuracies against a backdrop of general reliability and, presumably, facilitating their subsequent knowledge acquisition. However, it is unlikely that 4-year-olds suddenly mature in their ability to track, trust, and utilize others' testimony; rather, this transition is likely gradual. Einav and Robinson (2010), for example, reported age-related changes in children's sensitivity to magnitude of error. In their study, 6- and 7-year-olds showed greater trust in informants who provided answers that were nearly correct (e.g., calling a tiger a *lion*) than informants who provided answers that were less correct (e.g., calling a tiger a *mouse*). Four- and 5-year-olds, by contrast, were not as sensitive to such differences in magnitude of error. Their sensitivity, however, did appear to vary somewhat by domain, suggesting that their ability to reason critically about an informant's errors may be gated by their preexisting semantic and conceptual knowledge. Taken together, these results suggest that, with development, children become more sophisticated in their judgments about what are more and less acceptable errors, whether these errors affect an informant's credibility, and when to use this information to guide their learning.

Although the majority of testimony research has focused on children's learning of new object labels, children may also consider an informant's past accuracy when acquiring knowledge about other domains. Einav and Robinson (2010) demonstrated that children consider magnitude of error when learning about counting. Furthermore, Clément et al. (2004) showed that preschoolers considered prior accuracy when deciding whom to trust in regard to hidden objects' perceptual properties (e.g., color) and functions (Birch et al., 2008; Clément et al., 2004; Koenig & Harris, 2005). Children may also extend selective trust to speakers with a history of morphological accuracy. Using the standard selective-trust paradigm, Corriveau, Pickard, and Harris (2011) demonstrated speakers' accuracy or inaccuracy through morphological errors (e.g., "Here is a *spoon*" vs. "Here is a *spoons*"). When the two informants each presented children with novel morphological forms (e.g., "Yesterday he *glang*" vs. "Yesterday he *glung*"), 4-year-old children preferred the informant with a history of using correct morphological forms.

Testimony research has shown that young children are not passive or overly credulous recipients of new knowledge; rather, they critically evaluate what they are told and selectively trust informants with a past history of reliability and accuracy. As children age and acquire greater conceptual knowledge, their selective trust becomes increasingly sophisticated and nuanced. Due to these abilities, young children appear to be remarkably resilient to learning erroneous information provided by others. They may strategically decide which information to trust and which to ignore, thereby serving as active participants in the learning process.

The Significance of Inaccuracy

As the work reviewed thus far demonstrates, inaccuracy seems to be an especially salient cue for children when deciding whether to trust the information provided by other people. Why is prior inaccuracy so significant for young children? In this section, we review several possible reasons: epistemic significance, group membership, moral significance of inaccuracy, and negativity bias. Although these reasons are likely not mutually exclusive, each has important implications for children's knowledge development.

Epistemic Significance

Inaccurate statements may have direct epistemic significance for children in that they signal or reflect erroneous states of mind. Past inaccuracy may signal to children that an informant either lacks knowledge or is incorrect in their beliefs about a particular domain. This possibility is consistent with research demonstrating that children are more likely to trust knowledgeable informants. When children are told that one informant was knowledgeable and another is not, they are more likely to accept new information provided by the knowledgeable informant (Kushnir, Wellman, & Gelman, 2008). Children are also more likely to accept new words and object functions from speakers who previously demonstrated knowledge about familiar objects (e.g., "It's a ball") than a speaker who demonstrated ignorance (e.g., "I don't know what that is") (Koenig & Harris, 2005; Sabbagh & Baldwin, 2001). Such research suggests that children extend selective trust on the basis of an informant's knowledge. When an informant has a history of inaccuracy, perhaps children interpret this inaccuracy as indicating benevolent ignorance rather than willful deception (Mascaro & Sperber, 2009) and are more likely to treat the informant as an unreliable source of information.

Given that children are generally sensitive to cues that indicate what an informant knows or fails to know, it is perhaps unsurprising that children appear more likely to trust informants who demonstrate expertise in a relevant domain. For example, young children accept that doctors are a better source of information about the causes of runny noses than mechanics (Lutz & Keil, 2002), and adults are better sources of information about the nutritional content of food than children (VanderBorght & Jaswal, 2009). Children also seem to understand that knowledge can be domain specific, and an informant's expertise does not necessarily extend across domains. In recent work, Koenig and Jaswal (2011) contrasted a domain-specific expert (e.g., dog expert) with a nonexpert to examine the boundaries of what children expect experts to know. When asked to identify the breed of an unfamiliar dog, both 3- and 4-year-old children were more likely to endorse a label provided by the dog expert than the nonexpert. Importantly, when asked to identify the name of a novel artifact, children endorsed labels by both speakers equally. These results suggest that children understand that just because someone is an expert in a particular domain does not mean he or she is an expert in all domains.

Although young children may understand that expertise does not extend across domains, they do appear to believe that ignorance in one domain indicates general ignorance. In a second experiment, Koenig and Jaswal (2011) contrasted inexpert informants (e.g., calls a dog *cat*) with neutral speakers. When asked to identify an unfamiliar dog breed, children were more likely to trust the testimony of the neutral speaker. Moreover, they were also more likely to trust the neutral speaker when identifying the name of a novel artifact. This suggests that children may approach unknowledgeable individuals with skepticism, regardless of the type of information being learned. When informants make domain-specific errors, children may interpret this as indicating a lack of knowledge in a more general sense (see also Sobel & Corriveau, 2010).

In addition to considering informants' general expertise, children may also use verbal reports of informational access to guide their learning. Koenig (2012) found that 3- and 4-year-old children selectively trust informants based on the reasons they provide for their responses. For example, one speaker provided a good reason for believing that a particular object was hidden in a box (e.g., "Because I saw it") while a second speaker provided a bad reason for believing a different object was in a box (e.g., "Because I want it to be there"). Children were more likely to believe speakers who provided good epistemic reasons for their beliefs than those who provided bad reasons. This work provides evidence that children consider how informants came to know something when deciding whether to trust the information being provided.

Research on expertise suggests that children may consider an informant's domain-specific knowledge when extending selective trust. Children may also consider an informant's specific knowledge, such as whether he or she has perceptual access to relevant information. Although children demonstrate a greater degree of trust in an expert informant than an ignorant informant, they show undifferentiated trust between the two informants when both are blindfolded and thus denied perceptual access (Kushnir et al., 2008). Children may also excuse past inaccuracy if perceptual access is limited. For example, Nurmsoo and Robinson (2009) presented children with one puppet that was repeatedly inaccurate. The puppet had either limited perceptual access (i.e., could not see the target object) and had an excuse to be inaccurate, or had full perceptual access and thus had no such excuse. Children were more likely to trust the puppet with limited perceptual access, indicating that they are able to use evidence of perceptual access to determine what an informant should or should not know and use this information to guide learning (see also Robinson & Whitcombe, 2003).

Research suggests that children are sensitive to differences in individuals' knowledge and use these differences to guide their subsequent learning. Children are thus active learners who selectively gather information from informants who are most likely to have accurate or reliable knowledge. Children may rely on a heuristic to selectively avoid informants with histories of inaccuracy to improve the likelihood of gaining knowledge that is both reliable and credible.

Group Membership

In addition to evaluating the epistemic knowledge of an informant, children are sensitive to the group membership of informants, such that they are more likely to trust people they judge as being members of their in-group. For example, Kinzler, Corriveau, and Harris (2011) found that children were more likely to trust the testimony of adult speaking in children's native accent than an adult speaking with a foreign accent. This held when both the native and foreign speaker used nonsense words when familiarizing themselves with children. Similarly, children appear more willing to trust a family member than a stranger (Corriveau, Harris, et al., 2009). These findings suggest that children may have a natural tendency to trust people they judge to be a part of their group.

Interestingly, MacDonald (2010) showed that children trust in-group members even for seemingly arbitrary groups. Four-year-olds observed two informants: one informant was correct either 100% or 75% of the time and the other was correct only 25% or 0% of the time. Unlike Pasquini et al. (2007), however, this study also manipulated group membership by assigning children to teams indicated by different shirt colors. Children showed a tendency to trust the more accurate informant when both informants wore the same color shirt, indicating that they were part of the in-group. But when the more reliable informant wore a shirt different from the child (i.e., out-group member) and the less reliable informant wore the same color shirt as the child (i.e., in-group member), children were more likely to trust the in-group informant over the out-group informant regardless of their relative accuracy. Group membership may thus be a possible explanation why children consider an informant's past accuracy to be a salient cue. When an informant incorrectly labels a familiar object, children may interpret this as a signal that the speaker is unaware of the conventions of the child's in-group and is, therefore, a member of a different or unfamiliar social group.

However, children do sometimes privilege past accuracy even when it contrasts with group status. Although children may typically trust family members over strangers, for example, they are more likely to trust labels provided by a previously accurate stranger than labels provided by their previously incorrect parent (Corriveau, Harris, et al., 2009). Importantly, children's attachment security moderated their willingness to extend selective trust toward the more accurate stranger. Secure children were more likely to show flexibility in their trust, initially trusting their parent until he or she proved to be inaccurate. Resistant children, by contrast, were more likely to continue to trust their parent despite their past inaccuracy, whereas avoidant children extended the least amount of trust in their parent, regardless of past accuracy. These findings suggest that children's social-emotional characteristics may influence the flexibility with which they extend selective trust to non-group members.

Collectively, these findings provide evidence that children may prefer information provided by members of their in-group over information provided by members of an out-group. Moreover, under certain conditions, children may even privilege group status over an informant's past accuracy. Given that group status appears to be a salient cue for children, perhaps this accounts for the significance children place on inaccuracy: inaccuracy may be interpreted as a violation of the conventions of the child's group. Future research is necessary to examine this possibility.

Moral Significance

A third possibility is that children interpret inaccurate statements as signaling malevolent intentions and the possibility of being misled. Children may be wary of someone who provides incorrect information because they recognize, on some level, that inaccuracy may signal deliberate lying. Evidence supporting this possibility is provided by Mascaro and Sperber (2009), who demonstrated that 3-year-old children are more likely to endorse new labels provided by a "nice" informant than by a "mean" informant. Furthermore, 5- to 6-year-olds were more likely to describe a "mean" informant who provided wrong information as a "liar" than as being mistaken.

More recently, Doebel and Koenig (in press) asked whether children's learning would be guided by the informant's moral behavior, without being told explicitly that a character was "nice" or "mean." Three-, 4-, and 5-year-old children were presented with two informants: one informant was neutral and the other informant showed either benevolent behavior (e.g., helping a friend pick up a toy) or malevolent behavior (e.g., preventing a friend from reaching a toy). When pitted against the neutral informant, children were more likely to remember the behavior of a malevolent informant than a benevolent one. Furthermore, they were more likely to endorse information provided by a neutral speaker than a malevolent speaker. There were no such learning differences found between neutral speakers and benevolent speakers.

These studies suggest that children use evidence of moral behavior in deciding whom to trust. This pattern is consistent with other research in early cognitive development showing a keen sensitivity to moral information from very early in life. Even infants track moral behavior and prefer an agent who helps another over one who hinders

(Hamlin, Wynn, & Bloom, 2007, 2010). Preschoolers use moral behavioral and trait information to guide their behavioral and trait predictions (Boseovski & Lee, 2006), psychological inferences (Heyman & Gelman, 1999) and moral actions (Vaish, Carpenter, & Tomasello, 2010). Taken together, this research suggests a general aversion to trusting people who exhibit duplicitous behavior. Such early skepticism toward morally problematic sources of information may indeed help children avoid being misled, which may contribute to an overall high standard of quality in the knowledge base.

Negativity Bias

Finally, children may value inaccuracy because of a more general negativity bias, or positive–negative asymmetry (see Koenig & Doebel, in press, for a discussion). Partially because positive events are more likely than negative events, humans tend to be more sensitive to negative events than positive ones, and give greater weight to negative than positive circumstances (e.g., Peeters, 1971; Peeters & Czapinski, 1990; Rozin & Royzman, 2001). Furthermore, negative information and events may be salient for adaptive purposes—negative events tend to be more urgent than positive ones (Peeters & Czapinski, 1990). In the case of deciding which of a pair of informants to trust, children may attend to inaccuracy because of this general bias to attend to the negative.

Evidence of this can be seen in very young children. For example, Koenig and Echols (2003) found that 16-month-old infants look longer at inaccurate informants than at accurate informants. This suggests that children of this age found negative information (i.e., inaccurate labeling) as more worthy of their attention than positive information (i.e., accurate labeling). Furthermore, 3-year-olds systematically avoided an informant who erred only once in labeling familiar objects (Pasquini et al., 2007) and also avoided an inaccurate informant in favor of both an accurate source and a neutral one (Corriveau, Meints, & Harris, 2009). Furthermore, Corriveau, Meints, et al. (2009) demonstrated that when 3-year-old children were presented with a previously accurate informant and one who made neutral comments (i.e., "Look at that one"), they treated them as equally good informants, suggesting that being accurate did not confer any special status to a potential informant. That is, being inaccurate taints trust in an informant's statements, but being accurate is no different from having said nothing—positive information is expected, but negative information has more consequences.

In addition, Koenig and Jaswal (2011) found that children applied a domain-specific filter when receiving information from experts, in that they expected a dog expert to be an expert about dogs only, not artifacts. However, when an informant proved ignorant about dogs, children expected them to be also ignorant about artifacts. That is, children applied a domain-general avoidance of incompetent sources, with no corresponding domain-general belief in competent sources. Furthermore, Doebel and Koenig's (in press) study, mentioned above, also provides evidence for a negativity bias. They found that, when presented with a malevolent (i.e., is unkind to a friend) and a neutral (i.e., engages in parallel play with a friend) informant, children are more likely to trust information provided by the neutral speaker. However, if presented with a benevolent (i.e., is kind to a friend) and a neutral informant, children are no more likely to endorse labels provided by the benevolent speaker than by the neutral speaker. Again, these findings suggest a distinction in the weight that children apply to negative and positive events, and may indicate that children's attention to inaccuracy may be a result of an overall negativity bias.

In summary, although children do attend to positive evidence in their selective trust decisions, children also seem to pay particular attention to evidence that weighs against an informant's moral character or epistemic competence. This tendency to attend to the negative may be one reason that children focus on inaccuracy and track the inaccuracy of individuals. In turn, tracking the inaccuracy of individuals may lead children avoid informants associated with any negative event.

Mechanisms Underlying Selective Trust

The research summarized thus far suggests that young children track an impressive range of behaviors and make use of them in selective learning. However, it is not clear what mechanisms underlie the process by which children go from simply tracking these cues to making a decision about the reliability of a speaker. *How* do children use cues like inaccuracy, malevolent behavior, and group status to determine whom to trust?

There are two major ways to interpret the mechanism by which children determine whom to trust. First, a "rich" interpretation argues that children's use of these cues may be the product of some kind of inferential process concerning the knowledge and intentional states of informants. That is, children may track certain behaviors because they shed light on whether the informant has the capacity, or intention, to provide accurate information. By contrast, a more "lean" interpretation of the extant research would be that children attend to and are guided by behavioral information only, and do not make any inferences about the underlying mental states of their informants (Birch et al., 2008; Lucas &

Lewis, 2010). That is, in avoiding an inaccurate speaker, children may not be exercising mistrust based on their interpretation of the internal state of the informant; they may simply find the informant strange and aversive. For example, when a speaker points out familiar objects and mislabels them (e.g., calling a shoe a *duck*), children may be at a loss to make sense of how the speaker could make such an error, and may simply find them odd. From this perspective, children may not make mental inferences in selective learning, but instead rely solely on behavioral information to guide their trust, such as avoiding an informant whose past behavior has been incomprehensible.

Evidence for the lean view comes from studies that suggest that infants avoid learning from unconventional or incompetent models in general (Chow, Poulin-Dubois, & Lewis, 2008; Zmyj, Buttelmann, Carpenter, & Daum, 2010). For example, Chow et al. (2008) presented infants with individuals who varied on the "reliability" of their gaze. The individuals peered into a container, smiled and exclaimed "Wow!," and then gave the infant an opportunity to inspect. In the unreliable looker condition, the container was empty, whereas in the reliable one it contained a toy. The researchers found that 14-month-old infants were less likely to follow the gaze of an unreliable looker when she looked behind a barrier than when she looked in front of a barrier at an object in full view. This pattern indicates that infants are selective in whom they take cues from when tracking others' gaze. According to the lean view, their tendency to differentially follow the gaze of a reliable versus an unreliable looker is not likely to reflect a deeper understanding of the unreliable looker as epistemically deficient; rather, children are likely to avoid following her gaze because she's strange.

Another interpretation offered by proponents of the lean view is that children use a simple inductive strategy in determining selective trust. They track the output of the speaker and use this information to make a best guess about the quality of future outputs (Birch et al., 2008). In this case, children do not need to make inferences about underlying mental states in order to respond selectively on these tasks; they only have to ignore the informant with a low-quality signal output. According to this interpretation, if an informant's output was bad (i.e., they were incorrect in the familiar labeling trials), they ought to be ignored in subsequent trials in order to avoid further bad input.

Evidence for the rich interpretation of infant behavior in selective trust tasks includes Chow and Poulin-Dubois (2009), who found that infants looked longer when a reliable looker acted in a way that was incongruent versus congruent with their beliefs. Conversely, they showed no such differential looking in the case of an unreliable looker. This pattern suggests that infants appear to predict that a reliable looker acts in accordance with their beliefs, indicating that infants may indeed be making deeper interpretations of the source's behavior (i.e., in terms of the underlying belief states).

Further evidence for the rich interpretation of children's selective trust comes from the many cues children have been shown to use in determining whom to trust. The range of cues that children are sensitive to, which are known to indicate what an informant *knows*, would seem to speak against lean interpretations of selective trust. Specifically, children's sensitivity to domain expertise, perceptual access, and speaker intentions are not easily accounted for under interpretations that make no reference to epistemic understanding. For example, Koenig and Jaswal's (2011) finding that children preferred to learn novel dog names, but not artifacts, from a dog expert suggests that children are not simply avoiding a bizarre informant. In this study, neither speaker was making incorrect claims about the target object. Rather, one informant was providing more specific information than the other, suggesting that they had a greater degree of knowledge about that object. There is nothing odd about a speaker who knows an ordinary amount about dogs (i.e., provides nonspecific labels to different types of dogs) versus one who knows a lot (i.e., provides very specific labels), yet children differentially trust the latter. Furthermore, this study also suggests that children are not using a purely inductive strategy. If children had been only attending to the highest quality signal, they should be more likely to attend to the informant who gave the best information in the first task, no matter the context of the second task. However, children did not overgeneralize their trust in the dog expert to the domain of artifacts, which indicates that they are sensitive to the fact that knowledge in one domain is not a good basis for expecting knowledge in an unrelated one. Finally, when children defer to the testimony of a speaker who had perceptual access over one who did not (Kurshnir et al., 2008; Nurmsoo & Robinson, 2009), it is best explained by children's sensitivity to the link between seeing and knowing.

On the other hand, an example of a selective trust strategy that seems to implicate a low-level bias in children's selective learning is their inclination to prefer the testimony of a familiar informant to that of an unfamiliar one (Corriveau & Harris, 2009; Corriveau et al., 2009). Evidence that children prefer to trust an informant based on familiarity alone suggests that knowledgability does not necessarily need to be a factor in trust, which favors a lean interpretation. However, it is possible that children prefer testimony from a familiar source for reasons other than a low-level familiarity bias, including an extended relationship history that would likely confer some confidence on the part of the child about the informant's general quality as a source of knowledge.

In general, evidence suggesting that children make use of low-level or non-epistemic cues in selective learning does not imply that children do not engage in more sophisticated reasoning about the knowledge states of informants. These two types of strategies, though differing in richness, are not mutually exclusive. In other words, children may use both low-level and higher-level information in selective trust. For example, Corriveau et al. (2009) found that when the mother's testimony conflicted with information that was perceptually available, children deferred to the stranger and rejected their mother's claims. Similarly, children's default trust in an adult shifted to an accurate child when that adult proved previously unreliable (Jaswal & Neely, 2006). Such flexible use of cues to reliability suggests that children actively evaluate information from others rather than passively react to it.

Conclusion

In summary, the experimental work reviewed here has established a great deal of insight into children's ability to selectively learn from informants based on various cues indicating the relative trustworthiness of individuals (e.g., Fusaro & Harris, 2008; Jaswal & Malone, 2007; Pasquini et al., 2007). However, many important issues remain in need of greater attention. For example, the role of children's prior knowledge in how they selectively learn from others needs further investigation. A teacher, parent, or peer may often say things that conflict with children's prior knowledge, which would require some ability to evaluate and compare the prior knowledge against the testimony from others.

In addition, outside of an experimental setting, it is more likely that children receive information by a single source (e.g., a parent or a teacher) than by two conflicting informants. In this case, children must evaluate whether to trust that informant individually, rather than in direct comparison to another. Further investigation of how children make these decisions will have implications for how children receive testimonial information at varying ages, in different learning situations.

Finally, the finding that a positive relationship moderated, to some degree, the flexibility of a child's trust in her mother (Corriveau et al., 2009) has important classroom implications. The presence of positive (or negative) relationships with a teacher may have a direct bearing on the degree to which a child may trust and on how much they may learn from that person. If future work elucidates the importance of the child–teacher relationship in learning, interventions may be developed to help foster this relationship and potentially increase academic success.

Overall, this chapter has provided evidence that children are rather sophisticated in their ability to evaluate the testimony provided by others, whether it be a parent, educator, or even another child. Children use a variety of cues, weighing some more heavily than others, to decide from whom they are willing to learn information. Future work will provide insight as to how our knowledge of children's ability to use testimony in learning can be used to promote learning in a variety of contexts.

REFERENCES

Birch, S. A. J., Vauthier, S. A., & Bloom, P. (2008). Three- and four-year-olds spontaneously use others' past performance to guide their learning. *Cognition, 107*(3), 1018–1034.

Boseovski, J. J., & Lee, K. (2006). Children's use of frequency information for trait categorization and behavioral prediction. *Developmental Psychology, 42*(3), 500–513.

Chow, V., & Poulin-Dubois, D. (2009). The effect of a looker's past reliability on infants' reasoning about beliefs. *Developmental Psychology, 45*(6), 1576–1582.

Chow, V., Poulin-Dubois, D., & Lewis, J. (2008). To see or not to see: Infants prefer to follow the gaze of a reliable looker. *Developmental Science, 11*(5), 761–770.

Clément, F., Koenig, M., & Harris, P. (2004). The ontogenesis of trust. *Mind and Language, 19*(4), 360–379.

Corriveau, K., & Harris, P. L. (2009). Choosing your informant: Weighing familiarity and recent accuracy. *Developmental Science, 12*(3), 426–437.

Corriveau, K. H., Harris, P. L., Meints, E., Fernyhough, C., Arnott, B., Elliott, L., et al. (2009). Young children's trust in their mother's claims: Longitudinal links with attachment security in infancy. *Child Development, 80*(3), 750–761.

Corriveau, K. H., Meints, K., & Harris, P. L. (2009). Early tracking of informant accuracy and inaccuracy. *British Journal of Developmental Psychology, 27*(2), 331–342.

Corriveau, K. H., Pickard, K., & Harris, P. L. (2011). Preschoolers trust particular informants when learning new names and new morphological forms. *British Journal of Developmental Psychology, 29*(1), 46–63.

Doebel, S., & Koenig, M. (in press). Children's use of moral behavior in selective learning: Evidence for a negativity bias. *Developmental Psychology.*

Einav, S., & Robinson, E. J. (2010). Children's sensitivity to error magnitude when evaluating informants. *Cognitive Development, 25*(3), 218–232.

Fusaro, M., & Harris, P. L. (2008). Children assess informant reliability using bystanders' non-verbal cues. *Developmental Science, 11*(5), 771–777.

Ganea, P. A., Koenig, M. A., & Millet, K. G. (2011). Changing your mind about things unseen: Toddler's sensitivity to prior reliability. *Journal of Experimental Child Psychology, 109*(4), 445–453.

Hamlin, J. K., Wynn, K., & Bloom, P. (2007). Social evaluation by preverbal infants. *Nature, 450,* 557–559.

Hamlin, J. K., Wyann, K., & Bloom, P. (2010). Three-month-olds show a negativity bias in their social evaluations. *Developmental Science, 13*(6), 923–929.

Harris, P. L., & Koenig, M. A. (2006). Trust in testimony: How children learn about science and religion. *Child Development, 77*(3), 505–524.

Heyman, G. D., & Gelman, S. A. (1999). The use of trait labels in making psychological inferences. *Child Development, 70*(3), 604–619.

Jaswal, V., & Malone, L. S. (2007). Turning believers into skeptics: 3-year-olds' sensitivity to cues to speaker credibility. *Journal of Cognition and Development, 8*(3), 263–283.

Jaswal, V. K., & Neely, L. A. (2006). Adults don't always know best: Preschoolers use past reliability over age when learning new words. *Psychological Science, 17*(9), 757–758.

Kinzler, K. D., Corriveau, K. H., & Harris, P. L. (2011). Children's selective trust in native-accented speakers. *Developmental Science, 14*(1), 106–111.

Koenig, M. A. (2012). Beyond semantic accuracy: Preschoolers evaluate a speaker's reasons. *Child Development,* 1–13.

Koenig, M. A., Clément, F., & Harris, P. L. (2004). Trust in testimony: Children's use of true and false statements. *Psychological Science, 15*(10), 694–698.

Koenig, M. A., & Doebel, S. (in press). Children's understanding of unreliability: Evidence for a negativity bias. In S. Gelman, & M. Banaji (Eds.), *The development of social cognition.*

Koenig, M. A., & Echols, C. H. (2003). Infants' understanding of false labeling events: The referential roles of words and the speakers who use them. *Cognition, 87*(3), 179–208.

Koenig, M. A., & Harris, P. L. (2005). Preschoolers mistrust ignorant and inaccurate speakers. *Child Development, 76*(6), 1261–1277.

Koenig, M. A., & Jaswal, V. K. (2011). Characterizing children's expectations about expertise and incompetence: Halo or pitchfork effects? *Child Development, 82*(5), 1634–1647.

Koenig, M. A., & Woodward, A. L. (2010). Sensitivity of 24-month-olds to the prior inaccuracy of the source: Possible mechanisms. *Developmental Psychology, 46*(4), 815–826.

Kushnir, T., Wellman, H. M., & Gelman, S. A. (2008). The role of preschoolers' social understanding in evaluating the informativeness of causal interventions. *Cognition, 107*(3), 1084–1092.

Lucas, A. J., & Lewis, C. (2010). Should we trust experiments on trust? *Human Development, 53*(4), 167–172.

Lutz, D. J., & Keil, F. C. (2002). Early understanding of the division of cognitive labor. *Child Development, 73*(4), 1073–1084.

MacDonald, K. (2010). *The influence of group membership on preschoolers' selective trust.* Unpublished manuscript, Psychology Department, Wesleyan University, Middletown, CT.

Mascaro, O., & Sperber, D. (2009). The moral, epistemic, and mindreading components of children's vigilance towards deception. *Cognition, 112*(3), 367–380.

Nurmsoo, E., & Robinson, E. J. (2009). Children's trust in previously inaccurate informants who were well or poorly informed: When past errors can be excused. *Child Development, 80*(1), 23–27.

Pasquini, E. S., Corriveau, K. H., Koenig, M., & Harris, P. L. (2007). Preschoolers monitor the relative accuracy of informants. *Developmental Psychology, 43*(5), 1216–1226.

Peeters, G. (1971). The positive–negative asymmetry: On cognitive consistency and positivity bias. *European Journal of Social Psychology, 1*(4), 455–474.

Peeters, G., & Czapinski, J. (1990). Positive–negative asymmetry in evaluations: The distinction between affective and informational negativity effects. *European Review of Social Psychology, 1,* 33–60.

Piaget, J. (1970). Piaget's theory. In P. H. Mussen (Ed.), *Carmichael's manual of child psychology* (pp. 703–732). New York: Wiley.

Robinson, E. J., & Whitcombe, E. L. (2003). Children's suggestibility in relation to their understanding about sources of knowledge. *Child Development, 74*(1), 48–62.

Rozin, P., & Royzman, E. B. (2001). Negativity bias, negativity dominance, and contagion. *Personality and Social Psychology Review, 5*(4), 296–320.

Sabbagh, M. A., & Baldwin, D. A. (2001). Learning words from knowledgeable versus ignorant speakers: Links between preschoolers' theory of mind and semantic development. *Child Development, 72*(4), 1054–1070.

Scofield, J., & Behrend, D. A. (2008). Learning words from reliable and unreliable speakers. *Cognitive Development, 23*(2), 278–290.

Sobel, D. M., & Corriveau, K. H. (2010). Children monitor individuals' expertise for word learning. *Child Development, 81*(2), 669–679.

Vaish, A., Carpenter, M., & Tomasello, M. (2010). Young children selectively avoid helping people with harmful intentions. *Child Development, 81*(6), 1661–1669.

VanderBorght, M., & Jaswal, V. K. (2009). Who knows best? Preschoolers sometimes prefer child informants over adult informants. *Infant and Child Development, 18*(1), 61–71.

Vygotsky, L. S. (1978). *Mind in society.* Cambridge, MA: Harvard University Press.

Zmyj, N., Buttelmann, D., Carpenter, M., & Daum, M. M. (2010). The reliability of a model influences 14-month-olds' imitation. *Journal of Experimental Child Psychology, 106*(4), 208–220.

CHAPTER 4

■ ■ ■ ■ ■

Beyond Pedagogy

HOW CHILDREN'S KNOWLEDGE DEVELOPS IN THE
CONTEXT OF EVERYDAY
PARENT–CHILD CONVERSATIONS

Maureen Callanan
Jennifer Rigney
Charlotte Nolan-Reyes
Graciela Solis

Everyday conversation is a crucial context in which children first express their intuitive ideas about the natural world and learn by hearing how others respond to these ideas. In contrast to the constructivist focus on children's learning *from* others' directive teaching (e.g., Piaget, 1929), researchers in the sociocultural tradition have argued for many years that development is embedded in the context of social interactions and cultural communities and that learning is not solely an individual cognitive pursuit but socially constructed within communities and through interactions (Cole, 1998; Rogoff, 2003; Tomasello, 2001; Wertsch, 1998). Building on Vygotsky's (1978) insights, recent research has shown that, through social participation in the cultural practices of their community, children may develop not only different content knowledge, but also different ways of thinking (Bang & Medin, 2010; Rogoff et al., 2007). The sociocultural approach thus focuses on how children learn *through* participation with others rather than how they directly appropriate knowledge *from* others.

In our research, we focus on integrating constructivist and sociocultural approaches by examining everyday family conversation as a key setting for children's learning. Our goal in this chapter is to discuss how we have integrated these approaches, taking seriously the proposal that knowledge development is always social and cultural, while also considering how preschool-age children's thinking about the natural world develops in the social context of conversations with others. We specifically focus on two types of parent–child conversations: (1) conversations that guide children in forming domain boundaries, such as the boundary between living and nonliving things; and (2) conversations that focus on causal questions and explanations within science-relevant domains. Focusing on conversation is a way to consider children's thinking in action. Everyday conversations provide opportunities for children to learn not only terms and explanations, but also views about the nature of knowledge and about how best to reach an understanding of the natural world. Although young children are not likely to be aware of "science" as a domain, considerable evidence demonstrates that they often spontaneously wonder about some of the same sorts of scientific questions that scientists pursue and are capable of sophisticated reasoning about meaningful events that they encounter in everyday life (Callanan & Oakes, 1992; National Research Council, 2009; Tizard & Hughes, 1984).

In this chapter, we first discuss our basic theoretical approach and the importance of the social context of children's thinking. Next we present two lines of research focused on two types of parents' conversations with children about science domains. We first consider conversations about naming and describing biological and physical objects that guide children, either in explicit or subtle ways, to draw boundaries between domains. Our second line of research involves the role of questioning and explaining in family science talk. This research clearly links everyday family conversation to the wide-ranging work on inquiry in science learning, as well as to the studies of causal thinking and "theory theory" in developmental psychology (e.g., Gopnik & Wellman, 1994). Finally, we end the chapter by raising questions about implications of our work and important future directions.

Social Contexts of Cognitive Development

Although the social nature of learning has always been fundamental to sociocultural approaches, recent attention to the social context of children's thinking and learning has also emerged within constructivist traditions. Two recent programs of research have taken seriously the notion of social influences on cognitive development. In particular, there has been a recent focus on *pedagogy* and *testimony* as ways in which the social world influences children's thinking and cognitive development.

According to Csibra and Gergely's (2009) theory of natural pedagogy, children are innately biased to attend to certain gaze, gesture, and prosody cues that reveal adults' intentions to teach them something new. In pedagogical contexts, children may learn information easily and expect it to be generalizable. For example, children as young as 13 months are attentive to adults' gaze direction when learning a name for a novel object (Baldwin, 1993; Vaish, Demir, & Baldwin, 2011), and they attend differently to intentional actions than to accidental actions (Carpenter, Akhtar, & Tomasello, 1998). Children's tendency to imitate an unusual action depends on whether there is a rational explanation why a more conventional action was not used: young children would imitate an adult turning on a touch-activated light by tapping it with her head, but they were more likely to turn the light on with their hands if the adult's hands were occupied (Gergely, Bekkering, & Király, 2002). Research exploring children's attention to pedagogical cues is breaking new ground in the study of language and conceptual development.

Research on testimony also highlights the importance of social interactions in development. Testimony is defined as information provided by other people in contrast to information acquired through observation (Harris, 2002; Harris & Koenig, 2006). There are certain entities and processes that children cannot directly observe or figure out on their own, and for which they must take the word or testimony of other people. It is only through conversations with others that many children learn about names for things, germs, God, where babies come from, and the shape of the earth, for example. Experimental work has demonstrated that children show selective trust in testimony depending on a speaker's past accuracy and knowledge (Koenig & Harris, 2005; Sabbagh & Baldwin, 2001). In this growing area of research, investigators are expanding our understanding of the conditions under which children display trust in others' testimony (see Corrow, Cowell, Doebel, & Koenig, Chapter 3, this volume).

At the same time, recent studies have explored the limits of pedagogy and testimony. Pinkham and Jaswal (2011), for example, found an intriguing result using a simple modification of previous tasks. If children were first allowed to explore a touch-activated light, then they were much less likely to follow the unusual pedagogical action of turning the light on with their heads. Furthermore, Bonawitz et al. (2011) discussed the "double-edged sword of pedagogy," providing evidence that pedagogical teaching can sometimes limit children's exploratory behavior. Children showed lower subsequent engagement in exploration of a novel toy when an adult deliberately taught children its function (e.g., "I'm going to show you how my toy works. Watch this!") as compared to when an adult seemed surprised to discover the same function. These studies highlight the important distinction between children's learning *through* observing an adult's actions versus learning something in a directive and linear way *from* an adult.

Although both the pedagogy and testimony approaches have inspired important new conceptual questions and valuable research findings, there are two potential shortcomings to these approaches. First, both approaches assume that parents and others are typically engaged in relatively deliberate and conscious teaching. Second, little attention is typically placed on actual everyday parent–child interactions (but see Henderson & Sabbagh, 2010). An important piece of the puzzle concerns the typical interactions that children engage in with adults, even when adults are focused on everyday goals and not deliberately trying to teach something to their child.

In order to establish the ways that children's learning is supported by social interaction, it is critical to identify how everyday experiences relate to children's thinking, and how these experiences vary for children from diverse backgrounds. Influenced by the sociocultural approach, our research has focused on exploring the conversations parents and children have about topics and processes related to understanding the physical and biological world, with a special focus on the diversity in family conversations, related not only to culture and ethnicity, but also to parents' science background and beliefs about the nature of knowledge. Just as studies of cognitive development must be principled with regard to children's abilities, they must also be principled with regard to the social and pragmatic realities within which children learn and gain knowledge (Callanan & Sabbagh, 2004).

Delineating Domains in Parent–Child Everyday Talk

In the development of language, the words children hear others speak undoubtedly play a crucial role in the learning process. Parents' naming of objects is crucial for early word learning and may invite children to make many inferences, even about unfamiliar objects (Gelman, 2003; Waxman & Markow, 1995). In early work, we found that parents' naming of objects may contribute to children's understanding of conceptual organization, such as hierarchies of concepts and their associated words (Callanan & Jipson, 2001; Callanan & Sabbagh, 2004). Names for objects can also signal important domain boundaries for children. For instance, cultural naming patterns may influence children's concepts of "animal" versus "living thing," leading to variation in their understanding of the animate/inanimate distinction (Angorro, Medin, & Waxman, 2010). However, naming objects is not the only way that parents communicate information about domain boundaries to their children. Subtle use of pronouns (e.g., *he* vs. *it*) and verbs (e.g., *grows, thinks*), for example, can also signal boundaries between physical, biological, and psychological domains.

Children's understanding of such domain distinctions is critical to their later science understanding. In our research on parent–child conversation, we ask whether information is present in conversations that could support children's developing understanding of domain distinctions and domain-specific theories. Clearly, children can learn a great deal through their own exploration (see Kaefer, Chapter 1, this volume); however, not everything can be figured out through observation. Many phenomena are complex and may require verbal explanation, such as the fact that the earth is round even though it looks flat, or that robots are not alive even though they have faces and move around. Parent–child conversations may be particularly informative for the unclear cases of entities that straddle the typical boundaries (Jipson & Gelman, 2007a, 2007b).

Family conversations likely play an important role in guiding children's concepts of both where to draw domain boundaries and the theories that apply to those domains. For example, Jipson and Callanan (2003) examined mothers' use of the word *grow* for things from several different domains that get bigger over time (e.g., a plant growing, a balloon getting bigger, a crystal getting larger). Mothers tended to restrict their use of *grow* to biological increases in size when talking with their children, and tended to use biological explanations when discussing these items (e.g., "He grew because he ate a lot of food"). Although mothers did sometimes use *grow* for nonbiological items such as crystals, in these cases they hedged their use of the term (e.g., "This kinda grows"), did not use biological explanations, and tried to explain this growth in some other way (e.g., chemicals). When children used *grow* for nonbiological items, their mothers tended to gently correct them. These results suggest that mothers' spontaneous use (and qualification) of the word *grow* could help their children better understand biological and nonbiological domains, particularly when cases seemed to straddle domain boundaries.

The broader research on children's naïve biology also makes clear the importance of examining sociocultural contexts of development. Early research on children's naïve biological development showed that children, up to around age 10, seemed to reason about animals and plants using humans as an inductive base ("anthropocentrism"; Carey,

1985). Recently, however, Herrmann, Waxman, and Medin (2010) found that urban 3-year-old children did not show anthropocentric reasoning, suggesting that anthropocentrism may be learned. Furthermore, cross-cultural research has revealed that anthropocentrism is not the predominant way of thinking about living things for many children. For example, both Menominee Native American and European American children growing up in rural areas reasoned using biological or ecological categories as early as age 6 (Medin & Atran, 2004; Medin, Waxman, Woodring, & Washinawatok, 2010; Ross, Medin, Coley, & Atran, 2003). These findings suggest that middle-class suburban or urban children's anthropocentric reasoning may be a learned way of thinking related to their lack of direct experience with nature as well as the testimony they experience.

Given this, we were interested in whether patterns in conversation with others may lead children to an anthropocentric view of the living world. Rigney and Callanan (2011) explored how families visiting a marine science center talked about living things that were categorized as typical animals (e.g., sharks, eels, and other fish having eyes and obvious locomotion), atypical animals (e.g., sea anemones, sea stars, and other animals without faces), and plants. We found that parents rarely referred to the plants in the tank and were often concerned with figuring out the "scientific" names of the animals. Interestingly, they also framed the animals' activity using psychological language and masculine pronouns (e.g., "He likes you" or "He's hiding from us"). Perhaps children learn to think about the world anthropocentrically through hearing this psychological/anthropomorphic language. This type of talk, along with similar representations of animals in the media, may be partly responsible for children's developing reliance on similarity with humans as a gauge for the attributes of living creatures.

It is important to note that these anthropomorphic patterns in parents' talk were found only in reference to the typical animals; parents rarely used masculine pronouns or intentional language when discussing atypical animals (Rigney & Callanan, 2011). Thus, in addition to guiding children to think about animals anthropomorphically, these conversations may blur some of the boundaries between psychological and nonpsychological entities as well as animate and inanimate things. Parents drew a domain boundary between fish and sea stars through subtle cues in their speech; this talk rarely seemed pedagogical. Parents' incidental use of intentional language and animate pronouns for the typical (but not atypical) animals may suggest to children that these animals are like humans in some ways and thus invite comparisons. Indeed, research has shown that through comparing unfamiliar animals to humans (or other familiar animals), children can come to understand much about these unfamiliar animals (Inagaki & Hatano, 2002). Even though parents' restricting anthropomorphic language to typical animals may encourage children to exclude invertebrates from their concept of "living things," parents' talk may have provided a category structure that makes sense for everyday reasoning and supports children's developing theories about the living world.

Parents' anthropomorphic talk about animals might provide their children with culturally relevant "ways of knowing" about the living world (Bang & Medin, 2010). At the same time, children will be exposed to "scientific" (as well as "everyday") ways of thinking about living things in school science or when engaged with parents in more overtly scientific activities (Vygotsky, 1962). Experimental work shows that children can flexibly use different frameworks for thinking about the same phenomena (Bang & Medin, 2010; Gutheil, Vera, & Keil, 1998; Harris, 2011); however, children may benefit from parental guidance in recognizing when to use a particular way of knowing.

Questioning and Explaining in Parent–Child Conversation

Explanation has been called a "ubiquitous" aspect of human cognition (Keil, 2006; Lombrozo, 2012). Children and adults alike are compelled to both offer and request causal explanations for surprising events around them and express a sense of satisfaction when adequate answers are obtained (Frazier, Gelman, & Wellman, 2009; Gopnik, 1998). We argue that scientific thinking appears even in very young children's spontaneous questions about the world, and that parents offer different forms of explanatory guidance to their children as they develop scientific thinking. Depending on how parents respond to children's questions, they may communicate to children subtle messages about which topics are worth discussing, and about how to find answers.

Children's questions often focus on unusual or puzzling events, and they often initiate explanatory conversations with parents and other adults. In a diary study, we asked parents to keep track of the "why" and "how" questions asked by their preschool-age children for 2 weeks. Children asked many sophisticated questions about science domains, and the conversations following these questions are opportunities for children to revise their understanding of domains that interest them (Callanan & Oakes, 1992; see also Tizard & Hughes, 1984). Children are often persistent in obtaining answers to their questions, and even seem to search for answers that provide causal information. For example, Frazier et al. (2009) found that children typically did not stop asking "why" questions until they received an explanatory answer. In addition, children may better remember information obtained as a result of their own curiosity than information spontaneously provided by adults (Chouinard, 2007). These findings suggest that children's questions may be a mechanism that aids their conceptual development.

Some research has suggested, however, that children's tendency to ask questions varies across cultural communities. For example, Rogoff et al. (2007) identified "intent community participation" as a common style of learning among indigenous groups of the Americas whose communities tend not to have a history of formal schooling. Intent community participation emphasizes learning and communication focused on observation and other nonverbal strategies, rather than the primarily verbal style of many middle-class European American families. Morever, an emphasis on asking questions may be connected to schooling (Laosa, 1980), such that children whose parents have less formal schooling may utilize more nonverbal strategies, including keen attention, when interacting with adults, and may ask fewer questions (Rogoff, Paradise, Mejía Arauz, Correa-Chávez, & Angelillo, 2003). Question-asking also may not be equally valued by all cultural groups. For example, the Mexican cultural value of *respeto* emphasizes politeness and discourages challenging authority (Ruvalcaba, Rogoff, López, Correa-Chávez, & Gutiérrez, 2011); asking questions could be seen as a violation of this value, possibly making children of Mexican descent less likely to ask questions (Delgado-Gaitan, 1994).

In contrast to the idea that Mexican culture discourages children's questions, however, we have recently found evidence of rich spontaneous "why" questions in a diary study with Mexican-descent children (Callanan, Perez-Granados, Barajas, & Goldberg, 2012). Two groups of families of Mexican heritage were asked to keep track of their children's "why" and "how" questions for 2 weeks. Parents in one group were immigrants to the United States with an average of 7 years of formal schooling; the other group was born in the United States and had graduated from high school. We found no difference in frequency of questions between the two schooling groups; moreover, children in this study were just as likely to ask "why" and "how" questions as were the mostly middle-class European American children in the Callanan and Oakes (1992) study. In contrast to the notion that questions would be discouraged, parents in this study welcomed their children's questions and provided informative explanations; the two groups did not differ in their tendency to provide causal answers despite differences in formal schooling experience.

Recent work in our lab supports the idea that children from a variety of backgrounds use questions as an information-seeking strategy. Solis and Callanan (2012) asked Mexican-descent children and their parents to engage in a science-related task: predicting, then testing, whether a variety of objects would sink or float in a tub of water (see also Siegel, Esterly, Callanan, Wright, & Navarro, 2007; Tenenbaum & Callanan, 2008). As in our previous research, no differences were found in the frequency of questions children asked as a function of their parents' schooling background. However, children whose parents had less experience with formal schooling asked more conceptual questions (e.g., "Why does this sink when it's so small?"), whereas those whose parents had more schooling asked more procedural questions (e.g., "Is it my turn to test it now?"). These surprising findings suggest an intriguing link between parental schooling experience and the types of questions children ask, which in turn may be related to children's understanding of and goals for their current task. Future research is needed to further explore this possibility.

In addition to considering children's questions, parents' explanations to children, children's reactions to the explanations they receive, and children's developing ability to provide their own explanations are also important. In a variety of studies, we have explored the explanations that parents provide to children in museum visits, at home, and in lab activities (e.g., Crowley, Callanan, Jipson, et al., 2001; Tenenbaum & Callanan, 2008). We found that children who visited a museum exhibit with a parent were more likely to experience events that may help them understand phenomena. In a study of a zoetrope exhibit, for example, children who attended with a parent were more likely to experience all four states of the zoetrope (i.e., moving, stationary, viewed from above, viewed through the slots) than were children who engaged with the exhibit on their own (Crowley et al., 2001a).

Much of our research has also shown that different families may approach science learning in very different ways. Tenenbaum and Callanan (2008) explored family conversations in a museum setting and at home, working with the same data as Solis and Callanan (2012). Two groups of families of Mexican descent visited a children's museum and completed several tasks at home. Although parents with higher formal schooling explained more in the museum, both groups of parents provided similar numbers of explanations during the sink-and-float task at home. Parents' goals for the museum also varied across the two groups: parents with basic schooling (many of whom had never been to a museum) had goals for their child to learn about museums, whereas parents with higher schooling had more specific goals for their child to learn about scientific concepts. Cultural variation in how parents talk to children about science topics and in the goals parents have for their children's learning are also evident in many other studies (e.g., Gaskins, 2008; Tenenbaum, Snow, Roach, & Kurland, 2005).

Even within middle-class European American populations, we have seen evidence of individual variation in conversation styles. Parents give many more causal explanations to boys than to girls in a museum setting (Crowley, Callanan, Tenenbaum, & Allen, 2001), and parents from different occupational backgrounds discuss conflicting claims (e.g., contrasting evaluations on food additives) differently with their children (Valle, 2005). More recently, we have also investigated personal epistemological variation in how much parents focus on evidence as a way to answer questions (Kuhn, Cheney, & Weinstock, 2000). We hypothesized that this strategy is likely related to parents' educational backgrounds, occupations, and attitudes about science. During a book-reading task in which families were presented with a number of science-relevant topics (e.g., global warming, extinction, the origin of gender differences), parents with different attitudes toward science or different epistemological stances about the nature of knowledge talked differently with their children. Importantly, these differences were correlated with variation in children's own understanding of the use of evidence (Luce, Callanan, & Smilovic, 2012). Further links between epistemological stance and pedagogical style would be a very fruitful direction to explore. We are also finding that parents' scores on the "Need for Cognition" personality measure (Cacioppo, Petty, Feinstein, & Jarvis, 1996) are correlated with their tendency to ask their children questions that encourage the use of evidence to investigate a set of fossils and other ambiguous objects (Luce et al., 2012). This exploratory finding points to the need for a broader set of parent variables, beyond schooling and ethnicity, to better understand the diversity of conversational styles with which children have experience.

In a new set of studies, we are exploring another aspect of parents' explanatory conversations with children: socialization of ways of thinking about unusual or improbable events. Although extensive research in cognitive development confirms that young children, even babies, can easily distinguish between ordinary and impossible events (Baillargeon, 1994; Wang & Baillargeon, 2008), preschoolers will nonetheless endorse the existence of magical and fantastical entities such as Santa Claus when there are cultural supports for doing so (for review, see Van Reet, Chapter 2, this volume). Yet children are often even more skeptical than adults when it comes to improbable and uncertain events. Shtulman and Carey (2007) looked at young children's reactions to both physically impossible events (e.g., walking on water) and conceptually improbable events (e.g., walking on a telephone wire). Surprisingly, children between the ages of 4 and 8 rarely acknowledged that improbable, but possible, events could possibly occur in real life (e.g., an alligator appearing under a bed); 4-year-olds were particularly likely to deny that these types of events could occur. Little is known however, about the social context in which such judgments may emerge.

In recent work (Nolan-Reyes & Callanan, 2012), we examined how parents talked to their children about the same types of improbable and impossible events used by Shtulman and Carey (2007), and found a relation between parental talk and children's reasoning about improbable events. In particular, parents' speculative causal talk about how unusual events could occur was correlated with children's tendency to agree (in a separate task) that unusual things can happen in real life. We argue that, when parents encourage speculative inferential reasoning by entertaining possible circumstances for an unusual event, parents and children are practicing speculation and hypothesis generation as creative ways of thinking about the world. Parents who restrict such thinking, in contrast, may guide children toward greater skepticism about unusual events. We intend to follow up on these intriguing findings by exploring variation in parents' encouragement of possibility thinking as related to educational background, occupation, and epistemological style.

Summary and Implications

It is clear from many studies of family conversation that parents and children sometimes spontaneously talk about scientific domains in everyday life, and they seek out, as well as construct, explanations for scientific and other unusual phenomena. The source of children's knowledge is not necessarily a mutually exclusive choice between direct observation versus "input" from others. There are brief moments of deliberate teaching, or "opportunistic guidance" (Valle, 2012), such as when a parent takes a passing opportunity to reinforce a value of healthy eating in a meandering conversation that touches on what to eat for a snack. However, the guidance that many parents naturally offer to children in everyday settings does not seem to be predominantly deliberate or directive. Instead, the talk often accompanies actions where there are multiple goals in play, and where parents' guidance seems more subtle and variable and cuts across multiple domains. In some cases, parents offer guidance that fits what formal and informal science educators advocate for scaffolding children's understanding of science. The causal explanations that encouraged thinking about possibilities in Nolan-Reyes and Callanan's (2012) study, for example, may support children's inquiry skills. In other cases, however, parents' guidance may arguably steer children away from the scientific view of a domain, as in Rigney and Callanan's (2011) finding that parents may subtly encourage anthropomorphic thinking about fish and discourage thinking of starfish as animals. Yet despite the mostly nonpedagogical nature of family conversation, our research and that of other scholars seems to support the notion that children are learning not only information, but also ways of thinking from these interactions. Children bring their prior knowledge to learning situations and learn from both explicit, directive speech (e.g., "This is tiger shark; it's an animal") and from implicit patterns in conversation (e.g., "He wants to find some food"). In addition, children may learn particular "ways of knowing" from the types of questioning and explaining practiced while discussing scientific phenomena, regardless of whether a task is framed as scientific.

Given the nondirective nature of many family conversations, museums seem to be an ideal setting for families to engage naturally in conversations about scientific topics. Recent research has examined how museums can develop more effective scaffolding for parents to give them the content-based grounding needed on a topic that allows them to engage with children in an open-ended and inquiry-based way (Callanan, Luce, Martin, DeAngelis, & Kawaratani, 2012; Van Schijndel, Franse, & Raijmakers, 2010). It is important to keep in mind, however, that visits to museums are an everyday part of life only for certain groups of families, and that even within that population, girls and boys may have a different experience (Crowley et al., 2001b). If museums are to be part of a plan to work toward equal access to science, there is still much work to be done.

Findings regarding the diversity in beliefs, knowledge, and attitudes that are expressed in family conversations are very important for teachers and educational designers to consider. Children's ways of thinking may not be predictable by their age or by other standard background variables, and the epistemological views that children are exposed to at home may have very important implications for their developing understanding of the nature of science (Luce et al., 2012; Sandoval, 2005), just as the cultural practices of children's families have important implications for their ways of learning (Rogoff et al., 2007). Finally, consistent with Bonawitz et al.'s (2011) experimental findings, we argue that it is a mistake to assume that parents' pedagogical talk is always most effective. Children often learn very effectively simply by observing and noticing subtle actions or patterns of speech—even when we do not want them to (e.g., Akhtar, Jipson, & Callanan, 2001). Future research is needed to understand more deeply the situations in which children learn from testimony or pedagogy, and the situations where they resist learning.

Future Directions

There are a number of exciting new directions in which we hope to take our work. First, there is a need for more exploration of diversity in family conversations and links to variations in how children learn about domain boundaries, causal mechanisms, evidence, and creative speculation as generated through word use and explanations. Central to our continuing work is the goal of furthering our understanding of the variety of different stances parents take when talking with their children, and the impact of these stances for children's learning. Parents are sometimes pedagogical or directly informative, and other times encourage more questioning and creative thinking. These different stances are likely to vary across parents, across cultural communities, and across contexts. Sometimes the same parent will take a pedagogical stance when discussing one topic and switch to a more co-constructive exploratory stance when discussing a different topic (Luce et al., 2012). Children may learn more about domains they are allowed or encouraged to question compared with domains that are not open for discussion in their families or communities (e.g., Goodnow, 1990, 2005; Hasan, 2002; Nucci & Weber, 1995). Understanding the diversity of verbal and nonverbal forms in which parents and children discuss science-related phenomena is therefore an important issue.

Another important future direction is to understand how children learn to coordinate their multiple frameworks for thinking about the world. Children have community or everyday ways of thinking about science-related phenomena (Bang & Medin, 2010), and it is important that science educators not dismiss these culturally relevant frameworks but instead consider ways to incorporate them into teaching and discussion. Further research is needed on the everyday knowledge that children bring to school topics, such as how everyday social and cultural understanding of food connects with scientific study of biology and nutrition. In future work, we also hope to further explore the important dimensions of individual differences among parents, including examining parents whose occupations, education, and values lean more toward the arts versus science. Scientist parents and artist parents are likely to be similar in many ways, but they may emphasize different ways of thinking about the world; perhaps scientist parents model more consistent use of logic and evidence when evaluating phenomena, whereas artist parents may model a more open-ended, speculative approach to consider many solutions to problems.

In conclusion, children participate in and learn from a variety of everyday conversations with their parents. Parents model different styles of thinking and speaking in these conversations; children's immersion in these conversational styles likely influences their thinking about the natural world. Although the current research attention to pedagogy and testimony has brought welcome focus to the social context of children's learning, sociocultural approaches demand closer attention to the everyday conversations in which children practice different forms of thinking and develop understanding. Children's real lives are not necessarily always analogous to the experimental settings that we utilize to systematically investigate children's thinking. We need to know more about how likely children are to follow testimony or pedagogical demonstrations, depending on their prior beliefs and experiences. Depending on the context, parents may engage in styles that look more or less pedagogical. Sometimes parents will take a pedagogical stance in order to be sure that an important fact or behavior is learned, perhaps especially in situations where safety is relevant. At other times, parents' goals may be more focused on encouraging curiosity in their children. At still other times parents are just trying to get things done and may only give children brief answers to their questions. What is clearly needed is a combination of experimental and more naturalistic methods to ensure our theories are true to the lived experiences of children.

REFERENCES

Akhtar, N., Jipson, J., & Callanan, M. (2001). Learning words through overhearing. *Child Development, 72*(2), 416–430.

Anggoro, F. K., Medin, D. L., & Waxman, S. R. (2010). Language and experience influence children's biological induction. *Journal of Cognition and Culture, 10*(1–2), 171–187.

Baillargeon, R. (1994). Physical reasoning in young infants: Seeking explanations for impossible events. *British Journal of Developmental Psychology, Special Issue: Magic, 12*(1), 9–33.

Baldwin, D. A. (1993). Early referential understanding: Infants' ability to recognize referential acts for what they are. *Developmental Psychology, 29*(5), 832–843.

Bang, M., & Medin, D. (2010). Cultural processes in science education: Supporting the navigation of multiple epistemologies. *Science Education, 94*(6), 1008–1026.

Bonawitz, L., Shafto, P., Gweon, H., Goodman, N., Spelke, E., & Schulz, L. (2011). The double-edged sword of pedagogy: Instruction limits spontaneous exploration and discovery. *Cognition, 120*(3), 322–330.

Cacioppo, J. T., Petty, R. E., Feinstein, J. A., & Jarvis, W. B. G. (1996). Dispositional differences in cognitive motivation: The life and times of individuals varying in need for cognition. *Psychological Bulletin, 119*(2), 197–253.

Callanan, M. A., & Jipson, J. (2001). Explanatory conversations and young children's developing scientific literacy. In K. S. Crowley, C. Schunn, & T. Okada (Eds.), *Designing for science: Implications from everyday, classroom, and professional settings* (pp. 21–49). Mahwah, NJ: Erlbaum.

Callanan, M., Luce, M., Martin, J., DeAngelis, S., & Kawaratani, L. (2012, April). *Hands-on museum components shape family science talk about fossils.* Paper presented at meeting of American Educational Research Association, Vancouver.

Callanan, M. A., & Oakes, L. M. (1992). Preschoolers' questions and parents' explanations: Causal thinking in everyday activity. *Cognitive Development, 7*(2), 213–233.

Callanan, M. A., Perez-Granados, D., Barajas, N., & Goldberg, J. (2012). *"Why" questions in Mexican-descent children's conversations with parents.* Unpublished manuscript, Psychology Department, University of California—Santa Cruz, Santa Cruz, CA.

Callanan, M. A., & Sabbagh, M. A. (2004). Multiple labels for objects in conversations with young children: Parents' language and children's developing expectations about word meanings. *Developmental Psychology, 40*(5), 746–763.

Carey, S. (1985). *Conceptual change in childhood.* Cambridge, MA: MIT Press/Bradford Books.

Carpenter, M., Akhtar, N., & Tomasello, M. (1998). Fourteen through 18-month-old infants differentially imitate intentional and accidental actions. *Infant Behavior and Development, 21*(2), 315–330.

Chouinard, M. M. (2007). Children's questions: A mechanism for cognitive development. *Monographs of the Society for Research in Child Development, 72*(1, Serial No. 286).

Cole, M. (1998). *Cultural psychology: A once and future discipline.* Cambridge, MA: Harvard University Press.

Crowley, K., Callanan, M., Jipson, J., Galco, J., Topping, K., & Shrager, J. (2001a). Shared scientific thinking in everyday parent–child activity. *Science Education, 85*(6), 712–732.

Crowley, K., Callanan, M. A., Tenenbaum, H. R., & Allen, E. (2001b). Parents explain more often to boys than to girls during shared scientific thinking. *Psychological Science, 12*(3), 258–261.

Csibra, G., & Gergely, G. (2009). Natural pedagogy. *Trends in Cognitive Science, 13*(4), 148–153.

Delgado-Gaitan, C. (1994). Socializing young children in Mexican American families: An intergenerational perspective. In P. Greenfield & R. Cocking (Eds.), *Cross-cultural roots of minority child development* (pp. 55–86). Hillsdale, NJ: Erlbaum.

Frazier, B. N., Gelman, S. A., & Wellman, H. M. (2009). Preschoolers' search for explanatory information within adult–child conversation. *Child Development, 80*(6), 1592–1611.

Gaskins, S. (2008). Designing exhibitions to support families' cultural understandings. *Exhibitionist, 27*(1), 10–19.

Gelman, S. (2003). *The essential child: Origins of essentialism in everyday thought*. New York: Oxford University Press.

Gergely, G., Bekkering, H., & Király, I. (2002). Rational imitation in preverbal infants. *Nature, 415,* 755.

Goodnow, J. J. (1990). The socialization of cognition: What's involved? In J. W. Stigler, R. A. Shweder, & G. H. Herdt (Eds.), *Cultural psychology: Essays on comparative human development* (pp. 259–286). New York: Cambridge University Press.

Goodnow, J. J. (2005). Family socialization: New moves and next steps. *New Directions for Child and Adolescent Development, 109,* 83–90.

Gopnik, A. (1998). Explanation as orgasm. *Minds and Machines, 8*(1), 101–118.

Gopnik, A., & Wellman, H. M. (1994). The theory theory. In L. A. Hirschfeld & S. A. Gelman (Eds.), *Mapping the mind: Domain specificity in cognition and culture* (pp. 257–293). New York: Cambridge University Press.

Gutheil, G., Vera, A., & Keil, F. C. (1998). Do houseflies think? Patterns of induction and biological beliefs in development. *Cognition, 66*(1), 33–49.

Harris, P. L. (2002). What do children learn from testimony? In P. Carruthers, S. Stich, & M. Siegal (Eds.), *The cognitive basis of science* (pp. 316–334). Cambridge, UK: Cambridge University Press.

Harris, P. L. (2011). Conflicting thoughts about death. *Human Development, 54*(3), 160–168.

Harris, P. L., & Koenig, M. A. (2006). Trust in testimony: How children learn about science and religion. *Child Development, 77*(3), 505–524.

Hasan, R. (2002). Semiotic mediation and mental development in pluralistic societies: Some implications for tomorrow's schooling. In G. Wells & G. Claxton (Eds.), *Learning for life in the 21st century: Sociocultural perspectives on the future of education* (pp. 112–126). Malden, MA: Blackwell.

Henderson, A. M. E., & Sabbagh, M. A. (2010). Parents' use of conventional and unconventional labels in conversations with their preschoolers. *Journal of Child Language, 37*(4), 793–816.

Herrmann, P., Waxman, S. R., & Medin, D. L. (2010). Anthropocentrism is not the first step in children's reasoning about the natural world. *Proceedings of the National Academy of Sciences, 107*(22), 9979–9984.

Inagaki, K., & Hatano, G. (2002). *Young children's naïve thinking about the biological world*. New York: Psychology Press.

Jipson, J. L., & Callanan, M. A. (2003). Mother–child conversations and children's understanding of biological and nonbiological changes in size. *Child Development, 74*(2), 629–644.

Jipson, J. L., & Gelman, S. A. (2007a, March). *Of mice and machines: How mothers' testimony influences children's inferences about living and nonliving kinds*. Paper presented at the biennial meeting of the Society for Research on Child Development, Boston, MA.

Jipson, J. L., & Gelman, S. A. (2007b). Robots and rodents: Children's inferences about living and nonliving kinds. *Child Development, 78*(6), 1675–1688.

Keil, F. (2006). Explanation and understanding. *Annual Review of Psychology, 57*, 227–254.

Koenig, M. A., & Harris, P. L. (2005). Preschoolers mistrust ignorant and inaccurate speakers. *Child Development, 76*(6), 1261–1277.

Kuhn, D., Cheney, R., &Weinstock, M. (2000). The development of epistemological understanding. *Cognitive Development, 15*(3), 309–328.

Laosa, L. (1980). Maternal teaching strategies in Chicano and Anglo-American families: The influence of culture and education on maternal behavior. *Child Development, 51*(3), 759–765.

Lombrozo, T. (2012). Explanation and abductive inference. In K. J. Holyoak & R. G. Morrison (Eds.), *Oxford handbook of thinking and reasoning* (pp. 260–276). New York: Oxford University Press.

Luce, M., Callanan, M., & Smilovic, S. (2012). *Children's learning in conversations with parents: Variations in using evidence to answer questions.* Manuscript submitted for publication.

Medin, D. L., & Atran, S. (2004). The native mind: Biological categorization and reasoning in development and across cultures. *Psychological Review, 111*(4), 960–983.

Medin, D., Waxman, S., Woodring, J., & Washinawatok, K. (2010). Human-centeredness is not a universal feature of young children's reasoning: Culture and experience matter when reasoning about biological entities. *Cognitive Development, 25*(3), 197–207.

National Research Council. (2009). *Learning science in informal environments: People, places, and pursuits. A report of the National Research Council of the National Academy of Science.* Washington, DC: National Academy Press.

Nolan-Reyes, C., & Callanan, M. A. (2012). *Practicing possibilities: Parents' explanations of unusual events and children's thinking.* Manuscript submitted for publication.

Nucci, L., & Weber, E. K. (1995). Social interactions in the home and the development of young children's conceptions of the personal. *Child Development, 66*(5), 1438–1452.

Piaget, J. (1929). *The child's conception of the world.* London: Paul, Trench, Trubner, & Co.

Pinkham, A. M., & Jaswal, V. K. (2011). Watch and learn? Infants privilege efficiency over pedagogy during imitative learning. *Infancy, 16*(5), 535–544.

Rigney, J. C., & Callanan, M. A. (2011). Patterns in parent–child conversations about animals at a marine science center. *Cognitive Development, 26*(2), 155–171.

Rogoff, B. (2003). *The cultural nature of cognitive development.* New York: Oxford University Press.

Rogoff, B., Moore, L., Najafi, B., Dexter, A., Correa-Chavez, M., & Solis, J. (2007). Children's development of cultural repertoires through participation in everyday routines and practices. In J. Grusec & P. Hastings (Eds.), *Handbook of socialization: Theory and research* (pp. 490–515). New York: Guilford Press.

Rogoff, B., Paradise, R., Mejía Arauz, R., Correa-Chávez, M., & Angelillo, C. (2003). Firsthand learning through intent participation. *Annual Review of Psychology, 54,* 175–203.

Ross, N., Medin, D. L., Coley, J. D., & Atran, S. (2003). Cultural and experiential differences in the development of folkbiological induction. *Cognitive Development, 18*(1), 25–47.

Ruvalcaba, O., Rogoff, B., López, A., Correa-Chávez, M., & Gutiérrez, K. (2011). *Use of nonverbal respeto in requests for help by Mexican-heritage and European-heritage children.* Unpublished manuscript, Psychology Department, University of California—Santa Cruz, Santa Cruz, CA.

Sabbagh, M. A., & Baldwin, D. A. (2001). Learning words from knowledgeable versus ignorant speakers: Links between preschoolers' theory of mind and semantic development. *Child Development, 72*(4), 1054–1070.

Sandoval, W. A. (2005). Understanding students' practical epistemologies and their influence on learning through inquiry. *Science Education, 89*(4), 634–656.

Shtulman, A., & Carey, S. (2007). Improbable or impossible? How children reason about the possibility of extraordinary events. *Child Development, 78*(3), 1015–1032.

Siegel, D., Esterly, J., Callanan, M., Wright, R., & Navarro, R. (2007). Conversations about science across activities in Mexican-descent families. *International Journal of Science Education, 29*(12), 1447–1466.

Solis, G., & Callanan, M. (2012). *Children's questions to parents: Navigating expertise.* Unpublished manuscript, Psychology Department, University of California—Santa Cruz, Santa Cruz, CA.

Tenenbaum, H., & Callanan, M. A. (2008). Parents' science talk to their children in Mexican-descent families residing in the USA. *International Journal of Behavioral Development, 32*(1), 1–12.

Tenenbaum, H. R., Snow, C. E., Roach, K. A., & Kurland, B. (2005). Talking and reading science: Longitudinal data on sex differences in mother–child conversations in low-income families. *Journal of Applied Developmental Psychology, 26*(1), 1–19.

Tizard, B., & Hughes, M. (1984). *Young children learning.* Cambridge, MA: Harvard University Press.

Tomasello, M. (2001). *The cultural origins of human cognition.* Cambridge, MA: Harvard University Press.

Vaish, A., Demir, Ö. E., & Baldwin, D. (2011). Thirteen- and 18-month-old infants recognize when they need information. *Social Development, 20*(3), 431–449.

Valle, A. (2005). *"How do you know?" Communicating ideas about science and scientific reasoning in parent-child conversations.* Doctoral dissertation. Available from the ProQuest Dissertations & Theses database (305004110).

Valle, A. (2012). *Opportunistic guidance in development.* Manuscript in preparation.

Van Schijndel, T. J. P., Franse, R. K., & Raijmakers, M. E. J. (2010). The exploratory behavior scale: Assessing young visitors' hands-on behavior in science museums. *Science Education, 94*(5), 794–809.

Vygotsky, L. S. (1962). *Thought and language.* Cambridge, MA: MIT Press.

Wang, S., & Baillargeon, R. (2008). Detecting impossible changes in infancy: A three-system account. *Trends in Cognitive Sciences, 12*(1), 17–23.

Waxman, S. R. & Markow, D. B. (1995). Words as invitations to form categories: Evidence from 12- to 13-month-old infants. *Cognitive Psychology, 29*(3), 257–302.

Wertsch, J. V. (1998). *Mind as action.* New York: Oxford University Press.

CHAPTER 5

■　■　■　■　■

Drawing on the Arts

LESS-TRAVELED PATHS
TOWARD A SCIENCE OF LEARNING?

Jessa Reed
Kathy Hirsh-Pasek
Roberta Michnick Golinkoff

A growing body of data suggests that connections between the art and science of learning are rigorously supportable by quantitative studies. Contemporary research is beginning to explore explicit neuroscientific hypotheses concerning the beneficial effects of activities such as musical performance, drawing, visual aesthetics and dance observation.
—TYLER, LEVITIN, AND LIKOVA (2009, p. 15)

In June 2008, the National Science Foundation convened a distinguished group of scientists and artists to ask whether it was now time to study the role of art in the science of learning. As noted above, this panel resolutely concluded that a "growing body of data" made this a frontier worth exploring. Mission statements from the field of education agree. When the U.S. Department of Education published its response to No Child Left Behind in March 2010, it suggested that college- and career-ready students require a well-rounded education that covers history and mathematics, science, *and* the arts. To date, this focus on the arts has not been realized. As a nation, 6% of elementary schools offer no music instruction and 13% lack visual arts instruction, while dance and theater are only offered to 20% and 19%, respectively (NCES, 2002). Furthermore, a recent survey of 254 classrooms in New York City and

Los Angeles mirrored this trend (Miller & Almon, 2009). In fact, 15% of schools in New York City and 13% of schools in Los Angeles had only enough art supplies for half of their classes. Music, dance, drama, and visual arts bring students to an understanding of social or historical events and satisfy the craving of beauty in its own right (Gardner, 2011). They might also prove to be a gateway to how we amass general knowledge in areas like reading, mathematics, and language and a route that supports the growth of attention and memory—skills that promote learning to learn.

This chapter reviews budding research suggesting that the arts might play a role in the science of learning. It asks more questions than it provides answers. For example, where might we find connections between the arts and general learning? What research exists to support connections between artistic training and learning outcomes? How can our theories of learning explain these nascent connections, and how might we build a new path toward learning that draws on the arts?

Finding Connections: Speculating on Links between the Arts and General Learning

The foundation for connecting learning to the arts comes largely from qualitative studies. Some of the research and theorizing asks us to consider learning processes that students use when engaged in the arts—when they are learning to draw, to sing, or to dance. In what has become a landmark study, Hetland, Winner, Veenema, and Sheridan (2007) observed 38 visual art classrooms throughout one academic year in two Boston high schools dedicated to the visual arts. Each class lasted approximately 2 or 3 hours. After observing students in these classrooms, they distilled a set of *studio habits,* or ways of thinking, that are fostered through arts instruction. While learning technique (i.e., *developing craft*) was a prominent activity in these classrooms, student–teacher interactions also isolated 7 additional skill sets that move beyond content and toward processes that support learning.

Among them was self-regulation (i.e., *engage and persist*). The assigned tasks were designed to challenge students. When frustrated, teachers encouraged students to be patient, acknowledging that the process was demanding. *Stretch and explore* is another habit fostered through the arts. Students were challenged to move beyond the familiar and to embrace mistakes. As one teacher described it, "You ask kids to play, and then in one-on-one conversations you name what they've stumbled upon" (Winner, Hetland, Veenema, Sheridan, & Palmer, 2006,

p. 74). Such discovery is a critical element in Eisner's (2002) thesis. He borrows Dewey's (1938) term, *flexible purposing,* to describe the importance of improvisation. He writes, "in choosing to pursue surprise, one selects an uncertain path" (p. 79). An unanticipated line on paper or movement on stage may be just the spark needed to move forward in a new direction, and the arts foster the courage to follow that lead. Students are also asked to suspend their usual ways of perceiving the world and instead notice the lines, patterns, colors, textures, and spatial relations in their work, developing the habit of *observation.* Viewfinders are but one tool to reinforce this habit.

The participants in Hetland et al.'s (2007) study were talented high school students. Yet some of our recent work suggests that many of the habits witnessed by Hetland and colleagues are also present when Head Start preschool children in an arts-enriched program within a Northeast metropolitan community participate in dance, music, and visual art classes during their school day (Reed, Fisher, Hirsh-Pasek, & Golinkoff, 2012). Preschool children attend music, visual art, and dance classes throughout the day, taught by artists and art instructors. Like Hetland and colleagues, we followed the four preschool classrooms as they attended their arts classes across a 6-month period. Preliminary analyses reveal that processes in these preschool arts classrooms parallel those in the Boston arts high schools. Our interest turned to whether the arts assist children in fine-tuning their attention and focus—in addition to any benefit the arts might yield for academic learning. That is, we asked how might an arts-enriched pedagogy foster executive function alongside content? By way of example, children receive a pair of drumsticks; at 3 and 4 years of age, their first instinct is to bang them together. The experience is structured, however, to reinforce self-regulation and inhibitory control as well as the practice of proper technique. Immediately after passing out the sticks, the teacher demonstrates "giving them a rest" through a series of fun movements that require the children to resist the urge to strike them together and instead follow the teacher's lead, pretending that the sticks are bug ears, among other things. Once the children are thoroughly immersed in the task, the teacher begins with soft taps and the students follow suite. This tapping becomes progressively more difficult, as the teacher integrates foot taps and body movement with the steady tapping. To succeed, students must focus, control themselves, and observe the teacher, who does not announce the next movement but simply acts so that students must monitor her behavior in addition to their own. In this way, even young "art" students build executive function habits like attention, self-regulation, and observation.

A second body of research linking the arts and learning comes from Gardiner (2000). He identifies the process of *mental stretching,* whereby a change in one's representation in one domain aids in the understanding of a different domain via analogous thinking. Take, for example, an elementary curriculum that focuses on pitch and melody. Because musical pitch and melody require attention to linear order and sequence, learning music might bolster children's understanding of the number line. Additionally, children who learn to compare high and low notes attend to spatial thinking in action. Some evidence adds credence to this theoretical perspective. First-graders in arts classrooms with a specific curricular focus on sequenced skill development outpaced their peers in control arts classrooms on a standardized assessment of mathematics (Gardiner, Fox, Knowles, & Jeffrey, 1996). Gardiner posits that participation in the arts builds the kinds of mental representations that reinforce learning in other domains. *In this sense, the medium itself leads learners to find abstract relationships that can be of broad use to their conceptualizations.* Such research offers a reconciliatory note with regard to the often elusive evidence of transfer (e.g., Winner & Hetland, 2000). Perhaps the arts foster a kind of learning to learn or what Katz (1995) called "dispositions for learning"—like the studio habits—that are critical for learning in all domains.

Schellenberg (2005) adds that music offers pointed lessons on abstraction. Analogous to logic and mathematics, music is a symbol system that does not depend on the individual notes in a tune, but rather on the *relations* between those notes as they spin a familiar melody. Even infants attend to the common melody line across key changes (e.g., Plantinga & Trainor, 2005; Trainor & Trehub, 1992). For older children, understanding how music is built on relations may offer a powerful analogue to mathematical thinking.

Children's drawings offer a similar foundation for building representations and learning skills. Kellogg (1979) collected and analyzed 2 million pieces of children's art from around the country. As she categorized the drawings of children between 24 and 40 months old, she found remarkable similarities in the kinds of scribbles they created, and in the way that the nonintentional marks of the infant transformed into the intentional fine-motor marks of the toddler, and then into the budding human form of the preschool child. Hirsh-Pasek and Golinkoff (2007) traced the development of children's scribbles from 9 months to 3 years and saw the expansion of children's representational capacity in action. Lowenfeld and Brittain (1987) examined similar drawings to explore the creative and mental growth of young children. Children move along a developmental continuum from making a mark on a page, to endowing scribbles with names (at around 3.5 to 4 years), through a preschematic phase of drawing recognizable geometric forms and nascent human fig-ures, to drawing two-dimensional spatial representations (7 to 9 years) and beyond. We note, however, that recent work, such as Kindler (2004), offers an alternative to this model, in which she contends that instead of "endpoints" in artistic development (i.e., from scribbles to three-dimensional representations), the progression should focus on "reper-toires," or advances in artistic thinking. Nevertheless, in traversing this continuum, we meet children who are forming visual representations, learning about space and sequencing, and mastering pattern production and recognition. Indeed, Gibson and Levin (1975, p. 235) called scrib-bling "the fundamental graphic act" noting that in the seemingly ran-dom marks of young children are found the rudiments of writing. When children as young as 15 months are offered a pencil or crayon that does not work, they throw it aside, knowing that these implements are meant to make marks on the page.

Gardner's (1980) book, *Artful Scribbles,* addresses why children's art is so appealing. He posits that "in striving for symmetry, the child instead achieves balance. . . . In striving for realism, he achieves charm-ing, recognizable deviations from a photographic likeness" (p. 141). Gardner argues that children's art is not simply a product of develop-ment; the art of drawing affords children opportunities to "explore in his own way" fears, worries, themes, and ideas (p. 115). As such, cre-ations reflect not only an emerging appreciation for realism as embraced by our culture but also an expressiveness of thought.

The connections between art and learning implied above are but speculative. Hetland et al.'s (2007) work gives us reason to suspect that students are learning more than still-life composition and sculpture when they enter the high school art classroom. The theories proposed by Gardiner (2000), Kellogg (1979), Lowenfeld and Brittain (1987), and Gardner (1980) force us to look beneath the surface to ask what children might be gleaning as they practice a rhythm or draw a self-portrait. To be sure, there is value in song and dance even if it only provides aes-thetic pleasure (Gardner, 2011; Kagan, 2009), but the works cited in the qualitative studies—admittedly descriptive in nature—suggest that art experiences may offer children more than meets the eye.

What Quantitative Research Supports Real Connections between Artistic Training and Learning Outcomes?

Recent research has begun to directly explore the hypothesis that expo-sure to and training in the arts are related to school outcomes. Most of this research comes from adults or elementary school children, and is composed of a smattering of observational, random assignment, and quasi-experimental field studies. This work is in its infancy; however, the available research suggests that exposure to the arts might foster reading and mathematical outcomes as well as promote executive function skills such as attention and memory.

The Arts Meet Language and Literacy

Musical notes and alphabet letters, rhythm and rhyme—the hypothesized links between the arts and language and literacy development depend on their shared structure. Indeed, for young children, the line between art and narrative is often blurred (e.g., Dyson, 1986; Thompson & Bales, 1991). Dyson (1986) urges educators to "allow time for the often messy, noisy, and colorful process of becoming literate" (p. 408). Johnson (2007) shares this sentiment, describing the "communicative significance" of creating art (p. 316). Harris's (2011) observations of parent–child dyads facilitated by a music specialist highlighted the shared reciprocity inherent to both language and music. Indeed, Kirschner and Tomasello's (2009) research on joint drumming posits a similar link between language and music through shared intentionality.

Research suggests that music participation may foster a variety of emerging literacy skills, such as reading fluency (Wandell, Dougherty, Ben-Shachar, Deutsch, & Tsang, 2008), receptive vocabulary (Brown, Benedett, & Armistead, 2010), understanding and comprehension (Phillips, Gorton, Pinciotti, & Sachdev, 2010), and phonological awareness (Bolduc, 2009; Anvari, Trainor, Woodside, & Levy, 2002). For example, 4- and 5-year-old children completed a battery of musical (e.g., rhythm, melody, and chord discrimination tasks) and literacy assessments (Anvari, Trainor, Woodside, & Levy, 2002). Hierarchical regression analyses revealed that musical scores predicted reading scores, even after controlling for the child's phonological awareness. In addition, Moreno, Bialystok, Barac, Schellenberg, Cepeda, and Chau (2011) reported tht children's vocabulary scores improved after a 20-day computerized musical listening intervention.

Drama may also support children's literacy development (Moore & Caldwell, 1993; Nicolopoulou, de Sá, Ilgaz, & Brockmeyer, 2009; Nicolopoulou & Richner, 2007). Utilizing Paley's (1990) storytelling method, Nicolopoulou and colleagues found that the process of dictating and then acting out their stories fostered narrative development (Nicolopoulou & Richner, 2007), as well as story comprehension and print and word awareness (Nicolopoulou et al., 2009). In this line of research, children dictate stories and their peers become actors as these stories are then performed live. In her theorizing about the role of dramatization in the Paley storytelling method, Cooper (2005) describes the process as the "psychomotor embodiment of narrative text" (p. 246) that allows children to engage with the material in ways not possible when the story is simply in written form. Cooper describes how teachers may make inferences more salient to students when the plot is unfolding before them. For example, the teacher may pause the performance to ask students how a particular character is feeling, given the circumstances. These opportunities for reflection allow students to read beneath the surface, fostering the very competencies that will mature into critical thinking. Indeed, new research on "embodiment" (e.g., Glenberg, Gutierrez, Levin, Japuntich, & Kaschak, 2004) suggests that activity can enhance children's reading comprehension and understanding of narrative.

Moore and Caldwell (1993) draw upon the theorized links between the visual arts, drama, and narrative in their intervention study. Second- and third-grade lower-middle-class participants in the Rocky Mountains were randomly assigned to one of three conditions—a drama group, a reading group, and a discussion control group. An initial assessment of writing level revealed no differences among the groups prior to the intervention. After 15 weeks, both the drama and drawing groups had superior scores on the writing assessment relative to the children in the control condition. Moore and Caldwell suggest that planning through the arts scaffolds writing development.

The Arts and Mathematics and Spatial Development

The arts are inherently spatial. Music notation is represented graphically; we hum melodies based on the relations among notes. Patterns emerge in rhythm and paintings. Although there is relatively less literature linking art with mathematical and spatial thinking as compared to language and literacy, research suggests that participating in the arts bolsters performance on measures of mathematics and spatial thinking (e.g., Gardiner, Fox, Knowles, & Jeffrey, 1996). Edens and Potter (2007) analyzed fourth- and fifth-grade children's artwork for spatial relations, and this score correlated with their performance on a mathematical problem-solving task. While Spelke (2008) did not find a link for younger participants, adolescents with intensive music training excelled at a geometrical reasoning task relative to their nonmusician peers.

Fischer, Moeller, Bientzle, Cress, and Nuerk (2011) analyzed performance on a number line estimation task. Five- and 6-year-old children compared number magnitudes and responded, utilizing either a dance mat or computer tablet (nonspatial control). In the dance mat condition, images were projected on the ground and children compared one stimulus (e.g., a box with many squares inside) to an initial stimulus (e.g., a box with few squares inside). This initial stimulus was presented along a number line. If the new display was greater than the original, children moved to the right; if smaller, children moved to the left (corresponding to the principles of a number line). In the control condition, two stimuli were presented on the tablet's touch screen and children responded by clicking the larger one. These images were not presented spatially on the tablet's screen. Those children who worked with the dance mat outperformed their peers in the control condition on a 0–10 number line task (performance did not differ on a 0–20 task, postulated to be too difficult for this age). Furthermore, these children scored higher on the *counting principles* subtest of the TEDI-MATH assessment, but not for any other subtest (e.g., object counting, Arabic digits, number words, and calculation subtests), suggesting that this finding is not simply a result of heightened attention. A mediation analysis revealed that scores on the counting principles measure mediated the superior performance on the number line task. While the dance mat task was not inherently aesthetic or creative, the activity coupled movement with spatial relations, which facilitated performance on a number line task.

The Arts and School Readiness Skills

In addition to links with specific content areas, our research (Reed, Fisher, Hirsh-Pasek, & Golinkoff, 2011; Reed, Fisher, Hirsh-Pasek, & Golinkoff, 2012) suggests that arts experiences may also bolster school readiness skills. Fifteen children attending the arts-enriched preschool at the Settlement Music School and 16 children in a more traditional program were followed longitudinally from the fall to spring of an academic year. Both schools serve their local Head Start families, have earned the highest Pennsylvania Keystone Stars rating, and are accredited by National Association for the Education of Young Children (NAEYC). Because the two schools are matched for quality, the differential impact of an arts-enriched pedagogical approach can be explored. At both time points, participants completed several measures that tapped content knowledge (i.e., Woodcock–Johnson–R letter–word identification and applied math subtests). Additionally, a measure of executive function (*Grass/Snow*; Carlson, 2005) required children to pair the words *grass* and *snow* with the opposite colors (i.e., experimenter prompted *grass* and the child touched a white square). While children at both schools made similar gains in early literacy and numeracy skills across the school year, the children in the arts-enriched program outperformed their peers on the measure of sustained attention. Pedagogy (i.e., arts-enriched or traditional) was a significant predictor of the proportion of correct responses before children made their first mistake in the task, controlling for age and initial attention score.

This study is among the first to quantitatively test the *studio habits* thesis. Children spent several hours each day engaged in the arts—music, movement, and drawing. In these classes, letters and numbers were not the explicit focus; instead teachers instilled an appreciation for form, rhythm, color, and pattern across the different mediums. The arts then became the medium through which the academic content was integrated while also reinforcing such school readiness skills like attention and self-regulation. Similarly, Moreno et al. (2011) found that a 20-day musical listening intervention (but not the visual arts intervention) improved children's scores on a measure of executive function. This improvement was positively correlated with children's vocabulary difference scores.

How Can Our Theories of Learning Explain These Nascent Connections and How Might We Build a New Frontier for Learning Science That Draws on the Arts?

The available research is relatively limited, especially with respect to the lack of studies with true experimental designs and tight controls. Yet both the qualitative and quantitative work suggest that exposure to and training in the arts might augment children's general knowledge in ways that will also relate to school readiness and school outcomes. What are the psychological mechanisms through which the arts might exert their impact on learning? Several have been proposed. First, as Hetland et al. (2007) suggest, working in the arts might bolster basic learning processes that feed into later academic and social outcomes. Second, the arts themselves provide firsthand lessons in a variety of symbolic representations that can support later learning. Third, exploring a problem space through the arts (e.g., counting through rhythm and beat) uses the kinds of engaged, interactive, and meaningful pedagogical approaches known to foster optimal learning. Each of these areas is a frontier for future research.

On Basic Learning Processes

The Hetland et al. (2007) work and our follow-up study (Reed, Fisher, Hirsh-Pasek, & Golinkoff, 2012) describe some of the learning processes that children recruit when engaged in the arts. One of the most exciting new areas of research concerns processes like these that support general knowledge acquisition. Dubbed "approaches to learning" or "learning to learn," this research examines how skills like persistence, emotion regulation, and attentiveness are related to later outcomes in reading and mathematics, even up to fifth grade (Li-Grining, Votruba-Drzal, Maldonado-Carreno, & Haas, 2010). Similar findings emerge in the highly touted *Tools of the Mind* curriculum, which uses playful learning through dramatic play throughout the school day to help children practice and learn emotion regulation (Bodrova & Leong, 2007). Results from underprivileged Head Start children in a randomized study suggested that the *Tools* curriculum improved inhibitory control on two measures of executive function (Diamond, Barnett, Thomas, & Munro, 2007). Further, improved executive function skills were related to concurrent and latent academic outcomes. Correspondingly, using results from the Early Childhood Longitudinal Study (ECLS-K) Grissmer, Grimm, Aiyer, Murrah, and Steele (2010) find that approaches to learning (here defined as attention) is a better predictor of fourth-grade reading scores than are kindergarten reading scores.

Until recently, it was not clear whether approaches to learning skills were malleable (National Institute of Child Health and Human Development Early Child Care Research Network [NICHD ECCRN], 2005) but increasingly we are learning not only that the environment can alter the trajectories of these skills, but that these skills relate centrally to academic outcomes. Furthermore, the budding research from Hetland et al. (2007) suggests that exposure to and engagement in the arts may support children's development of these learning skills. In fact, a burgeoning focus on executive function in children (e.g., Blair, 2002; Diamond et al., 2007) has led researchers to hypothesize a direct link between the arts and such skills as attention (Posner, Rothbart, Sheese, & Kieras, 2008; Neville, Andersson, Bagdade, Bell, Currin, et al., 2008) and self-regulation (Winsler, Ducenne, & Koury, 2011). In the Dana Consortium Report on Arts and Cognition, for example, Posner, Rothbart, Sheese, and Kieras (2008) proposed that training in the arts might strengthen precisely those areas of the brain involved in attention, mediated by children's interest in and motivation to engage in the arts. Thus, while it remains an untested assumption, one might speculate that training in and exposure to the arts fosters precisely the kinds of skills that will support general knowledge development and specific outcomes that are related to school success.

On the Arts and Symbolic Representation

In his address to the Learning, Arts, and the Brain conference, Kagan (2009) emphasized the critical role that mental representations play in transforming children's knowledge, a position that is in line with Gardiner's (2000) thesis. The ability to think like an artist—spatially, visually, or in notes and keys—offers a perspective that can scaffold thinking in other areas. Eisner (2002) argues that, "representation stabilizes the idea or image . . . and makes possible a dialogue with it" (p. 6). Consequently, Eisner posits that the arts bolster one's attention to relationships through explorations of "the interactions among the qualities constituting the whole" (p. 76). The aesthetic perspective thus allows one to perceive qualities of an experience that may not be perceived with a scientific lens (e.g., Eisner, 2002; Gadsden, 2008; Seidel, Tishman, Winner, Hetland, & Palmer, 2009).

Kirsh, Muntanyola, Jao, Lew, and Sugihara (2009) describe a process in creative thinking called *tasking,* whereby a choreographer presents her dancers with a "choreographic problem or task." Dancers then respond to these problems through body movements. The director described the process as one whereby "assigning the dancers problems to solve they stretch their repertoire more effectively—they discover new ways of moving themselves; he, the choreographer, has the opportunity to see new things that the dancers can do" (Kirsh et al., 2009, p. 192). The process may be no different for children who lack the expert technique of professional artists but nevertheless are motivated to create within a new representational form.

Using Engaged, Interactive, and Meaningful Pedagogical Approaches

Another area where the arts might prove a powerful tool in education is through pedagogy. Teaching about math and science through the arts offers exciting cases of discovery learning—from rhythm to fractions as one student drums whole notes while another student overlaps with a four-quarter note pattern to demonstrate the concept of fractions to the use of space through preschool architecture. By way of example, the recently designed Imagination Playgrounds introduced by New York architect David Rockwell encourage children to be the construction team for their own mobile playgrounds. Equipped with large pieces of foam building blocks, these children fill blank spaces as they test the structure of tall towers and the slopes required for sliding objects down an incline. At the end of the day, the pieces are put away, only to be assembled anew by the next team of children.

A large research base supports the kind of learning that emerges when children are engaged and when the learning is meaningful. Chi (2009) reviews this literature, suggesting that the best learning occurs when children are *active, constructive,* and *interactive.* While active learning requires only that the learner engage with the material, constructive activities lead to the generation of new information not previously presented in the material, within a context that allows for active engagement. For example, the process of drawing connections between different storybooks may foster tolerance and empathy (e.g., Wan, 2006). Interactive learning involves a dialogue, with either a more knowledgeable partner (*instructional dialogue*) or a peer (*joint dialogue*). When paired with a teacher, the conversation lends itself to scaffolding, in which the child responds to prompts designed to spur thinking; the dialogue builds upon student responses and teacher elaborations. A joint dialogue is collaborative, as each partner builds upon the other's ideas and thoughts. Because interactive experiences offer individuals the opportunity to generate new knowledge together with a partner, Chi hypothesized that such activities will engender better learning outcomes than either constructive or active ones; all three types of activities are hypothesized to outperform passive ones. Research lends support to these ideas. Alfieri, Brooks, Aldrich, and Tenenbaum's (2011) meta-analysis reveals that enhanced discovery pedagogical approaches, such as elicited explanations and guided discovery, lead to better student outcomes in a variety of domains than does a direct instruction approach.

Critically, these experiences are *authentic,* such that the selected activities are indisputably connected to the curricular goals (e.g., Fink, 2003). Seidel, Tishman, Winner, Hetland, and Palmer (2009) interviewed 16 arts education theorists and practitioners and observed 16 programs nominated for their arts commitment in order to distill the essence of excellence in the arts and present their findings through one of four lenses (i.e., student learning, pedagogy, community dynamics, and the environment). Paramount from the pedagogical perspective is the authenticity of the experiences themselves. Authenticity is evident in the quality of the content presented to students; children must be exposed to a variety of exemplars in order to draw connections and pinpoint differences among the pieces, at which point a deeper understanding of a particular style or genre may be reached.

In addition, engagement and purposeful experiences are critically important when defining quality from the student's perspective. Creating art, regardless of medium, requires improvisation and surprise (Eisner, 2002). Drawing, choreography, and composition involve both imagination *and* problem solving; Seidel et al. (2009) parallel purposeful art experiences to that of project-based learning. The aim is clear and students understand the motivation behind the task, sustaining them through the revision process. Seidel and colleagues also describe how "many arts settings have almost a laboratory atmosphere" (p. 32); exploration and experimentation are key mechanisms linking the arts to learning.

It is notable that the arts also present the same possibilities for engagement that are discussed in the literature on playful learning (Hirsh-Pasek, Golinkoff, Berk, & Singer, 2009; Miller & Almon, 2009). Play activities are varied but, like visual art and music, share several defining features—they are fun, voluntary, flexible, and can have no extrinsic goals. They involve the child's active engagement and often contain an element of make believe (e.g., Pellegrini, 2009; Sutton-Smith, 2001). Both playful learning and the arts offer a forum for learning through guided play.

Guided play is a pedagogical approach to playful learning that incorporates both enriched environments and supportive adults as resources to promote children's general learning (Fisher, Hirsh-Pasek, Golinkoff, Singer, & Berk, 2011). First, teachers, parents, and other adults support children's learning when children's play areas are strategically peppered with materials designed to foster imagination through activities aligned with curricular goals. The presence of a supportive adult is another element of guided play as a pedagogical approach. Within an "empty vessel" philosophy, teachers are obliged to heap facts into children's minds; learning is but a process of accumulation, akin to assembling a prefabricated bookcase from IKEA. Guided play, by contrast, adheres to the constructivist philosophy, in which children create knowledge through their interactions with materials, teachers, and peers. How might guided play unfold in the domain of arts enrichment? The preschool program at the Settlement Music School offers us a portrait of just this kind of an educational supplement. For example, listening to fast and slow Celtic orchestral songs in music class highlights the concept of opposites that was earlier discussed with the homeroom teacher. In dance class, children creatively move their bodies to match the tempo and tone of the piece—sometimes emulating a thunderstorm's fervor, sometimes pretending to blossom to Vivaldi's *spring* concerto from *The Four Seasons*. As they match rhythm and tone, they learn patterns and practice counting the beats.

In summary, the arts are currently an underutilized resource for schools that would broaden children's general knowledge and offer a possible forum for introducing positive approaches to learning, new types of symbolic representations, and scaffolding for reinforcing the learning presented in other parts of the curriculum. In theory, training in and exposure to the arts provide potentially powerful supplements to current educational practices and a pedagogical tool that is consistent with best practices.

Looking Forward: From Theory to Research to Practice

Research on connections between the arts and the science of learning are, at this point, more suggestive than compelling. Yet, as the National

Science Foundation document proposes, there is indeed a "growing body of data" to suggest that exposure, training, and engagement in the arts might provide important pathways for learning (Tyler, Levitin, & Likova, 2009). Indeed, the literature on how young children might benefit from exposure to the arts and whether this exposure might be more or less potent for young children is still an open question. Furthermore, it is becoming increasingly clear that even talking about the "arts" as a unified construct will prove misleading. Exposure to and engagement in music are likely to offer different advantages and learning opportunities than exposure to and engagement in the visual arts or drama or dance.

Thus future research might focus on several areas of inquiry. First, in what ways does preschool exposure to various types of arts training translate into executive function skills and approaches to learning? For example, do kindergarteners who have visual arts every day for half an hour demonstrate more persistence or self-regulation in a nonartistic task? Second, we need to be more specific about the mechanisms that might link say, music training and mathematics. Within the domain of music, for example, is it only rhythmic training that relates to the number line, or might recognition of melody also support mathematical learning? Third, we need to research head-on claims that training in domains like music or drama promotes near and far transfer or mental stretching. Here there is a clear debate in the literature with scholars like Winner, Hetland, Veenema, Sheridan, and Palmer (2006) suggesting that there is near transfer from drama participation to verbal skills, but little transfer from visual arts or music. Gardiner (2000), on the other hand, expects the linkages between music or art and academic outcomes to be more transparent and broadly applicable. Fourth and finally, it would be interesting to see whether exposure to the arts might supplement current pedagogical practices in ways that encourage children to be more interactive and engaged in meaningful learning. Like guided play, the arts might provide a forum through which we can use best practices to expand children's general knowledge and to reinforce the learning that goes on in more traditional subjects.

Conclusion

Picasso once noted, "All children are artists. The problem is how to remain one once he grows up." When children hear music, they dance; their countless drawings (and murals) demonstrate their natural propensity to draw. Understanding how we may best harness children's motivation to engage in the arts has significant implications for children's development. Approaching a problem with an artist's mindset invokes certain dispositions for focus and engagement. Frustration is to be expected and mistakes may abound but glorious surprises can result. In this chapter, we reviewed not only potential links between the arts and other domains of content knowledge but also the processes that foster such learning. In a time when Google is now a verb, the kind of thinking promoted by the arts is no less imperative than knowing.

> Aaaarrrttt! Art is obviously one of the three R's.
> —PETER WILLIAM BROWN

REFERENCES

Alfieri, L., Brooks, P. J., Aldrich, N. J., & Tenenbaum, H. R. (2011). Does discovery-based instruction enhance learning? *Journal of Educational Psychology, 103,* 1–18.

Anvari, S. H., Trainor, L. J., Woodside, J., & Levy, B. A. (2002). Relations among musical skills, phonological processing, and early reading ability in preschool children. *Journal of Experimental Psychology, 83,* 111–130.

Blair, C. (2002). School readiness. *American Psychologist, 57,* 111–127.

Bodrova, E., & Leong, D. J. (2007) *Tools of the mind: The Vygotskian approach to early childhood education* (2nd ed.). Upper Saddle River, NJ: Prentice Hall.

Bolduc, J. (2009). Effects of a music programme on kindergartners' phonological awareness skills. *International Journal of Music Education, 21*(1), 37–47.

Brown, E. D., Benedett, B., & Armistead, M. E. (2010). Arts enrichment and school readiness for children at risk. *Early Childhood Research Quarterly, 25,* 112–124.

Carlson, S. M. (2005). Developmentally sensitive measures of executive function in preschool children. *Developmental Neuropsychology, 28*(2), 595–616.

Chi, M. T. H. (2009). Active-constructive-interactive: A conceptual framework for differentiating learning activities. *Topics in Cognitive Science, 1,* 73–105.

Cooper, P. M. (2005). Literacy learning and pedagogical purpose in Vivian Paley's "storytelling curriculum." *Journal of Early Childhood Literacy, 5*(3), 229–251.

Dewey, J. (1938). *Experience and education.* New York: Macmillan.

Diamond, A., Barnett, W. S., Thomas, J., & Munro, S. (2007). Preschool program improves cognitive control. *Science, 318,* 1387–1388.

Dyson, A. H. (1986). Transitions and tensions: Interrelationships between the drawing, talking, and dictating of young children. *Research in the Teaching of English, 20,* 379–409.

Edens, K., & Potter, E. (2007). The relationship of drawing and mathematical problem solving: "Draw for math" tasks. *Studies in Art Education, 48,* 282–298.

Eisner, E. (2002). *The arts and the creation of mind.* New Haven, CT: Yale University Press.

Fink, D. (2003). *Creating significant learning experiences: An integrated approach to designing college courses.* San Francisco, CA: Jossey-Bass.

Fisher, K., Hirsh-Pasek, K., Golinkoff, R. M., Singer, D., & Berk, L. E. (2011). Playing around in school: Implications for learning and educational policy. In A. Pellegrini (Ed.), *The Oxford handbook of the development of play* (pp. 341–360). New York: Oxford University Press.

Fischer, U., Moeller, K., Bientzle, M., Cress, U., & Nuerk, H. C. (2011). Sensori-motor spatial training of number magnitude representation. *Psychonomic Bulletin Review, 18,* 177–183.

Gadsden, V. L. (2008). The arts and education: Knowledge generation, pedagogy, and the discourse of learning. *Review of Research in Education, 32,* 29–61.

Gardiner, M. F. (2000). Music, learning, and behavior: A case for mental stretching. *Journal for Learning Through Music, 1,* 72–93.

Gardiner, M. F., Fox, A., Knowles, F., & Jeffrey, D. (1996). Learning improved by arts training. *Nature, 381,* 284.

Gardner, H. (1980). *Artful scribbles: The significance of children's drawings.* New York: Basic Books.

Gardner, H. (2011). *Truth, beauty, and goodness reframed: Educating for the virtues in the twenty-first century.* New York: Basic Books.

Gibson, E. J., & Levin, H. (1975). *The psychology of reading.* Cambridge, MA: MIT Press.

Glenberg, A., Gutierrez, T., Levin, J. R., Japuntich, S., & Kaschak, M. P. (2004). Activity and imagined activity can enhance young children's reading comprehension. *Journal of Educational Psychology, 96,* 424–463.

Grissmer, D., Grimm, K. J., Aiyer, S. M., Murrah, W. M., & Steele, J. S. (2010). Fine motor skills and early comprehension of the world: Two new school readiness indicators. *Developmental Psychology, 46*(5), 1008–1017.

Harris, D. J. (2011). Shake, rattle, and roll—can music be used by parents and practitioners to support communication, language and literacy within a pre-school setting. *Education 3–13, 39*(2), 139–151.

Hetland, L., Winner, E., Veenema, S., & Sheridan, K. (2007). *Studio habits: The real benefits of visual arts education.* New York: Teachers College Press.

Hirsh-Pasek, K., & Golinkoff, R. M. (2007). *Celebrate the scribble: Appreciating children's art.* Bethlehem, PA: Crayola Beginnings Press.

Hirsh-Pasek, K., Golinkoff, R. M., Berk, L. E., & Singer, D. G. (2009). *A mandate for playful learning in preschool: Presenting the evidence.* New York: Oxford University Press.

Johnson, H. L. (2007). Aesthetic experience and early language and literacy development. *Early Child Development and Care, 3,* 311–320.

Kagan, J. (2009, May). *Why the arts matter: Six good reasons for advocating the importance of the arts in schools.* Paper presented to the Learning, Arts, and the Brain conference, Baltimore, MD.

Katz, L. G. (1995). Dispositions in early childhood education. In L. G. Katz

(Ed.), *Talks with teachers of young children: A collection*. Norwood, NJ: Ablex.

Kellogg, R. (1979). *Children's drawings, children's minds*. New York: Avon.

Kindler, A. M. (2004). Researching impossible? Models of artistic development reconsidered. In E. W. Eisner & M. D. Day (Eds.), *Handbook of research and policy in art education* (pp. 233–252). Mahwah, NJ: Erlbaum.

Kirsh, D., Muntanyola, D., Jao, R. J., Lew, A., & Sugihara, M. (2009). *Choreographic methods for creating novel, high quality dance*. Paper presented at the 5th International workshop on Design and Semantics of Form and Movement, Taipei.

Kirschner, S., & Tomasello, M. (2009). Joint drumming: Social context facilitates synchronization in preschool children. *Journal of Experimental Child Psychology, 102*, 299–314.

Li-Grining, C., Votruba-Drzal, E., Maldonado-Carreno, C., & Haas, K. (2010). Children's early approaches to learning and academic trajectories through fifth grade. *Developmental Psychology, 46*(5), 1062–1078.

Lowenfeld, V., & Brittain, W. L. (1987). *Creative and mental growth* (8th ed.). New York: Macmillan.

Miller, E., & Almon, J. (2009). *Crisis in the kindergarten: Why children need to play in school*. College Park, MD: Alliance for Childhood.

Moore, B. H., & Caldwell, H. (1993). Drama and drawing for narrative writing in primary grades. *The Journal of Educational Research, 87*(2), 100–110.

Moreno, S., Bialystok, E., Barac, R., Schellenberg, E. G., Cepeda, N. J., & Chau, T. (2011). Short-term music training enhances verbal intelligence and executive function. *Psychological Science, 22*, 1425–1433.

National Center for Education Statistics, U.S. Department of Education, Office of Educational Research and Improvement. (2002). *Art education in public elementary and secondary schools: 1999–2000* (Statistical Analysis Report 2002-131). Retrieved from *nces.ed.gov/pubs2002/2002131.pdf*.

National Institute of Child Health and Human Development Early Child Care Research Network. (2005). Predicting individual differences in attention, memory, and planning in first graders from experiences at home, child care, and school. *Developmental Psychology, 41*, 99–114.

Neville, H., Andersson, A., Bagdade, O., Bell, T., Currin, J., Fanning, J., et al. (2008). Effects of music training on brain and cognitive development in under-privileged 3- to 5-year-old children: Preliminary results. In C. Asbury & B. Rich (Eds.), *Learning, arts, and the brain: The Dana Consortium Report on arts and cognition* (pp. 105–116). New York: Dana Press.

Nicolopoulou, A., de Sá, A., Ilgaz, H., & Brockmeyer, C. (2009). Using the transformative power of play to educate hearts and minds. *Mind, Culture, and Activity. Special Issue on Playworlds of Children and Adults: Cross Cultural Perspectives on Play Pedagogy, 17*, 42–58.

Nicolopoulou, A., & Richner, E. S. (2007). From actors to agents to persons: The development of character representation in young children's narratives. *Child Development, 78*, 412–429.

Paley, V. G. (1990). *The boy who would be a helicopter: The uses of storytelling in the classroom*. Cambridge, MA: Harvard University Press.

Pellegrini, A. D. (2009). Research and policy on children's play. *Child Development Perspectives, 3,* 131–136.

Phillips, R., Gorton, R., Pinciotti, P., & Sachdev, A. (2010). Promising findings on preschooler's emergent literacy and school readiness in arts-integrated early childhood settings. *Early Childhood Education Journal, 38,* 111–122.

Plantinga, J., & Trainor, L. J. (2005). Memory for melody: Infants use a relative pitch code. *Cognition, 98,* 1–11.

Posner, M., Rothbart, M. K., Sheese, B. E., & Kieras, J. (2008). How arts training influences cognition. In C. Asbury & B. Rich (Eds.), *Learning, arts, and the brain: The Dana Consortium Report on arts and cognition* (pp. 1–10). New York: Dana Press.

Reed, J., Fisher, K., Hirsh-Pasek, K., & Golinkoff, R. M. (2011, April). *The art of learning: The impact of arts-enriched pedagogy on school readiness skills in Head Start children.* Poster presented at the Society of Research in Child Development Biennial Meeting, Montreal, Canada.

Reed, J., Fisher, K., Hirsh-Pasek, K., & Golinkoff, R. M. (2012, April). *The art of the matter: Playful learning in an arts-enriched preschool.* Paper presented at the American Education Research Association meeting, Vancouver, Canada.

Schellenberg, E. G. (2005). Music and cognitive abilities. *Current Directions in Psychological Science, 14*(6), 317–320.

Seidel, S., Tishman, S., Winner, E., Hetland, L., & Palmer, P. (2009). *The qualities of quality: Understanding excellence in arts education.* Commissioned by the Wallace Foundation. Cambridge, MA: Project Zero, Harvard Graduate School of Education.

Spelke, E. (2008). Effects of music instruction on developing cognitive systems at the foundation of mathematics and science. In C. Asbury & B. Rich (Eds.), *Learning, arts, and the brain: The Dana Consortium Report on arts and cognition* (pp. 17–50). New York: Dana Press.

Sutton-Smith, B. (2001). *The ambiguity of play.* Cambridge, MA: Harvard University Press.

Thompson, C., & Bales, S. (1991). "Michael doesn't like my dinosaurs": Conversations in a preschool art class. *Studies in Art Education, 33,* 43–55.

Trainor, L. J., & Trehub, S. E. (1992). A comparison of infants' and adults' sensitivity to Western musical structure. *Journal of Experimental Psychology, 18,* 394–402.

Tyler, C., Levitin, D., & Likova, L. (2009). *Art, creativity, and learning* (Final workshop report). Washington, DC: National Science Foundation.

U.S. Department of Education, Office of Planning, Evaluation and Policy Development. (2010). *ESEA blueprint for reform.* Washington, DC.

Wan, G. (2006). Teaching diversity and tolerance in the classroom: A thematic storybook approach. *Education, 127*(1), 140–154.

Wandell, B., Dougherty, R. F., Ben-Shachar, M., Deutsch, G. K., & Tsang, J. (2008). Training in the arts, reading, and brain imaging. In C. Asbury & B. Rich (Eds.), *Learning, arts, and the brain: The Dana Consortium Report on arts and cognition* (pp. 51–60). New York: Dana Press.

Winner, E., & Hetland, L. (Eds.). (2000). The arts and academic achievement: What the evidence shows. *Journal of Aesthetic Education, 34*(3/4).

Winner, E., Hetland, L., Veenema, S., Sheridan, K., & Palmer, P. (2006). Studio thinking: How visual arts teaching can promote disciplined habits of mind. In P. Locher, C. Martindale, L. Dorfman, & D. Leontiev (Eds.), *New directions in aesthetics, creativity, and the arts* (pp. 189–205). Amityville, New York: Baywood.

Winsler, A., Ducenne, L., & Koury, A. (2011). Singing one's way to self-regulation: The role of early music and movement curricula and private speech. *Early Education and Development, 22*(2), 274–304.

CHAPTER 6

■　■　■　■　■

Learning by the Book

THE IMPORTANCE OF PICTURE BOOKS FOR YOUNG CHILDREN'S KNOWLEDGE ACQUISITION

Ashley M. Pinkham

Among parents and teachers in the United States, books are overwhelmingly endorsed as valuable resources for the development of young children's conceptual knowledge and literacy skills. These positive attitudes are perhaps best reflected in shared book-reading behaviors. Parents often begin to engage in shared-reading activities even before their infants are 7 months of age (DeBaryshe, 1993). By the time their children are toddlers, parents from both low-income (High, LaGasse, Becker, Ahlgren, & Gardner, 2000; Raikes et al., 2006) and more socioeconomically advantaged homes (Hardman & Jones, 1999; Rideout, Vandewater, & Wartella, 2003) report participating in book-centered interactions with their children at least three times per week. Furthermore, the majority of preschool and early elementary school teachers devote daily classroom time to shared book reading (Hoffman, Roser, & Battle, 1993).

Beyond simply providing entertainment, books are often considered important teaching tools. Books can extend human memory, allowing children to learn about things they may have never seen, places they may have never visited, and events that may have happened hundreds of years ago. Children who read more are often assumed to have greater opportunities to develop the breadth and depth of their world knowledge

(Cunningham & Stanovich, 1998). Moreover, children's early experiences with books are thought to promote their emergent literacy skills and foster lifelong positive attitudes toward reading (Bus, van IJzendoorn, & Pellegrini, 1995; Ezell & Justice, 2005; Neuman, 1999).

The vast majority of research on book reading has focused on the nature of the adult–child interaction. This is consistent with the perspective that learning is a socially mediated process (Rogoff, 2003), and that one of the primary functions of shared book reading is the co-construction of meaning through extratextual adult–child conversations (Morrow, 1988). But despite the research emphasis on shared-reading, recent meta-analyses have reported that the overall educational benefits of such experiences may be surprisingly limited, particularly for children under the age of 6 (Mol, Bus, de Jong, & Smeets, 2008; National Early Literacy Panel, 2008). One possibility is that, during these interactions, parents and teachers simply do not focus on scaffolding children's content knowledge. For example, Neuman (1996) proposed that the primary role of shared-reading, especially in home contexts, may not be the acquisition of content knowledge or general literacy skills, but rather the transmission of cultural values. As a result, such book-reading interactions may be more relevant to children's sociocultural outcomes than, for instance, their learning of new information.

Somewhat surprisingly, relatively little research has addressed what information young children may learn from books themselves. For older children and adults, book reading is indeed positively associated with content and general world knowledge (Cunningham & Stanovich, 1991; Stanovich, West, & Harrison, 1995). Therefore, a common assumption underlying book reading, particularly when the books are considered "educationally relevant," is that young children will also be able to acquire and generalize new information from the printed page to the real world. Yet the extent to which young children learn new content knowledge from books has rarely been systematically explored, likely due to a general assumption that the answer is obvious (e.g., Cunningham & Stanovich, 1998; Neuman, 1999; van Kleeck, Stahl, & Bauer, 2003).

In this chapter, I examine the role of books as a source of children's knowledge development. I first address the foundational skills and knowledge necessary for young children to learn new information from books, independent of the extratextual scaffolding provided by many adult readers. Next, I examine how books might help children build their real-world knowledge and discuss whether there are particular features that might help facilitate children's ability to acquire and generalize new knowledge. I then conclude by discussing possible implications for using books as learning tools and suggest new directions for research on children's knowledge acquisition and development.

What Knowledge Is Necessary to Learn from Books?

By the beginning of first grade, the average middle-class American child has already experienced approximately 1,000 hours of book reading (Adams, 1990). If books are considered tools for knowledge development, these hours spent reading books should provide children with lots of opportunities for learning. And yet, to truly impact children's knowledge development, sheer volume of reading is likely insufficient. What information children may learn from book-reading experiences also depends, at least in part, on the skills and knowledge they bring to the task. To use books as a source of new learning, children must first understand the fundamental properties of books, and they must possess appropriate background knowledge in order to make sense of the content.

Understanding of Books

For a tool to be truly useful, one must understand how it works. A hammer is only a useful carpentry tool if the user knows how to properly hold the handle, strike the head against a nail, and so forth. Similarly, a book may only be a useful source of new knowledge if the reader understands how books works in a general sense, as well as understands that particular book's content. Before books can serve as effective educational tools, children must first begin to understand the symbolic nature and structure of books.

Symbolic Understanding

Picture books are usually one of the first types of books that young children encounter, and a range of styles may be included in the category. Wordless picture books, for example, are often considered "pure" picture books: the entire story is told through the illustrations. Narrative storybooks designed for young children are also frequently referred to as picture books. These books tend to rely strongly on illustrations to help establish the setting, define and develop characters, extend the plot, and contribute to textual coherence (Fang, 1996), thereby reducing the processing demands and background knowledge needed to comprehend the narrative. Pictures and illustrations may, in fact, facilitate children's ability to remember specific and concrete information (Brookshire, Scharff, & Moses, 2002) and draw inferences (Pike, Barnes, & Barron, 2010) about a book's content. Children also appear to pay significantly more attention to the pictures than the narration (Simcock, Garrity & Barr, 2011) or print (Evans & Saint-Aubin, 2005) during book-reading experiences. Importantly, young children may be able to independently access the information depicted in illustrations even if they are unable to read the text by themselves.

Before young children can learn new information from books, they must first possess a certain level of symbolic understanding. Because picture books are inherently symbolic, to successfully gain new content knowledge from picture books, children must first master the "three R's": representation, referent, and relation (DeLoache, Pierroutsakos, & Troseth, 1996). Children must understand that a picture is a *representation* that displays information about a *referent*. When perceiving and interpreting a picture, children must not only see the representation (i.e., picture surface), but also "see through" the representation to its referent (i.e., what the picture surface symbolizes). When reading a picture book about a dog, for example, a child with full pictorial competence would consider both the properties of the illustration (e.g., glossy surface, two-dimensional) as well as the real-world properties of the dog depicted in the illustration (e.g., furry, animate). Children must also understand the nature of the *relation* between the representation and referent—for example, that the illustration of the dog is standing in for a real-world dog. Given this, children's symbolic understanding of books involves their perceptual abilities as well as their conceptual knowledge (DeLoache, Pierroutsakos, & Uttal, 2003).

Children's pictorial competence develops gradually over the first few years of life. This fact is sometimes overlooked, as the nature and utility of picture books may seem transparent to adults. Although infants can, for example, recognize familiar people and objects in photographs and illustrations, 9-month-olds nonetheless manually explore depicted objects (DeLoache, Pierroutsakos, Uttal, Rosengren, & Gottlieb, 1998), suggesting that they have yet to appreciate how pictures differ from their real-world referents. By 18 months of age, children's tendency to manually explore the surface of pictures is replaced by communication about the depicted referent. Preissler and Carey (2004), for instance, taught 18- and 24-month-olds a new label ("whisk") for a line drawing of an unfamiliar object. When subsequently shown both the drawing and the real object, the children all chose either the real object or both real object and the picture; none of them selected only the picture. Thus, young children appear to understand that new information, such as object labels, refers to real-world referents, not simply the pictures. This also suggests that, by at least the middle of children's second year, picture books may begin to serve as a valuable source of new knowledge.

Nevertheless, children's understanding of picture–referent relations may remain fragile for some time. For example, 2-year-olds have difficulty matching objects depicted in color photographs to their real-world referents (Harris, Kavanaugh, & Dowson, 1997), and 2.5-year-olds have difficulty remembering which of two objects matches a picture they have recently seen (Callaghan, 2000). Even preschoolers sometimes confuse the properties of pictures and real objects, claiming that a picture of ice cream will feel cold to the touch (Beilin & Pearlman, 1991) or that shaking a picture of stacked blocks will cause the blocks to tumble (Flavell, Flavell, Green, & Korfmacher, 1990). Although pictures and illustrations may provide valuable information independent of or complementary to the text of a book, such research suggests that the ability to acquire such knowledge continues to be tenuous throughout the early childhood years. As such, the role of picture books as a source of real-world knowledge may increase only gradually with children's experience and development.

Story Grammar

In addition to its illustrations, a picture book's text may also be a valuable source of new information. Thus, to gain the most from book reading, children must possess not only some understanding of the nature of pictures, but also the nature of the story they are listening to or reading. Narrative picture books are the most common type of books selected by adults to read with young children (Duke, 2000). Such narratives are typically defined as fictional stories possessing a common structure: setting, problem, response, and outcome. This common structure may facilitate children's construction of a "story schema," or a set of expectations about the parts of a typical narrative and the relationship among those parts (e.g., Johnson & Mandler, 1980; Rumelhart, 1975). As each part of a narrative is encountered, children's story schema may help them roughly predict what will happen next, which may then help them to form coherent representations of stories. As a result, story schema may help guide children's learning from books by providing them with a general framework through which new knowledge is inferred and subsequently remembered.

Even young children appear to possess relatively well-developed story schemas. When asked to "read" a picture book, for example, kindergartners frequently produce language characteristic of narrative books, such as the formulaic opening "once upon a time" (Purcell-Gates, 1988). They may also spontaneously reorder jumbled stories to preserve their temporal sequence, thereby increasing both comprehensibility and memorability (Low & Durkin, 2000). Importantly, children's story schema and knowledge development may be linked in a mutually reinforcing manner. Children with better comprehension skills tend to have stronger expectations about the structure and sequence of elements in stories (Cain, 2003), while those with a greater understanding of narrative structure tend to have stronger listening comprehension skills (Lynch et al., 2008). In fact, explicitly teaching children about narrative structure may improve their comprehension and recall of a book's content by helping them to recognize the important elements and draw appropriate inferences (Dimino, Taylor, & Gersten, 1995).

Prior Knowledge

In addition to understanding the fundamental properties of picture books, children must also possess the foundational knowledge necessary to interpret the content. Children's existing vocabulary and content knowledge may positively influence their acquisition of new information from books, possibly through facilitating both their comprehension and inferencing abilities (Pinkham & Neuman, 2012).

Vocabulary

Research has long established that the breadth and depth of children's vocabulary knowledge significantly predicts their comprehension skills (for review, see Neuman, Pinkham, & Kaefer, in press). When listening to or reading a book, young children must first derive the meanings of the individual words. Words must then be connected to form sentences, sentences connected to form events, and so forth, to derive key ideas and themes. In this way, children form a representation of the state of affairs described by the book. Accurate representations are necessary for both successful comprehension and knowledge acquisition.

Because the first step toward building an accurate representation involves discerning word meanings, children's overall learning may be significantly reduced if too many words in a book are unknown. Moreover, the relation between children's vocabulary knowledge and their comprehension of book content appears reciprocal in nature: greater vocabulary knowledge may lead to better comprehension, and better comprehension may lead to acquiring new knowledge (Stanovich, 1986). To understand a book's content, children must know approximately 95% of the words; the remaining 5% can typically be inferred from context. Children with proficient vocabularies may thus gain both new vocabulary and content knowledge from books, whereas children with more limited vocabularies may suffer a double loss: the book is puzzling because too many words are unknown and, as a result, a learning opportunity is missed. For infants and toddlers learning their first words and incrementally building their vocabularies, wordless or nearly wordless picture books may therefore be more beneficial learning tools than books composed of relatively sophisticated vocabulary or complex narratives, particularly when extratextual scaffolding is limited or absent. Similarly, preschoolers and older children may learn new information most readily from books with vocabulary demands consistent with their current level of vocabulary knowledge (see also Duke, Halvorsen, & Knight, Chapter 12, this volume).

Content Knowledge

In addition to understanding individual words, children must also understand a book's overall content. As a result, children's comprehension and learning may be driven, at least in part, by their preexisting content knowledge. Consider the following from the children's book *Is a Blue Whale the Biggest Thing There Is?*:

> If you put 100 blue whales in a really big jar, and then put two of those whale jars on an enormously large platform, that tower of whale jars would look quite small balanced on top of Mount Everest! (Wells, 1993)

Even if each word is familiar, only children with specific prior content knowledge (i.e., blue whales, Mount Everest) may fully comprehend the sentence's meaning and learn new information from the book (i.e., relative size of things on Earth).

Preexisting content knowledge may positively influence children's subsequent learning in a number of ways. First, prior knowledge about a book's content may create expectations, thereby directing children's attention toward information that is especially relevant or important. Second, content knowledge may facilitate comprehension by providing a stable framework for memory encoding and retrieval. Finally, content knowledge may benefit children's ability to fill in informational gaps to maintain coherence and enhance their representation of the book's content. Successful inferencing requires that new information be integrated with children's preexisting knowledge base. To interpret "Bobby grabbed his mitt and headed to first base," for example, children may use their content knowledge (e.g., mitts are used in baseball) to go beyond the explicitly stated information and form more detailed mental representations of the text (e.g., Bobby is the first baseman). When children possess accurate content knowledge about a topic, they may demonstrate superior inferencing and learning relative to instances in which such knowledge is incorrect, inaccessible, or lacking (see Pinkham & Neuman, 2012, for further discussion).

Having a broad knowledge base may thus positively contribute to children's ability to learn new information from books in at least two respects. In the more immediate sense, their extant content knowledge may help children encode, retrieve, and comprehend a book's content. More broadly, prior content knowledge may also help children learn how to interpret and apply the information they have just learned.

Do Young Children Gain Real-World Knowledge from Books?

Given the still-developing nature of young children's understanding of books and their general knowledge base, their ability to effectively use books as learning tools is likely also still developing. This does not mean, of course, that very young children cannot learn anything from books. Two-year-olds, for example, are able to correct parents if they deviate from the text of a familiar storybook (Sulzby, 1985), while infants as young as 8 months of age can recognize words from frequently read stories (Jusczyk & Hohne, 1997). Although compelling, such findings, however, do not necessarily provide evidence of young children acquiring knowledge from books; rather, this may simply be evidence of rote memorization. For books to be truly effective learning tools, children must be able not only to comprehend and recall the book's content; they must also be able to generalize and extend their knowledge between the book and the real world. In recent years, researchers have begun to examine the types of content young children may learn from books, particularly when the book-reading experience is not scaffolded by adults' extratextual comments or behaviors. This research has primarily focused on children's ability to learn two broad types of content: ways of acting on the world and knowledge about the real world.

Ways of Acting on the World

Through books, children may be exposed to new ways of acting on the world, including new behaviors (e.g., brushing teeth, potty training) and strategies (e.g., sharing, making friends). To examine whether young children can acquire such knowledge from picture books, researchers frequently utilize an imitation paradigm. In a typical imitation task, children encounter a novel action sequence, such as how to construct a toy rattle, in a picture book. Following a brief delay, they are then given the opportunity to complete the action themselves. There are at least two benefits to this paradigm: first, children have to both retain and generalize new knowledge to successfully complete the task; second, since knowledge is assessed through a behavioral measure, researchers can examine young children's learning without relying on their ability to verbalize what they know.

Using such an imitation paradigm, Simcock and DeLoache (2006) demonstrated that 18- and 24-month-old children are able to learn novel action sequences when depicted by realistic color photographs. Not until 30 months of age, however, are children able to reenact action sequences depicted by realistic line drawings. For young children, the iconicity of the illustrations within picture books may thus influence knowledge acquisition. This may be particularly important given children's tendency to pay more attention to a book's illustrations than its content (Evans & Saint-Aubin, 2005; Simcock et al., 2011).

In subsequent work, Simcock and colleagues investigated additional factors that may affect children's ability to learn from picture books. The influence of iconicity, for example, appears to decline after repeated exposure: both 18- and 24-month-olds are able to learn new action sequences depicted by realistic line drawings after four (but not two) exposures to a picture book (Simcock & DeLoache, 2008). The learning context also appears to be an important factor: although 18-month-olds appear able to learn new behaviors from book-reading interactions, they appear unable to generalize this knowledge to new contexts (e.g., different testing room) or slightly different materials (e.g., different-colored rattle). By at least 2 years of age, slight changes in context or stimuli may no longer disrupt children's ability to relate the contents of books to the real world; however, their ability to generalize new information may decline sharply after a delay of as little as 1 day (Simcock & Dooley, 2007).

Books may convey new behavioral information through text as well as illustrations. To learn such information, particularly from fictional narratives, children may have to reason by analogy. For analogical problem solving, children must be able to transfer a solution from a problem presented in one domain (e.g., a story about a genie who used a rolled-up magic carpet to move jewels from one bottle to another) to solve a similar problem presented in a new domain (e.g., children are asked to transfer balls from one bowl to another). Because children must recognize the similar relational structure of problems in different domains and contexts, analogical problem solving is often considered a relatively difficult task for children under the age of 10. Nonetheless, younger children may be able to transfer solutions to novel problems under certain conditions, such as a simple story structure (Holyoak, Junn, & Billman, 1984), repetition of goal-relevant features of the story (Brown, Kane, &

Echols, 1986), and familiarity with the characters in the original story (Richert, Shawber, Hoffman, & Taylor, 2009).

Knowledge about the Real World

Books also have the potential to serve as good sources of vocabulary and content knowledge. For example, children's books contain relatively more rare or sophisticated words than most oral language, including children's television and adult speech (Cunningham & Stanovich, 1998). But while a wealth of research on shared book-reading reports positive (although limited) effects on children's vocabulary knowledge (e.g., Mol et al., 2008), these studies are frequently confounded through using commercially available books, not accounting for whether children encounter the words outside the intervention, simultaneously teaching a large number of words, and/or confounding whether children learned new words from extratextual comments during the shared-reading interaction or from the books themselves.

Recent work, however, has attempted to control for many of these factors. Pinkham and Neuman (2011), for example, eliminated all extratextual conversation during a shared-reading interaction, focusing instead on the information children acquired incidentally from an experimenter-created storybook. The majority of preschoolers were able to learn at least one new word from the text, particularly if the new vocabulary was explicitly linked to their preexisting content knowledge. Moreover, their memory for new content knowledge was significantly above chance. In subsequent work, Kaefer, Pinkham, and Neuman (2011) reported that preschoolers' prior content knowledge may directly influence their ability to gain new vocabulary and content knowledge from storybooks (see also Barnes, Dennis, & Haefele-Kalvaitis, 1996; Cain, Oakhill, Barnes, & Bryant, 2001).

Although young children may be able to learn new words from books, their ability to generalize this knowledge may nonetheless be limited. Ganea, Pickard, and DeLoache (2008) found that 18-month-olds were able to extend newly learned object labels from books to the real world, but only when the objects were depicted by realistic photographs. They did not, by contrast, generalize new words from cartoons to real objects, suggesting that young children's knowledge acquisition may be best served by realistic illustrations. Children 24 months of age and younger also failed to extend newly learned words to slightly different category members (e.g., different color) (Ganea, Allen, Butler, Carey, & DeLoache, 2009). This is consistent with research demonstrating that children may need to be taught a label (e.g., *dog*) for multiple exemplars from a given category (e.g., illustrations of a beagle, dachshund, and Weimaraner) in order to effectively generalize their knowledge (e.g., Namy & Gentner, 2002). And as with their ability to learn new behaviors, contextual cues may affect children's ability to learn new words. For example, Horst, Parsons, and Bryan (2011) found that 3-year-olds were more likely to learn new words when the same story was read three times than when three different stories (each containing the same target words) were each read a single time. Moreover, children were better able to retain the new information in the former condition than in the latter.

In recent work, Ganea, Ma, and DeLoache (2011) specifically investigated the extent to which young children can learn new content knowledge through book reading. After listening to a book that illustrated and described color camouflage in frogs, 4- but not 3-year-olds were able to use the information to explain a similar situation in a book about butterflies. More intriguingly, 4-year-olds were able to extend their knowledge about color camouflage from book illustrations to live animals, such as lizards and crabs. This ability, however, appeared to be somewhat tenuous, consistent with evidence that altering the contextual cues present when information is initially learned may have a negative impact on children's later recall.

Summary

Overall, this growing body of research suggests that young children are able to learn both new ways of acting on the world and knowledge about the real world through incidental exposure in books, even when the extratextual features that characterize many shared-reading interactions are not present. Although their learning may appear tenuous, children's acquisition, retention, and generalization of new information may be facilitated through features such as story structure, consistent contextual cues, and repeated exposure. The next section addresses how these features may be utilized to help scaffold children's knowledge development.

How Can Books Best Scaffold Knowledge Development?

Thus far, this chapter has examined the extent to which young children can acquire new knowledge from books, particularly when the book's content is not scaffolded through interactions with an adult reader. Although young children may be able to learn some information from books as early as infancy, their ability to use books as a knowledge resource may be limited by their developing understanding of books and the depth and breadth of their extant knowledge base. Moreover, their learning may be disrupted through changes in context or stimuli—changes that may be integral to knowledge generalization and transfer.

Given that books can provide important learning opportunities, a crucial question is how to facilitate children's ability to acquire that knowledge. One answer—and one that perhaps appears most frequently in the research literature—is to focus on improving the quality of extra-textual interactions as a means of scaffolding children's comprehension and learning. As previously discussed, however, the effects of many such shared-reading interventions appear surprisingly limited. Furthermore, because adult readers possess varying skills and knowledge, their scaffolding may not be of uniformly high quality. Books themselves may thus be particularly important when extratextual comments are insufficient or nonexistent, such as during lower-quality shared-reading or independent reading experiences (Pinkham & Neuman, 2011, 2012). Given that children's ability to learn from books may be influenced by factors including the book structure, learning context, and amount of exposure, an alternative (although not necessarily mutually exclusive) strategy may be to utilize these factors to facilitate children's knowledge acquisition.

Book Structure

Books are an inherently symbolic medium, but it is often quite difficult for young children to simultaneously consider the two aspects of symbolic objects (i.e., as a concrete entity and in relation to its abstract referent) (DeLoache et al., 2003). In such situations, children's ability to understand and learn from books may be inhibited. This may particularly be the case when books are especially salient or interesting. Manipulative features intended to increase young children's engagement, for instance, may negatively affect learning. In recent work by Tare, Chiong, Ganea, and DeLoache (2010), 20-month-olds appeared less able to learn new words from books with salient manipulative features (e.g., pop-ups, pull tabs, textures) than from standard picture books, while 36-month-olds experienced greater difficulty learning new facts from the manipulative picture books. Similarly, children's learning may be impeded by less realistic images, such as cartoons. Because higher levels of perceptual similarity between books and their real-world referents may make the symbolic relationship more transparent (Callaghan, 2000), books with greater iconicity (i.e., realistic photographs and illustrations) and limited manipulative features may be considered preferable as learning tools.

A book's organizational structure may also influence children's learning. Children may benefit from books with a simple story structure

(Holyoak et al., 1984) and coherent story grammar (Dimino et al., 1995). In recent work, Pinkham and Neuman (2011) hypothesized that storybook texts can also be explicitly structured in a manner that will scaffold children's learning. Specifically, they examined whether story-books organized around a familiar taxonomic category (i.e., birds) could provide children with a general conceptual framework through which information could be readily encoded and subsequently remembered. Preschoolers learned significantly more words and content knowledge from taxonomically organized storybooks than traditional storybooks. Considered collectively, research suggests that books must be carefully structured to provide young children with every opportunity to acquire new knowledge.

Learning Context

In general, knowledge transfer may be facilitated by the similarity of the context in which new information is learned and the context in which that information is applied. Altering those contextual cues may thus have a negative impact on children's ability to generalize their knowledge (Barnett & Ceci, 2002). Even slight changes, such as altering the room in which a book is originally read, may disrupt children's knowledge transfer. Children may therefore benefit from opportunities to encounter a book's content across multiple contexts.

Books aimed at young children may sometimes further reduce the similarity between initial learning and transfer by using fantasy con-texts or characters to teach information meant to be applied in the real world. Almost by definition, however, fantasy worlds may be fundamen-tally dissimilar to the real world. In fact, children conceptualize fictional worlds (e.g., the worlds of SpongeBob or Batman) as distinct and sepa-rate from the real world (Skolnick & Bloom, 2006) and are significantly more likely to transfer knowledge learned from stories about real people than stories about fantasy characters (Richert et al., 2009). They are also more likely to trust information learned from scientific-looking books than books that appear fantastical (Woolley & Van Reet, 2006). This suggests that fictional or fantastical storybooks may be a relatively less effective resource for teaching young children real-world information than nonfiction or informational books.

Repeated Exposure

Repeated readings may also facilitate children's knowledge acquisition by providing additional opportunities to encode, associate, and store new information (Pinkham, Neuman, & Lillard, 2011). Children's learning of new action sequences (Simcock & DeLoache, 2008) and vocabulary words (Biemiller & Boote, 2006) from books, for example, increases significantly with additional readings. Repetition may also give children more chances to notice deeper conceptual similarities, thereby facilitating their ability to transfer knowledge to new situations (Ganea et al., 2011). Children may thus benefit more from several readings of a single book than from single readings of several books (see also Horst et al., 2011).

Implications and Future Directions

Books are essential resources for knowledge development. They can serve as invaluable teaching tools, exposing children to things, places, and events that are beyond their direct experience. Reading books can provide opportunities to encounter new ideas, consider alternative perspectives, and expand world knowledge. Providing all children with access to books is thus an important and worthy goal (e.g., High et al., 2000; Neuman, 1999). However, the mere availability of books is likely insufficient. To truly impact children's knowledge development, we need to also consider children's understanding of the books themselves, as well as the breadth and depth of their extant knowledge base. Books should be carefully selected to be consistent with children's current knowledge and abilities, and consideration should be given to book features that may facilitate children's learning, particularly in nondialogic contexts.

For books to serve as truly effective learning tools, children must be able to generalize and extend new knowledge from the pages of the book to the real world. Children who have read a book about insects need to be able use that knowledge when encountering a real ladybug. Moreover, they must be able to apply that knowledge regardless of whether the ladybug is in their classroom or on the playground, whether it is encountered the same day as the insect book or weeks later. To date, however, children's knowledge transfer over periods longer than 24 hours or across contexts has been largely unexamined (Barnett & Ceci, 2002).

It also remains unclear whether young children recognize books as good resources for learning. As adults, we may assume that books contain largely reliable knowledge and are less susceptible to inaccuracies (accidental or intentional) than information conveyed by other people. Young children also appear quite discriminating when evaluating sources of new information, judging some experiences (e.g., Pinkham & Jaswal, 2011) and informants (e.g., Corrow, Cowell, Doebel, & Koenig, Chapter 3, this volume) to be more reliable and trustworthy than others. But whether children are similarly discriminating when judging knowledge learned from books relative to other sources (e.g., other people, TV) or learned from some types of books versus others (e.g., fictional narrative, informational) remains an open question.

Conclusion

Parents and teachers often consider books to be important resources for children's development. On average, they spend a considerable amount of time reading to children and engaging them in book-reading activities. Children may derive many benefits from these shared-reading interactions. However, we must also remember that the nature and utility of books as knowledge resources may not seem intuitive to children, and that their symbolic understanding and world knowledge are still developing. In addition to providing children with opportunities to interact with books, we must also foster the skills and knowledge necessary to learn how to learn.

REFERENCES

Adams, M. (1990). *Beginning to read*. Cambridge, MA: MIT Press.

Barnes, M. A., Dennis, M., & Haefele-Kalvaitis, J. (1996). The effects of knowledge availability and knowledge accessibility on coherence and elaborative inferencing in children from six to fifteen years of age. *Journal of Experimental Child Psychology, 61*(3), 216–241.

Barnett, S. M., & Ceci, S. J. (2002). When and where do we apply what we learn? A taxonomy for far transfer. *Psychological Bulletin, 128*(4), 612–637.

Beilin, H., & Pearlman, E. G. (1991). Children's iconic realism: Object versus property realism. In H. W. Reese (Ed.), *Advances in child development and behavior* (Vol. 23, pp. 73–111). New York: Academic Press.

Biemiller, A., & Boote, C. (2006). An effective method for building meaning vocabulary in primary grades. *Journal of Educational Psychology, 98*(1), 44–62.

Brookshire, J., Scharff, L. F. V., & Moses, L. E. (2002). The influence of illustrations on children's book preferences and comprehension. *Reading Psychology, 23*(4), 323–339.

Brown, A. L., Kane, M. J., & Echols, C. H. (1986). Young children's mental models determine analogical transfer across problems with a common goal structure. *Cognitive Development, 1*(2), 103–121.

Bus, A. G., van IJzendoorn, M. H., & Pellegrini, A. D. (1995). Joint book reading makes for success in learning to read: A meta-analysis on intergenerational transmission of literacy. *Review of Educational Research, 65*(1), 1–21.

Cain, K. (2003). Text comprehension and its relation to coherence and cohesion in children's fictional narratives. *British Journal of Developmental Psychology, 21,* 335–351.

Cain, K., Oakhill, J. V., Barnes, M. A., & Bryant, P. E. (2001). Comprehension skill, inference-making ability, and their relation to knowledge. *Memory & Cognition, 29*(6), 850–859.

Callaghan, T. C. (2000). Factors affecting children's graphic symbol use in the third year: Language, similarity, and iconicity. *Cognitive Development, 15*(2), 185–214.

Cunningham, A. E., & Stanovich, K. E. (1991). Tracking the unique effects of print exposure in children: Associations with vocabulary, general knowledge, and spelling. *Journal of Educational Psychology, 83*(2), 264–274.

Cunningham, A. E., & Stanovich, K. E. (1998). What reading does for the mind. *American Educator, 22*(1–2), 8–15.

DeBaryshe, B. D. (1993). Joint picture-book reading correlates of early oral language skill. *Journal of Child Language, 20,* 455–461.

DeLoache, J. S., Pierroutsakos, S. L., & Troseth, G. L. (1996). The three "R's" of pictorial competence. In R. Vasta (Ed.), *Annals of child development* (Vol. 12, pp. 1–48). Bristol, UK: Kingsley.

DeLoache, J. S., Pierroutsakos, S. L., & Uttal, D. H. (2003). The origins of pictorial competence. *Current Directions in Psychological Science, 12*(4), 114–118.

DeLoache, J. S., Pierroutsakos, S. L., Uttal, D. H., Rosengren, K. S., & Gottlieb, A. (1998). Grasping the nature of pictures. *Psychological Science, 9*(3), 205–210.

Dimino, J., Taylor, R. M., & Gersten, R. M. (1995). Synthesis of the research on story grammar as a means to increase comprehension. *Reading & Writing Quarterly: Overcoming Learning Difficulties, 11,* 53–72.

Duke, N. K. (2000). 3.6 minutes per day: The scarcity of informational texts in first grade. *Reading Research Quarterly, 35,* 202–224.

Evans, M. A., & Saint-Aubin, J. (2005). What children are looking at during shared storybook reading: Evidence from eye movement monitoring. *Psychological Science, 16*(11), 913–920.

Ezell, H. K., & Justice, L. M. (2005). *Shared storybook reading: Building young children's language and emergent literacy skills.* Baltimore, MD: Brookes.

Fang, Z. (1996). Illustrations, text, and the child reader: What are pictures in children's storybooks for? *Reading Horizons, 37*(2), 130–142.

Flavell, J. H., Flavell, E. R., Green, F. L., & Korfmacher, J. E. (1990). Do young children think of television images as pictures or real objects? *Journal of Broadcasting & Electronic Media, 34*(4), 399–419.

Ganea, P. A., Allen, M. L., Butler, L., Carey, S., & DeLoache, J. S. (2009). Toddlers' referential understanding of pictures. *Journal of Experimental Child Psychology, 104*(3), 283–295.

Ganea, P. A., Ma, L., & DeLoache, J. S. (2011). Young children's learning and transfer of biological information from picture books to real animals. *Child Development, 82*(5), 1421–1433.

Ganea, P. A., Pickard, M. B., & DeLoache, J. S. (2008). Transfer between picture books and the real world by very young children. *Journal of Cognition and Development, 9*, 46–66.

Hardman, M., & Jones, L. (1999). Sharing books with babies: Evaluation of an early literacy intervention. *Educational Review, 51*(3), 221–229.

Harris, P. L., Kavanaugh, R. D., & Dowson, L. (1997). The depiction of imaginary transformations: Early comprehension of a symbolic function. *Cognitive Development, 12*(1), 1–19.

High, P. C., LaGasse, L., Becker, S., Ahlgren, I., & Gardner, A. (2000). Literacy promotion in primary care pediatrics: Can we make a difference? *Pediatrics, 105*(3), 927–934.

Hoffman, J. V., Roser, N. L., & Battle, N. (1993). Reading aloud in classrooms: From the modal toward a "model." *The Reading Teacher, 46*(6), 496–503.

Holyoak, K. J., Junn, E. N., & Billman, D. O. (1984). Development of analogical problem-solving skill. *Child Development, 55*(6), 2042–2055.

Horst, J. S., Parsons, K. L., & Bryan, N. M. (2011). Get the story straight: Contextual repetition promotes word learning from storybooks. *Frontiers in Psychology, 2*, 1–11.

Johnson, N. S., & Mandler, J. M. (1980). A tale of two structures: Underlying and surface forms in stories. *Poetics, 9*, 51–86.

Jusczyk, P. W., & Hohne, E. A. (1997). Infants' memory for spoken words. *Science, 277*(5334), 1984–1986.

Kaefer, T., Pinkham, A. M., & Neuman, S. B. (2011, March). *Taxonomic organization scaffolds young children's learning from storybooks: A design experiment.* Paper presented at the semiannual meeting of the Society for Research on Educational Effectiveness, Washington, DC.

Low, J., & Durkin, K. (2000). Event knowledge and children's recall of television based narratives. *British Journal of Developmental Psychology, 18*, 247–267.

Lynch, J. S., van den Broek, P., Kremer, K. E., Kendeou, P., White, M. J., & Lorch, E. P. (2008). The development of narrative comprehension and its relation to other early reading skills. *Reading Psychology, 29*, 327–365.

Mol, S. E., Bus, A. G., de Jong, M. T., & Smeets, D. J. H. (2008). Added value of dialogic parent–child book readings: A meta-analysis. *Early Education and Development, 19*(1), 7–26.

Morrow, L. M. (1988). Young children's responses to one-to-one story readings in school settings. *Reading Research Quarterly, 23*(1), 89–107.

Namy, L. L., & Gentner, D. (2002). Making a silk purse out of two sow's ears: Young children's use of comparisons in category learning. *Journal of Experimental Psychology: General, 131*(1), 5–15.

National Early Literacy Panel. (2008). *Developing early literacy.* Washington, DC: National Institute for Literacy.

Neuman, S. B. (1996). Children engaging in storybook reading: The influence of access to print resources, opportunity, and parental interaction. *Early Childhood Research Quarterly, 11*(4), 495–513.

Neuman, S. B. (1999). Books make a difference: A study of access to literacy. *Reading Research Quarterly, 34*(3), 286–311.

Neuman, S. B., Pinkham, A. M., & Kaefer, T. (in press). Building word and world knowledge in the early years. In K. Hall, T. Cremin, B. Comber, & L. Moll (Eds.), *International handbook of research on children's literacy, learning and culture*. Malden, MA: Wiley-Blackwell.

Pike, M. M., Barnes, M. A., & Barron, R. W. (2010). The role of illustrations in children's inferential comprehension. *Journal of Experimental Child Psychology, 105*(3), 243–255.

Pinkham, A. M., & Jaswal, V. K. (2011). Watch and learn? Infants privilege efficiency over pedagogy during imitative learning. *Infancy, 16*(5), 535–544.

Pinkham, A. M., & Neuman, S. B. (in press). Early literacy development. In B. H. Wasik & B. Van Horn (Eds.), *Handbook of family literacy* (Vol. 2). New York: Routledge.

Pinkham, A. M., & Neuman, S. B. (2011, November). *Taxonomically organized storybooks for vocabulary and concept development.* Paper presented at the annual meeting of the Literacy Research Association, Jacksonville, FL.

Pinkham, A. M., Neuman, S. B., & Lillard, A. S. (2011, November). *Have we underestimated repetition? Repeated exposures to promote vocabulary development.* Paper presented at the annual meeting of the Literacy Research Association, Jacksonville, FL.

Preissler, M. A., & Carey, S. (2004). Do both pictures and words function as symbols for 18- and 24-month-old children? *Journal of Cognition and Development, 5*(2), 185–212.

Purcell-Gates, V. (1988). Lexical and syntactic knowledge of written narrative held by well-read-to kindergartners and second graders. *Research in the Teaching of English, 22,* 128–160.

Raikes, H., Pan, B. A., Luze, G., Tamis-LeMonda, C. S., Brooks-Gunn, J., Constantine, J., et al. (2006). Mother–child bookreading in low-income families: Correlates and outcomes during the first three years of life. *Child Development, 77,* 803–1128.

Richert, R. A., Shawber, A. B., Hoffman, R. E., & Taylor, M. (2009). Learning from fantasy and real characters in preschool and kindergarten. *Journal of Cognition and Development, 10*(1–2), 41–66.

Rideout, V. J., Vandewater, E. A., & Wartella, E. A. (2003). *Zero to six: Electronic media in the lives of infants, toddlers, and preschoolers.* Menlo Park, CA: Kaiser Family Foundation.

Rogoff, B. (2003). *The cultural nature of human development.* New York: Oxford University Press.

Rumelhart, D. E. (1975). Notes on a schema for stories. In D. G. Bobrow & A. Collins (Eds.), *Representation and understanding: Studies in cognitive science* (pp. 211–236). New York: Academic Press.

Simcock, G., & DeLoache, J. S. (2006). Get the picture? The effects of iconicity on toddlers' reenactment from picture books. *Developmental Psychology, 42*(6), 1352–1357.

Simcock, G., & DeLoache, J. S. (2008). The effect of repetition on infants' imitation from picture books varying in iconicity. *Infancy, 13*(6), 687–697.

Simcock, G., & Dooley, M. (2007). Generalization of learning from picture books to novel test conditions by 18- and 24-month-old children. *Developmental Psychology, 43*(6), 1568–1578.

Simcock, G., Garrity, K., & Barr, R. (2011). The effect of narrative cues on infants' imitation from television and picture books. *Child Development, 82*(5), 1607–1619.

Skolnick, D., & Bloom, P. (2006). What does Batman think about SpongeBob? Children's understanding of the fantasy/fantasy distinction. *Cognition, 101*(1), B9–B18.

Stanovich, K. E. (1986). Matthew effects in reading: Some consequence of individual differences in the acquisition of literacy. *Reading Research Quarterly, 21*(4), 360–407.

Stanovich, K. E., West, R. F., & Harrison, M. R. (1995). Knowledge growth and maintenance across the life span: The role of print exposure. *Developmental Psychology, 31*(5), 811–826.

Sulzby, E. (1985). Children's emergent reading of favorite storybooks: A developmental study. *Reading Research Quarterly, 20*(4), 458–481.

Tare, M., Chiong, C., Ganea, P., & DeLoache, J. (2010). Less is more: How manipulative features affect children's learning from picture books. *Journal of Applied Developmental Psychology, 31*(5), 395–400.

van Kleeck, A., Stahl, S. A., & Bauer, E. B. (Eds.) (2003). *On reading books to children: Parents and teachers.* Mahwah, NJ: Erlbaum.

Wells, R. E. (1993). *Is a blue whale the biggest thing there is?* Morton Grove, IL: Albert Whitman & Company.

Woolley, J. D., & Van Reet, J. (2006). Effects of context on judgments concerning the reality status of novel entities. *Child Development, 77*(6), 1778–1793.

CHAPTER 7

■ ■ ■ ■ ■

Television and Children's Knowledge

Heather J. Lavigne
Daniel R. Anderson

Children are not born knowing how to watch television. Before 2 years of age, young children suffer from a video deficit, such that information displayed through live demonstration is more meaningful to them than the same demonstration shown on video (for reviews, see Anderson & Hanson, 2010; Anderson & Pempek, 2005). There is currently no evidence that, in infancy, television has any substantial influence on children's knowledge development. Around 30 months of age, however, children's relationship to television changes. Children's increasing sequential and linguistic comprehension allows them to begin to use television as a source of information about the real world. Once this developmental shift occurs, television can be a powerful means of knowledge acquisition and behavioral change. But, of course, the power of television to teach cuts two ways: television can be a source of misinformation and negative behaviors, or it can be a window to the world of education and knowledge.

Children's Relationship with Television

From an early age, the majority of American children are exposed to television. According to recent Nielsen research, children 2 to 8 years of age spend an average of 25 hours 48 minutes watching television on traditional TV sets each week (Nielsen Company, 2010). This same report estimated that children ages 2 through 11 comprise 10% of the total American viewing audience. In 2008 the average U.S. home owned 2.86 television sets, indicating the physical presence of a television in multiple rooms in the home (Nielsen Company, 2009). Moreover, 46% of preschool children ages 4–6 have a television set in their bedrooms, putting more control of what and how much to watch within children's reach (Rideout & Hamel, 2006).

As children mature and gain experience with the medium, their TV viewing behaviors change considerably. Children's attention to and time spent with television increases substantially from infancy until about 11 years of age (Anderson & Levin, 1976; Anderson, Lorch, Collins, Field, & Nathan, 1986). Around 30 months of age, their comprehension of child-directed TV programs improves alongside the development of attention skills, increases in language comprehension, increases in the ability to appreciate the meaning of transitions between shots, and other aspects of cognitive development. Children subsequently develop sophisticated television-viewing skills, including the ability to multitask between television viewing and other activities while losing little or nothing in comprehension of the TV program (Lorch, Anderson, & Levin, 1979). When watching TV, children do not simply stare at the screen; rather, they frequently look at and away from the screen, often also playing with toys or engaging with other viewers. Children then use audio and visual indicators to guide their attention back to the television at important points. These indicators, referred to as "formal features," take the shape of various production elements like editing techniques, cuts, pans, zooms, sound effects, changes in character voices, signature musical cues, activity level, and program pacing; they also include character features, such as puppet, animal, adult human, and so on. Through these formal features, children learn to look at the TV when their attention is likely to be rewarded by important, entertaining, and comprehensible content (for review, see Anderson & Kirkorian, 2006).

A number of influential theories have been developed to account for television's impact on children's knowledge and behavior. Bandura's (1971) social learning theory, for example, proposes that children learn through observing models. While watching television, children formulate action schemas based on TV character behaviors and subsequently use this encoded information to guide their own future behaviors. According to Gerbner and colleagues' cultivation theory (e.g., Gerbner, Gross, Morgan, Signorielli, & Shanahan, 2002), by contrast, children's time spent watching television contributes to their perceptions of the world beyond their immediate experience. Cultivation theory posits that the effects of television vary based on frequency of viewing; thus lighter viewers' sense of reality might be less guided by television content than that of more regular viewers. Heavy viewing of violent content, for instance, might contribute to beliefs about the world as being dangerous and scary.

However, children's knowledge acquisition can go much further than the imitation or encoded message frequency proposed by these theories; complex, conceptual learning can also occur. This is perhaps best demonstrated through children's "knowledge transfer," or their ability to take information gathered under one scenario, extract abstract conceptual understanding, and successfully apply the newly acquired conceptual understanding to different but analogous situations. One theoretical model that characterizes children's conceptual learning and knowledge transfer from television is Fisch's (2000) capacity model. For successful knowledge acquisition, the demands of a learning task (the "cognitive load") cannot exceed available working memory. According to the capacity model, children's comprehension and learning of messages from television is directly related to their strategic use of available working memory resources relative to the narrative and educational content of the show. More specifically, the capacity model suggests that successful comprehension occurs when the distance between educational and narrative content is small; that is, the learning objectives are closely tied to the program's story. If the distance between educational and narrative content becomes too great, however, the two goals may end up in competition. In this case, narrative comprehension may consume children's working memory resources, resulting in a sacrifice of encoding and learning the educational content. Moreover, because, unlike book reading, children cannot control how quickly information is presented on television, quickly paced programs may additionally tax children's working memory resources. For learning to occur, educational (and, presumably, entertainment) programs must therefore take into account the complexity of knowledge being presented in relation to viewers' cognitive abilities.

Knowledge Acquired from Entertainment versus Educational Programming

The potential educational benefit of television is often a polarizing issue. Some may argue that all TV viewing is in some way educational. This is an important issue, particularly for television networks, given the Federal Communication Commission's regulations requiring broadcasters to provide a certain amount of educational programming for children in order to renew their licensure. Television programming, however, is not monolithic. Some programs are intentionally created for educational purposes, whereas others are intended primarily as entertainment. For the purposes of this discussion, we refer to "educational television" as that which "contributes to children's healthy development by addressing their cognitive/intellectual or social/emotional needs" (Jordan, 2000, p. 5). Although learning may occur from both entertainment and educational programs, this demarcation allows us to distinguish between learning that occurs incidentally from entertainment programs and knowledge obtained from intentionally designed educational television.

Entertainment Programming

The majority of programming broadcast on any given day is, by our standards, entertainment. Most entertainment programming developed specifically for children is narrative and often presented as animated short stories or live-action situation comedies. Children may also watch entertainment programs developed for more general audiences; the content of these programs is not directed toward any particular age group and may be considered enjoyable for both children and adults. Given the prevalence of entertainment programming, much of children's learning from television is incidental insofar as there may have been no producer-intended goal of teaching particular content. For example, children may correctly infer the meaning of an unfamiliar word by observing the context in which it is used on TV. However, their observations may also lead to erroneous conclusions, such as believing that vampires or monsters are real. Entertainment programs can thus present children with a great deal of information, accurate or skewed, about the real world, as well as about worlds that have little relationship to reality.

For children, entertainment programs may be a readily available source of general knowledge about the world. One important component of children's general knowledge is their vocabulary. In their classic study comparing two towns, one with television and another without, Schramm, Lyle, and Parker (1961) found that children in the town with television had better vocabularies than children in the town without television. Subsequent research by Lemish and Rice (1986) found that parent–child television co-viewing was associated with increased vocabulary development, suggesting that children may add vocabulary contained in television programs to their knowledge base. Noble (1983) also found that school-age children learned more general factual information from watching entertainment programming. Other research, however, has not found links between the availability of television and children's vocabulary or general knowledge (e.g., Harrison & Williams, 1986).

Therefore, although possible, the nature of television's contribution to children's general knowledge acquisition remains an open issue.

It is clear, however, that watching television can influence children's beliefs. For example, entertainment programs may influence children's sense of personal identity. Gender stereotypes may be created and reinforced, such as men are strong and women are sexy (Reichert & Carpenter, 2004). Content analyses reveal that in most entertainment TV programs, male characters are typically represented as being more dominant in social interactions, as well as more adventurous and aggressive, whereas female characters are typically more emotional and passive (e.g., Glascock, 2001). In a study of interactions between male and female scientists in popular films, for instance, researchers found frequent events that undermined women's authority, as well as both overt and subtle gender stereotypes (Steinke, 2005). Consistent with the notion that television can influence personal identity, some research has found that heavy TV viewers are more likely than light viewers to hold gender-stereotyped views of themselves and others (e.g., Ross, Anderson, & Wisocki, 1982). Similarly, children's perceptions and knowledge about their own or others' race may be affected by television. In particular, television has been found in numerous content analyses to present children with a distorted view of people in their world (e.g., Woodard, 1999).

Entertainment programs may also influence children's beliefs about families. Children often believe that portrayals of family life on television are realistic (Weiss & Wilson, 1998) and may use television to inform their understanding of how families should interact and operate as a unit (Douglas, 2003). They may, for example, base their perceptions of their own families on what is represented on television. After they viewed a negative emotional event in the context of a realistic family sitcom, Weiss and Wilson (1998) found that elementary school-age children altered their real-world perceptions to be more comparable to what they viewed on television. In the last several decades, more diverse families are being represented in entertainment programs, including adopted youth, same-sex parent families, or single-parent households. By seeing families that are more representative of American culture, television may help children form more diverse beliefs and complex norms and values about family life.

Children's real-world beliefs may also be affected by advertising aired during entertainment programming. Televised food marketing, for example, has been linked to nutritional beliefs and food consumption patterns that are generally detrimental to child health (Institute of Medicine, 2006). However, children may also learn from public-service announcements (PSAs), which use the techniques of advertising to positively influence health-related knowledge and behavior. Linebarger and

Piotrowski (2009a), for example, found that preschool-age children learned health messages about nutrition, physical activity, and hand washing from health-related PSAs. Importantly, children were able to retain this new knowledge and transfer it to novel situations.

In addition to acquiring new facts and beliefs, children may also acquire knowledge about behavior from television. For instance, children may learn to imitate character behaviors through watching TV. Perhaps the most studied aspect of imitative learning concerns aggressive portrayals. In one of the best-known demonstrations of such work, Bandura, Ross, and Ross (1963) exposed preschool-age children to a televised demonstration of aggressive behavior to a Bobo doll. After the exposure period, children were allowed to play with a replica of the doll, as well as other, more neutral toys. Results showed that children imitated the actions of the aggressive model on the Bobo doll (e.g., hitting, kicking, punching) and also transferred their knowledge to novel ways of abusing the doll (e.g., hitting it with toys).

Huesmann (1998) further suggested that children can learn aggressive or violent scripts from exposure to violent television. He argued that if children are frequently exposed to aggressive models, they may be more likely to adopt cognitive-behavioral scripts for dealing with problems in an aggressive way. This implies that frequent exposure to violence over long periods of time may have a cumulative effect on children's knowledge of how to solve problems in real-life situations. Because children may be exposed to a wide variety of social scripts from television, it is worth noting that they presumably may learn positive behaviors, not just those involving violence.

In addition to programs that glorify aggressive or violent behaviors, depictions of real-world violence or scary programs may also affect children's perceptions of the real world. In no other context is this more evident than in viewing news programming. Many young children are exposed to news content on a weekly basis, with about 27% of kindergarten children watching "frequently" (Roberts, Foehr, & Rideout, 2005; Simon & Merrill, 1997). At this age, however, it is still difficult for children to understand important features of the news, like geographic relevance, or make appropriate inferences, such as the level of danger (Cantor, Wilson, & Hoffner, 1986). Only with maturity are children better able to take into account the context of news stories in order to determine the likelihood of events actually occurring in their lives (Smith & Wilson, 2002). Thus, although news programming can be beneficial to children by creating awareness and a global perspective, it may also contribute to the formation of children's fears (Calvert, 1999). For example, children who are heavy viewers of television may see a dangerous and real event (e.g., the planes crashing into buildings on September 11,

2001) replayed many times, leading them to believe that it is a frequent occurrence and thus creating unrealistic fears.

Taken together, this research suggests that children may learn new fact, beliefs, and behaviors by watching entertainment programming. One of the most important unresolved questions is how children tag particular information within entertainment programs as being relevant to their own lives. Entertainment programs, particularly those created specifically for children, are, on the whole, fictitious, if not downright fantastic. Yet most of these programs do contain some information that is both accurate and applicable to the real world. How do children decide what is relevant and what is inaccurate or unusable? Future research is needed to address this question.

Educational Programming

We consider programs to be educational if they are deliberately and systematically designed to enhance children's cognitive, academic, and/or social development. Series of this nature are ideally developed through an extended period of curriculum development, research, and formative assessment. Unlike children's entertainment programming, educational shows are typically laid out in the form of a "bible": a guiding document that outlines program structure, characters, storylines, an educational philosophy, and content objectives. Developmental specialists, educators, and content specialists may be involved in an advisory capacity, and formative assessment is often conducted throughout the production process. Formative assessments typically involve a research team working with children representing the target audience in order to determine what aspects of the program are successful or unsuccessful in achieving both audience interest and learning. These results are then used by the producer and writers to guide script revision or other aspects of the production. Summative evaluations may also be conducted following production to measure whether the series achieves the objectives set forth in preproduction (see Fisch & Truglio, 2001, for further discussion).

Formative and summative evaluations show that children's programs can influence knowledge acquisition and behaviors. For instance, research has reported positive associations between educational programming and children's literacy development. Programs focused on enhancing literacy skills, such as *Between the Lions* and *Martha Speaks,* have been reported to improve preschool and kindergarten viewers' oral language skills, including word recognition and vocabulary knowledge, as compared to nonviewers (Linebarger, Kosanic, Greenwood, & Doku, 2004; Linebarger, Moses, & McMenamin, 2010). After an 8-week period of exposure to *Super Why!,* another program geared to support early literacy skills, viewers performed significantly better on tests of early reading achievement as compared to nonviewers (Linebarger, McMenamin, & Wainright, 2008). After periods of in-school viewing, the original production of *The Electric Company* positively affected reading achievement and literacy skills in 18 content areas for children in first through fourth grade (Ball & Bogatz, 1973). In recent years, a modern adaptation of *The Electric Company* has adopted a similar literacy curriculum while specifically focusing on literacy proficiency in low-income children. Kindergarten through fourth-grade students who were exposed to 50 episodes over a span of 10 weeks performed better on measures of vocabulary and phonics skills than nonviewers (Garity, Piotrowski, McMenamin, & Linebarger, 2010). Educational programming may be particularly beneficial for young children's comprehension skills through exposure to narrative structure (Linebarger & Piotrowski, 2009b). Collectively, these studies suggest that educational programming may be an important resource for children's literacy development (see also Silverman & Hines, Chapter 14, this volume).

The benefits of educational programs may also extend to STEM (i.e., science, technology, engineering, and mathematics) content areas. Preschoolers learned about concepts like measurement, counting, and strategies for problem solving from *Peep and the Big Wide World* (a program intended to introduce basic math and science skills) (Goodman Research Group, 2007), while *Sid the Science Kid* (a program modeled after the Preschool Pathway to Science curriculum) taught preschool viewers to identify science tools and ask questions that prompted further investigation beyond the concept demonstrated in the program (Goodman Research Group, 2010). Furthermore, after viewing *Square One TV,* children showed significant recall of demonstrated problems and solutions and were able to extend their knowledge of math content to new problems (Peel, Rockwell, Esty, & Gonzer, 1987). In addition to contributing to new knowledge acquisition, these studies suggest that programs focused on the STEM areas may also promote children's interest in furthering their own learning.

In addition to academic content, educational programming may positively influence children's beliefs and behaviors. Prosocial programs, for instance, focus on modeling positive behavior in the hope of teaching children how to behave during social interactions. For example, a protagonist may be put in a situation in which he believes he must lie to another character to avoid conflict. Throughout the episode, he may encounter the consequences of the lie and then explore alternatives to lying. Programs with prosocial themes have indeed been found effective. After multiple exposures to the animated *Dragon Tales* series, preschoolers showed higher levels of initiating organized play with others, choosing challenging tasks, sharing, and cooperation as compared to children who did not watch prosocial programming (Rust, 2001). Moreover, kindergarteners who viewed *Mister Rogers' Neighborhood* demonstrated higher levels of social skills like task persistence, rule obedience, and delay tolerance (Friedrich & Stein, 1973).

Sesame Street, one of the pioneers of children's educational programming, provides a wide-ranging curriculum that includes both academic and prosocial content. Perhaps the most intensively studied educational program on television, numerous evaluations have found that the series can enhance children's knowledge of numbers and the alphabet, relational terms, sorting and classification, roles of community members, naming of body parts, and knowledge about members of their community (e.g., Ball & Bogatz, 1970; Bogatz & Ball, 1971; Lesser, 1974). Research has also found positive relationships between children's viewing and their vocabulary development (Rice, Huston, Truglio, & Wright, 1990), problem-solving behaviors (Hodapp, 1977), increased inclusion of children of other races during play (Gorn, Goldberg, & Kanungo, 1976), and reduced aggression during free play for both girls and boys (Bankart & Anderson, 1979).

Building on the Viewing Experience

Contemporary children are increasingly able to experience the content of their favorite TV programs on multiple platforms such as websites, game consoles, e-readers, and mobile devices. Do children experience the benefits of educational programming across these platforms? To investigate, Linebarger and Jennings (2011) conducted a school intervention using the *Super Why!* series. Kindergarten classrooms were assigned to a TV-only group, a TV-plus-Internet group, or a control group that received no media. After 4 weeks of exposure, children were tested for performance on literacy skills. Children in the TV-only group showed more sophisticated letter-sound skills than children in the control group. Children in the TV-plus-Internet group, however, displayed gains on letter sounds as well as lower-case knowledge and rhyme awareness. In a study with slightly older children, Fisch, Lesh, Motoki, Crespo, and Melfi (2010) also examined the impacts of cross-platform learning on children's mathematical problem solving using *Cyberchase*. Assigning children to DVD, Web, DVD and Web, hands-on, all materials, or a control condition, the study found the strongest effects for children in the DVD and Web condition, suggesting that multiplatform media work in powerful ways when used in an intentional way. Educational television may also be supported by hands-on activities using materials provided for home and classroom use. For many years, the Corporation for Public Broadcasting (CPB) spearheaded Ready to Learn, an early childhood program dedicated to using public television programs and hands-on resources to support early learning. Evaluation work suggests that this program has had important positive effects on children's literacy skills, particularly for disadvantaged families (CPB, 2011). Taken together, these results suggest that children may especially benefit from cross-platform learning.

Understanding the cumulative impact of television on children's knowledge and school achievement requires longitudinal assessment. One such investigation was the Recontact Study, in which children's television-viewing habits were assessed during the early childhood and high school years. Children who watched more educational programming (in particular, *Sesame Street*) during the preschool years had higher grades in high school English, mathematics, and science courses. Importantly, these results held even when controlling for socioeconomic factors like parent education and family size (Anderson, Huston, Schmitt, Linebarger, & Wright, 2001). When these findings are considered with many studies reporting shorter-term effects of educational TV on school readiness (e.g., Zill, 2001), the evidence for a positive impact of educational television is strong.

Moderators of Learning from Television

Based on research examining how children learn best from television, we suggest that there are at least four important moderating factors to consider when determining how knowledge acquisition occurs: children's prior knowledge, repeated exposure, the involvement of adults in the viewing experience, and the mental effort associated with viewing.

First, child characteristics, including their prior experience and knowledge, may have a profound impact on the influence of television. For example, negative impacts of television viewing are stronger for girls and for individuals with higher IQ scores (Keith, Reimers, Fehrmann, Pottebaum, & Aubey, 1986; Williams, Haertel, Walberg, & Haertel, 1982). Furthermore, the Recontact Study found that the relationship between early exposure to educational television and high school academic achievement was stronger for boys than girls (Anderson et al., 2001). Because American girls may be better prepared for school by their preschool experiences, the benefits of watching educational TV may be relatively greater for American boys. Children's reading ability may also influence television's impact. For example, Linebarger et al. (2004) found that the effectiveness of *Between the Lions* was differentiated by children's reading risk status. Specifically, non-risk and moderately at-risk children benefitted from viewing, whereas at-risk children did not demonstrate the same benefits. Due to at-risk children's unfamiliarity with basic literacy skills, educational programs may have too advanced a curriculum for this group.

Second, repeated exposure may influence children's learning from television. Almost every parent who has read a storybook to a child has heard the command "again." Preschool children appreciate story repetition, and repetition improves their comprehension of story elements (Peracchio, 1993). This holds true for television viewing as well. After 5 consecutive days of viewing a single episode of *Blue's Clues,* children's comprehension of the problem-solving strategies shown in the episode increased, attention was sustained, and audience participation increased (Crawley, Anderson, Wilder, Williams, & Santomero, 1999).

Adult co-viewers may also influence children's learning from television. Similar to storybook reading experiences, parents, educators, and other caregivers can enhance the impact of educational programs by drawing children's attention to crucial moments in the program and answering questions about what they see (e.g., Kerr & Mason, 1994; Silverman & Hines, Chapter 14, this volume). For example, Friedrich and Stein (1975) found that children who viewed *Mister Rogers' Neighborhood* with an active, co-viewing adult were more likely to successfully acquire target knowledge from the show and transfer their knowledge to novel situations. Preschoolers were also better able to use literacy and numeracy skills demonstrated on video if an adult co-viewer asked them to identify letters and numbers while watching (Reiser, Tessmer, & Phelps, 1984).

Finally, it is worth noting the impact of socialization on children's relationship with media. In his classic work, Salomon (1983) suggested that children's perception of the mental effort required for viewing television is influenced by how parents and teachers use television. If children are taught that television is simply an entertainment medium that requires very little mental effort, they may not use television as a source of useful information. If television is seen as an "easy" medium, Salomon argued, learning achieved from viewing may be of lesser impact than that achieved through other media such as books.

Recommendations to Support Learning from Television

How can the most be made of children's screen time? As Fisch's (2000) capacity model describes, the further away a child feels from the show's narrative, the greater the processing resources are needed to understand the story, leaving less working memory for the educational content. Ideally, educational programs should somewhat mirror what children see in their daily lives. If programs are set in a fantasy world, the educational content should be directly connected to the program's narrative.

Parents can also support children's knowledge acquisition by committing to co-viewing programs and actively participating in learning experiences that extend beyond the viewing time with their children. Adults can support learning by being aware of program content and answering children's questions about any frightening or hard-to-comprehend content. TV content can have a powerful influence on children, and parents should not relinquish control over that power. In addition, parents and educators should consider how television is referenced and how value is imposed on the medium. If television always seems to be a place in front of which the family "checks out" from reality or avoids discussion, then children may see television purely as an escape and where little mental effort is needed. Consequently, they may not treat television as an important resource for learning about the larger world.

Parents, educators, and program producers have an obligation to educate children not only about television, but also about the potential of media more generally and how to use media in appropriate ways. By learning media literacy skills from a very early age, children can become informed, intelligent consumers. When curricula are designed to teach children how to interpret media images, they become more critical evaluators of the content and can utilize coping strategies for disturbing or frightening content (Abelman, 1995; Singer, Zuckerman, & Singer, 1980).

Conclusion

Children are capable of engaging in a thoughtful and cognitively active relationship with television. Content determines most of the impact that television has on its young viewers. Although entertainment content can result in violent, fearful, or distorted views of the world, it can also contribute to diversifying children's knowledge and perspectives beyond their immediate surroundings. Educational programs can also introduce and support children's academic and prosocial skills. By the time children graduate from high school, they will have spent more time engaged in informal learning with media than in formal educational settings. It is thus crucial that parents, TV production and distribution companies, and government, through support of noncommercial alternatives, maximize the enormous positive potential—as well as minimize the negative—inherent in the media that children use every day.

ACKNOWLEDGMENTS

Preparation of this chapter was supported in part by Research Grant No. 0921173 from the National Science Foundation.

REFERENCES

Abelman, R. (1995). *Reclaiming the wasteland.* Cresskill, NJ: Hampton Press.

Anderson, D. R., & Hanson, K. G. (2010). From blooming, buzzing confusion to media literacy: The early development of television viewing. *Developmental Review, 30*(2), 239–255.

Anderson, D. R., Huston, A. C., Schmitt, K. L., Linebarger, D. L., & Wright, J. C. (2001). Early childhood television viewing and adolescent behavior: The Recontact study. *Monographs of the Society for Research in Child Development, 68*(1), 1–143.

Anderson, D. R., & Kirkorian, H. L. (2006). Attention and television. In J. Bryant & P. Vorderer (Eds.), *The psychology of entertainment* (pp. 35–54). Mahwah, NJ: Erlbaum.

Anderson, D. R., & Levin, S. R. (1976). Young children's attention to Sesame Street. *Child Development, 47*(3), 806–811.

Anderson, D. R., Lorch, E. P., Collins, P. A., Field, D. E., & Nathan, J. G. (1986). Television viewing at home: Age trends in visual attention and time with TV. *Child Development, 57*(4), 1024–1033.

Anderson, D. R., & Pempek, T. A. (2005). Television and very young children. *American Behavioral Scientist, 48*(5), 505–522.

Ball, S. J., & Bogatz, G. A. (1970). *The first year of* Sesame Street: *An evaluation.* Princeton, NJ: Educational Testing Service.

Ball, S., & Bogatz, G. A. (1973). *Reading with television: An evaluation of* The Electric Company. Princeton, NJ: Educational Testing Service.

Bandura, A. (1971). *Social learning theory.* New York: General Learning Press.

Bandura, A., Ross, D., & Ross, S. A. (1963). Imitation of film-mediated aggressive models. *Journal of Abnormal and Social Psychology, 66*(1), 3–11.

Bankart, P., & Anderson, C. C. (1979). Short-term effects of prosocial television viewing on play of preschool boys and girls. *Psychological Reports, 44*(3), 935–941.

Bogatz, G. A., & Ball, S. (1971). *The second year of* Sesame Street: *A continuing evaluation.* Princeton, NJ: Educational Testing Service.

Calvert, S. (1999). *Children's journeys through the information age.* Boston: McGraw-Hill.

Cantor, J., Wilson, B. J., & Hoffner, C. (1986). Emotional responses to a televised nuclear holocaust film. *Communication Research, 13*(2), 257–277.

Corporation for Public Broadcasting. (2011). *Findings from Ready To Learn 2005–2010.*

Crawley, A. M., Anderson, D. R., Wilder, A., Williams, M., & Santomero, A.

(1999). Effects of repeated exposures to a single episode of the television program *Blue's Clues* on the viewing behaviors and comprehension of preschool children. *Journal of Educational Psychology, 91,* 630–637.

Douglas, W. (2003). *Television families: Is something wrong in suburbia?* Mahwah, NJ: Erlbaum.

Fisch, S. M. (2000). A capacity model of children's comprehension of educational content on television. *Media Psychology, 2*(1), 63–91.

Fisch, S. M., Lesh, R., Motoki, E., Crespo, S., & Melfi, V. (2010). *Children's learning from multiple media in informal mathematics education.* Teaneck, NJ: MediaKidz Research & Consulting.

Fisch, S. M., & Truglio, R. T. (2001). *"G" is for "growing": Thirty years of research on children and* Sesame Street. Mahwah, NJ: Erlbaum.

Friedrich, L. K., & Stein, A. H. (1973). Aggressive and prosocial television programs and the natural behavior of preschool children. *Monographs of the Society for Research in Child Development, 38*(4), 1–64.

Friedrich, L. K., & Stein, A. H. (1975). Prosocial television and young children's behavior: The effect of verbal labeling and role playing training. *Child Development, 46*(1), 27–38.

Garrity, K., Piotrowski, J. T., McMenamin, K., & Linebarger, D. L. (2010). *A summative evaluation of* The Electric Company: *A final report prepared for the Corporation for Public Broadcasting.* Philadelphia: Annenberg School for Communication, University of Pennsylvania.

Gerbner, G., Gross, L., Morgan, M., Signorielli, N., & Shanahan, J. (2002). Growing up with television: Cultivation processes. In J. Bryant & D. Zillman (Eds.), *Media effects: Advances in theory and research* (2nd ed., pp. 43–67). Mahwah, NJ: Erlbaum.

Glascock, J. (2001). Gender roles on prime-time network television: Demographics and behaviors. *Journal of Broadcasting and Electronic Media, 45*(4), 656–669.

Goodman Research Group. (2007). Peep *season IV executive summary.* Cambridge, MA: Author.

Goodman Research Group. (2010). Sid the Science Kid *season 1 outreach evaluation.* Cambridge, MA: Author.

Gorn, G. J., Goldber, M. E., & Kanungo, R. N. (1976). The role of educational television in changing the intergroup attitudes of children. *Child Development, 47*(1), 277–280.

Harrison, L. F., & Williams, T. M. (1986). Television and cognitive development. In T. M. Williams (Ed.), *The impact of television: A natural experiment in three communities* (pp. 87–138). Orlando, FL: Academic Press.

Hodapp, T. V. (1977). Children's ability to learn problem-solving strategies from television. *The Alberta Journal of Educational Research, 23*(3), 171–177.

Huesmann, L. R. (1998). The role of social information processing and cognitive schema in the acquisition and maintenance of habitual aggressive behavior. In R. G. Geen & E. Donnerstein (Eds.), *Human aggression: Theories, research, and implications for policy* (pp. 73–109). New York: Academic Press.

Institute of Medicine. (2006). *Food marketing to children and youth: Threat or opportunity?* Washington, DC: The National Academies Press.

Jordan, A. B. (2000). *Is the three-hour rule living up to its potential? An analysis of educational television for children in the 1999/2000 broadcast season* (Report No. 34). Philadelphia: Annenberg Public Policy Center, University of Pennsylvania.

Keith, T. Z., Reimers, T. M., Fehrmann, P. G., Pottebaum, S. M., & Aubey, L. W. (1986). Parental involvement, homework, and television time: Direct and indirect effects on high school achievement. *Journal of Educational Psychology, 78*(5), 373–380.

Kerr, B. M., & Mason, J. M. (1994). Awakening literacy through interactive story reading. In F. Lehr & J. Osborn (Eds.), *Reading, language, and literacy: Instruction for the twenty-first century* (pp. 133–148). Hillsdale, NJ: Erlbaum.

Lemish, D., & Rice, M. L. (1986). Television as a talking picture book: A prop for language acquisition. *Journal of Child Language, 13,* 251–274.

Lesser, G. (1974). *Children and television lessons from* Sesame Street. New York: Random House.

Linebarger, D. L., & Jennings, N. (2011, March). *Access, use, content, and convergence across multiple media and characters.* Paper presented at the biennial meeting of the Society for Research in Child Development, Montreal, Canada.

Linebarger, D. L., Kosanic, A., Greenwood, C. R., & Doku, N. S. (2004). Effects of viewing the television program *Between the Lions* on the emergent literacy skills of young children. *Journal of Educational Psychology, 96*(2), 297–308.

Linebarger, D. L., McMenamin, K., & Wainright, D. K. (2008). *Summative evaluation of* Super Why!: *Outcomes, dose, and appeal.* Philadelphia: Children's Media Lab, Annenberg School for Communication, University of Pennsylvania.

Linebarger, D. L., Moses, A., & McMenamin, K. (2010). *Vocabulary learning from educational television: Can children learn new words from* Martha Speaks? Philadelphia: Annenberg School for Communication, University of Pennsylvania.

Linebarger, D. L., & Piotrowski, J. T. (2009a). Evaluating the educational potential of health PSAs with preschoolers. *Health Communication, 23*(6), 516–525.

Linebarger, D. L., & Piotrowski, J. T. (2009b). TV as storyteller: How exposure to television narratives impacts at-risk preschoolers' story knowledge and narrative skills. *British Journal of Developmental Psychology, 27,* 47–69.

Lorch, E. P., Anderson, D. R., & Levin, S. R. (1979). The relationship of visual attention to children's comprehension of television. *Child Development, 50*(3), 722–727.

Nielsen Company. (2009). *Television audience 2008.* Retrieved June 13, 2011, from *http://blog.nielsen.com/nielsenwire/wpcontent/uploads/2009/07/tva_2008_071709.pdf.*

Nielsen Company. (2010). *Three screen report: Television, Internet, and mobile usage in the U.S.* (Report No. 8). Retrieved June 13, 2011, from *www.nielsen.com/us/en/insights/reports-downloads/2010/three-screen-report-q1-2010.html*.

Noble, G. (1983). Social learning from everyday television. In M. J. A. Howe (Ed.), *Learning from television: Psychological and educational research* (pp. 101–124). London: Academic Press.

Peel, T., Rockwell, A., Esty, E., & Gonzer, K. (1987). *Square One television: The comprehension and problem solving study.* New York: Children's Television Workshop.

Peracchio, L. (1993). Young children's processing of a televised narrative: Is a picture really worth a thousand words? *Journal of Consumer Research, 20*(2), 281–293.

Reichert, T., & Carpenter, C. (2004). An update on sex in magazine advertising: 1983 to 2003. *Journalism and Mass Communication Quarterly, 81*(4), 823–837.

Reiser, R. A., Tessmer, M. A., & Phelps, P. C. (1984). Adult–child interaction in children's learning from Sesame Street. *Educational Communication and Technology Journal, 32*(4), 217–223.

Rice, M. L., Huston, A. C., Truglio, R., & Wright, J. (1990). Words from *Sesame Street*: Learning vocabulary while viewing. *Developmental Psychology, 26*(3), 421–428.

Rideout, V., & Hamel, E. (2006). *The media family: Electronic media in the lives of infants, toddlers, preschoolers, and their parents.* Menlo Park, CA: Henry J. Kaiser Family Foundation.

Roberts, D. F., Foehr, U. G., & Rideout, V. J. (2005). *Generation M: Media in the lives of 8–18-year-olds.* Washington DC: Henry J. Kaiser Family Foundation.

Ross, L., Anderson, D. R., & Wisocki, P. A. (1982). Adult television viewing and sex-role attitudes. *Sex Roles, 8*(6), 589–592.

Rust, L. W. (2001). *Summative evaluation of* Dragon Tales: *Final report.* Briarcliff Manor, NY: Langbourne Rust Research, Inc.

Salomon, G. (1983). Television watching and mental effort: A social psychological view. In J. Bryant & D. R. Anderson (Eds.), *Children's understanding of television: Research on attention and comprehension* (pp. 181–198). New York: Academic Press.

Schramm, W., Lyle, J., & Parker, E. B. (1961). *Television in the lives of our children.* Stanford, CA: Stanford University Press.

Simon, J., & Merrill, B. D. (1997). The next generation of news consumers: Children's news media choices in an election campaign. *Political Communication, 14*(3), 307–321.

Singer, D., Zuckerman, D. M., & Singer, J. L. (1980). Helping elementary school children learn about TV. *Journal of Communication, 30*(3), 84–93.

Smith, S. L., & Wilson, B. J. (2002). Children's exposure to, comprehension of, and fear reactions to television news. *Media Psychology, 4*(1), 1–26.

Steinke, J. (2005). Cultural representations of gender and science: Portrayals of female scientists and engineers in popular films. *Science Communication,* 27(1), 27–63.

Weiss, A. J., & Wilson, B. J. (1998). Children's cognitive and emotional responses to the portrayal of negative emotions in family-formatted situation comedies. *Human Communication Research, 24*(4), 584–609.

Williams, P. A., Haertel, E. H., Walberg, H. J., & Haertel, G. D. (1982). The impact of leisure-time television on school learning: A research synthesis. *American Educational Research Journal, 19*(1), 19–50.

Woodard, E. (1999). *The 1999 state of children's television report: Programming for children over broadcast and cable television.* Philadelphia: Annenberg Public Policy Center, University of Pennsylvania.

Zill, N. (2001). Does Sesame Street enhance school readiness?: Evidence from a national survey of children. In S. M. Fisch & R. T. Truglio (Eds.), *"G" is for "growing": Thirty years of research on children and* Sesame Street (pp. 115–130). Mahwah: NJ: Erlbaum.

PART II

PROMOTING KNOWLEDGE DEVELOPMENT IN THE CLASSROOM

CHAPTER 8

■　■　■　■　■

Four Play Pedagogies and a Promise for Children's Learning

Kathleen Roskos
James Christie

> Play . . . is a right of every child.
> —UNITED NATIONS HIGH COMMISSION FOR HUMAN RIGHTS

All children need time and opportunity for play in childcare and school because play is a natural tool for learning in the early years. It is in active play that children develop knowledge, creativity, problem solving, self-reliance, and resilience. They learn through their playful interactions with ideas, objects, and others. But play is changing in a changing world. There is less time for play; now, children play less than 16% of the time that they did in 1981. There is less opportunity for play at home, in neighborhoods, and at school due to hectic and overscheduled family life, a lack of safe places to play, and academic pressure to learn the 3R's at an earlier age. Play, some argue, is "under siege" by strong curricular forces focused on cognitive development, literacy, and mathematics that have dramatically reduced children's opportunities to play at childcare or school or even at home (Zigler & Bishop-Josef, 2004). Adults cannot let this happen to children; we must invest in play as a foundation for learning, especially for poor children whose access to playful learning may be seriously limited. Educators can help by providing rich opportunities for indoor and outdoor play at childcare and school.

In this chapter, we focus on play's contribution to conceptual and content knowledge. Children's storehouse of knowledge and basic concepts increases dramatically during the early years, and play can facilitate this process. Immature concepts of space, time, probability, and causality can be tested and revised during play (Johnson, Christie, & Wardle, 2007). The abstract concept of time, for example, comes to have meaning within the context of play. When children wait for their turn to use a toy or to perform their part in a script, expressions such as "in a few minutes," "a little while," "tomorrow," and even "next week" come to make more sense. Although time and space often are altered in play episodes, sequence and structure often are preserved and can become better understood.

To promote play's contribution in children's learning, we describe, in some detail, several play pedagogies that should be in every early childhood classroom for children ages 3–7. We focus first on a rationale for the pedagogy—why it is important for children's development and well-being, and how it builds their capacity for play as an opportunity for knowledge acquisition—and then describe what each looks like in real-world settings, describing what is essential for good effect on learning potential. What we hope to show is how play can *support* children, and not only teach them important knowledge about the world, but also to help them to be kind, generous, happy, creative, and engaged in meaningful work.

Four Pedagogies

Brian to his young pal, Michael: "We're pretendin' we're police. There's a fire. We gotta get every cop we have—and we need that fire 'stinguisher, too—the heavy-duty one! Huh, Michael?"

This brief exchange reminds us that learning is *in* the play. Adults create the conditions for rich play, perhaps nudge it along a bit, but then must step back to let children take charge. When children are in charge, they experience the satisfying power of play and immediately see the results of their own decisions and actions. This sense of agency taps the learning potential of play activity; it allows children to explore ideas, and to talk and listen in deeply focused ways.

The child at play and in charge, however, presents educators with a "Goldilocks" problem. Too much may result in frivolous, nonproductive activity that does not support deep conceptual learning; too little may stifle engagement, exploration, and creativity, turning play into academic work. What seems to be "just right" for classroom purposes is a proper mix of content, structure, and process that involves children with ideas, concepts, and language in a playful way. The four play pedagogies presented below reflect this proper mix, providing instructional frameworks for meaningful actions in play contexts that lay the foundations for academic learning.

Story Drama

> *Grandmother to teacher: "Alex just loves all books about animals. He loves* The Three Little Pigs *'cause I'll go, 'I'll huff and I'll puff and I'll blow your house down!' And Alex will look at me and he'll say: 'Let's play!' "*

Although this grandmother may not realize it, in reenacting *The Three Little Pigs,* which can be delightfully scary, she is helping young Alex to learn important literary concepts and skills found in most early learning content standards (e.g., the concept of character as a story element). Solid research evidence shows that children learn narrative structure and elements through story drama (i.e., the playful reenactment of stories). Saltz, Dixon, and Johnson (1977), for example, found that story drama helped preschool children connect separate events into logical sequences: what happens first, next, and last. Related research on story comprehension (e.g., Pellegrini, 1984) showed gains in both *specific* story comprehension (i.e., understanding of the story that was reenacted) and *generalized* story comprehension (i.e., understanding of other stories), suggesting that story drama may enhance children's knowledge of narrative story structure. As play pedagogy, story drama is easy to implement because it replicates traditional story retelling using creative drama techniques. The basic approach is to act out a familiar piece of literature: (1) a story is read and discussed, (2) props are made, (3) roles assigned, and (4) the reenactment occurs.

Let's take a look at story drama in Ms. Campbell's Head Start class. For the past few weeks the children have been studying gardens and flowers—reading books, exploring online sites, discovering gardens and flowers in the neighborhood, and growing plants on their own. They have read and discussed *Zinnia's Flower Garden* by Monica Wellington (2005) several times, and Ms. Campbell thinks the children might enjoy reenacting this story to deepen their understanding of plant growth. At Circle Time, she sets the stage for a story drama, indicating areas of the room where major scenes will occur, assigning roles to small groups or pairs of children, and providing a few simple props for each scene (e.g., seeds made out of construction paper; a watering can; a picture of the sun). After a brief review of the story, she positions the children in the room for a reenactment. This time she reads the story aloud and directs children to "act out" the scenes: (1) planting the seeds; (2) watering, fertilizing, and tending; (3) making bouquets of beautiful flowers; and (4) collecting flower seeds to grow new flowers. Next time, she will phase out her assistance, asking the children to enact each scene and retell the story on their own for their peers.

One of the beauties of story drama as a play pedagogy is its adaptability. It can be used before or after storybook reading and with small or large groups. It can be used, for example, to prepare children for a book by introducing it and asking children to predict what it might be about; then, while reading short segments, children improvise actions (James, 1967). Or a whole-group story drama technique can be applied, using character props that consist of "necklaces" (e.g., a string with a picture of the character's face, worn around the neck) or stick puppets with pictures of the character (McGee, 2007). Children are assigned parts, and as the story is read aloud they act out their parts. The next time, the children can both speak and act their parts, thus promoting oral language expression and listening comprehension. Placing the character necklaces and the book in the library corner encourages children to enact the story yet again on their own or with friends.

Story drama not only appeals to young children's love of make-believe, it also provides an excellent means for them to explore and interpret characters and plots, problems and issues, cycles and processes, at deeper levels of meaning. Listening to a story with the idea of acting it out encourages them to listen carefully and imaginatively, and to try to understand what is meant as well as what is plainly stated. As children engage in more story dramas, they develop an awareness of how stories are structured: the setting, a problem, the sequence of events, and a resolution. As text structures become internalized they provide conceptual frameworks around which children can build their own accounts and stories both orally and in writing.

Topic-Oriented Play

Children develop passions around topics they are curious about and often pursue them in their play with intensity and duration. Henry, now 5 years old, for example, is keenly interested in all things *Star Wars*—an interest that has progressed from narrative role play to movies and books about space and space travel broadly, and, more recently, to constellations and telescopes. Educators can identify children's passions in topic-oriented play that can be aligned with curricular goals in science, mathematics, social studies, and the arts. This is not unfamiliar play pedagogy in early childhood, although it goes by many names (e.g., theme-based play, sociodramatic play, play centers, play-based curriculum). It is also widely accepted in professional practice, although evidence of its direct impact on children's content learning remains rather thin (Smith, 2010). Certainly, children's natural interactions with toys, objects, and people are interleaved with disciplinary content that children may pick up. Manipulating puzzles, nesting cups, and dollhouse furniture, for example, nurtures nascent mathematical concepts, such as spatial reasoning, one-to-one correspondence, and counting, among others (Sarama & Clements, 2009). Still, play is different from being taught. It is an autotelic activity that can introduce children to disciplinary concepts, but it is not set up to explain them, nor does it take into account children's often scientifically incorrect ideas, based on their natural interactions with their environment. It can help children discover that certain objects sink and others float, for example, but not necessarily help them discover *why* or *how* the principle of buoyancy works. In play, misconceptions and inaccuracies may go unchallenged, becoming more deeply embedded and making future learning more difficult. The real benefit of topic-centered play, therefore, may be more affective than academic, developing wonder, curiosity, interest, eagerness to learn, "liking science or math," or "wanting to become a scientist"—all important drivers in the pursuit of content knowledge (Rix & McSorley, 1999).

Topic-oriented play works best when aligned with curricular goals related to academic content in science, mathematics, social studies, or the arts (Roskos & Christie, 2007). For example, in large- and small-group instruction, children are taught academic content that fits with a topic (e.g., buildings, water pipes and pumps, communities), and in play they are encouraged to further explore these new ideas and to literally play with their meanings through talk and action. The instruction primes the play by tapping prior knowledge, sorting out confusions, and introducing relevant vocabulary and facts. The theoretical assumption is that the play context then affords focused and sustained attention to content and language use that contributes to understanding (Kounin & Doyle, 1975); it also provides conditions for joint participation, which stimulates talk about content and procedures, thus creating opportunities to express and request content information (Callanan, Rigney, Nolan-Reyes, & Solis, Chapter 4, this volume; Rogoff, 1990). Effective topic-oriented play depends heavily on play-setting design, where the teacher deliberately extends ideas, language, and objects from the instructional setting to the play setting. What does this look like? Here are a few examples that highlight different content learning areas.

Adding Props

One of the simplest ways to connect instruction to topic-oriented play is to add relevant props to popular centers, such as dramatic play. In this example, a teacher added numeracy props to a grocery store play center in order to help her students meet the school district's kindergarten mathematics standards:

> According to her district's kindergarten math curriculum, Marilyn is expected to teach rote counting and recognition of numerals from 1–20. She also decides to experiment with turning the dramatic play center into a store. In addition to a balance scale, she is lucky enough to obtain an old hanging scale. She includes a Bates stamp with numbers that the children can rotate and change. She has several hand calculators and an old adding machine borrowed from a third-grade teacher. She also includes tubs of small objects, like Unifix cubes, that can be sold. She is delighted to find that she now has a use for out-of-date coupons and the weekly ads from local supermarkets. The pictures and numbers make the messages understandable for customers. The store is now open for business! On opening day, workers and customers discover that Marilyn has forgotten an important component: they need money. This leads to a group project making bills and coins. (Van Hourn, Scales, Nourot, & Alward, 1999, p. 175)

Marilyn has designed a play setting that provides opportunities for children to recognize numbers and to count—important objectives in her kindergarten math curriculum. She uses this play center as an alternative to more traditional forms of instruction, such as direct instruction and worksheets. The addition of math-related props transformed the center into an authentic environment for her students to learn about numbers and counting.

Extending Vocabulary

Along with concrete props, the teacher can deliberately link language and vocabulary to a topic-centered play area, such as a garage or a flower shop, to support content learning. Christie (2008) provided an example from a topic study of building and construction in a preschool classroom that highlights this technique. The teacher was teaching about construction tools. She began Circle Time with the shared reading of a rhyme poster. While the primary function of the poster was to teach rhyme identification, the teacher also focused the children's attention on two tool words in the rhyme. She had children make a hand motion when *hammer* was mentioned and use their fingers to show how small the *tiny little nails* were. Next, the teacher did a shared reading of a big book about building a doghouse. This informational book had very few text words but contained several photographs that contained tools. Even though the tools were not mentioned in the text, the teacher paused to discuss them. After the story was read, the children transitioned to center time. The teacher had arranged the play environment to provide additional opportunity to encounter and use tool words. The dramatic play center had a cardboard frame that resembled a doghouse and contained toy replicas of many of the tools mentioned in the doghouse book: plastic hammers, "nails" (actually wooden golf tees), a circular saw that made a whizzing noise, measuring tape, and safety goggles. Several children spent nearly 30 minutes playing together, pretending to build the doghouse. In the course of their play, the names of tools were used frequently, and the children reminded each other how to properly use each tool (e.g., to put on safety goggles before using the power saw). The intentional integration of props, language, and vocabulary words in the topic-oriented play setting provided children with opportunities to practice and consolidate the vocabulary and concepts being taught in the instructional part of the curriculum.

Structuring Tasks

Scaffolding for playful learning increases when specific tasks are embedded in the topic-oriented play setting. The combination of props + language + task creates an activity setting that can be a deliberate extension of direct instruction (Roskos, 1994). For example, during a 6-week topic study on winter, two kindergarten teachers taught children how to read thermometers and how to record this information, using the symbol for degrees. To connect this content with play, the teachers supplied the discovery play center (science labs) with various types of thermometers, note pads and pencils for recording data, materials for an experiment measuring the temperature of water under different conditions (e.g., warm water, tap water, ice water), lab coats for dress-up, and printed directions related to the experiment. Children's play was videotaped and analyzed for academic talk and social behavioral talk. Results showed that a majority of the children's interactions were related to the content activity available in the center (e.g., using thermometers). What was more impressive, the children's engagement in these content activities persisted across the entire play period. The children did not shift to "off-task" activities such as visiting with friends or other forms of play. The combination of setting cues (the "lab"), objects (scientific tools), task (measuring), and peer talk around a common goal (to measure water temperature) engaged and "pinned" children's attention to the content.

Game Play

Four-year-old Claudia is organizing her friends to play a board game. But who will be first? Claudia has a way to decide, using her own version of "One Potato, Two Potato," which goes something like this while tapping her friends' outstretched hands: "Hola vicka, sola nicka, boo, boo, boo / Hola vicka, sola nicka, I pick you."

Claudia's bid for play with friends hints at the primary features of game play: rules, roles, challenge, and, above all, social interaction (Baines & Blachford, 2011). The literature on the role of games in children's social and cognitive development at home, in school, and on the playground is wide ranging, so we limit our description of game play as a pedagogy to the use of board and digital games in early childhood education settings to support curriculum goals. That game play in the early years is related to content learning (e.g., the "hard" skills of mathematics and science) rests largely on correlational evidence, and any evidence of transfer across contexts is questionable (Goldstein, 2011; Okita, 2004). The "more research needed" refrain is often repeated to show the effects of game play on content knowledge, yet perhaps the impact of game play on "soft" skills, such as social understanding, perspective taking, self-regulation, and sustained attention, is a better bet and more relevant to the 21st-century learning skills children need (e.g., collaboration; Baines & Blachford, 2011). We don't know yet, and thus in the meantime encourage a game-play pedagogy that creates opportunities for practicing cognitive *and* behavioral skills. So what's involved?

Board games both commercial and teacher made are ubiquitous in early childhood classrooms—the likes of *Candy Land, Chutes and Ladders, Memory Game, Connect Four, Scrabble,* and *Monopoly,* to name a few. Use of board games for content learning is perhaps most prevalent in early mathematics, where research in general shows positive effects (e.g., Ramani & Siegler, 2008). Much of this research points to three essentials in the effective use of board games to promote content learning (Schuler & Wittmann, 2009): (1) teacher awareness of the content potential in the board game; (2) teacher presence to explain rules and goals, help children to follow rules, solve conflicts, and facilitate a sense of competence; and (3) substantive conversations that stimulate explanations, encourage reflections on action and thought, and challenge assumptions and hypotheses. Some of these features are illustrated in the following interchange between a teacher and her preschoolers:

Beth has just finished reading Snow Day! *by Devra Speregen (2005) to a small group of children and engages them in a teacher-made board game to practice new words introduced in the story. The board game consists of a winding road, a toy tractor (Barney Backhoe), and cotton balls to represent snow. Along the road are picture cards for the target vocabulary words and stop signs. She places the cotton balls on the road, and asks, "What am I doing here?" The children respond in a chorus of "Putting snow on the road." She confirms and demonstrates the game, "Yes, I'm putting snow on the road. I'm going to take my little tractor, and I'm going to push the snow off the road. When I get to a stop sign what should I do?" All respond, "Stop!" She says, "Stop . . . that's right. And then we're going to tell where we're at and the signs will help us remember." The children take turns pushing the toy tractor along the road, plowing pretend snow, until they come to a stop sign. Then they say the word that is represented by the picture near the sign. For example, the first child to play pushes the tractor and "snow" a little bit past the stop sign by the picture of a town. "Did you get to a stop sign?" she asks. "What do you need to do?" The child backs the tractor up to the stop sign and says, "Stop," "And where are you?" she queries. And the child looks at the sign (which has the word* town *and an accompanying photo) and says, "That's a city." Beth explains, "It's a city, or another name is a* town *[a target word]. Look at the word it starts with a* t: /t/ /t/ /t/ /t/ town." *The child leans into the sign, looks at the word, and says, "Town!"*

Board games like this one are excellent for the playful learning of important content. They cost next to nothing (parents, in fact, are often eager to donate or make board games), are easy to assemble and store, and can be easily inserted into daily routines. And they are highly motivating for students as learning contexts: we have not yet met a child who does not relish board game play, participating with sustained attention and considerable control, especially when it comes to selecting tokens, spinning spinners, and tossing dice.

In game play, access to electronic games is rapidly increasing in early childhood classrooms via SMART boards, touch-screen computers, and mobile devices. While educators often worry that electronic game playing may lead to social isolation, passivity, limited imagination, and aggressive behaviors, so far research evidence does not give grounds for these fears (Goldstein, 2011). Digital games, in fact, keep children and youth on task longer, improving the chances that what they have to offer may take hold in active minds (Owston, Wideman, Lotherington, Ronda, & Brown, 2007). Well-designed "educationally relevant" games incorporate fundamental principles for playful learning—putting learners in control, confronting them with challenges, encouraging different ways of thinking—and have been found to promote knowledge and cognitive processing among students of all ages (British Educational Communications and Technology Agency, 2001; McFarlane, Sparrowhawk, & Heald, 2002).

What do these digital games look like? Here is a research-based case example from early literacy. *Living Letters* (Letters in Beweging from Bereslim) is a digital game, developed in the Netherlands (Kegel, van der Kooy-Hofland, & Bus, 2009), which uses a child's proper name as a stimulus to prime knowledge of the alphabetic principle. Its design is modeled on name-writing research and includes three building blocks to the alphabetic principle: (1) recognizing the name in print, (2) associating the initial name letter with its sound, and (3) identifying the sound of the initial name letter in other orally presented words. The game automatically adapts to the child's proper name or defaults to the word *mama* and provides the child with targeted instruction on sound–letter relationships, modeled after parental instruction (see Anderson, Boyle, & Reiser, 1985). The game automatically registers the player's immediate responses to tailor the game to individual differences. Three skill levels are built into the game, each more difficult than the last. Level 1 (i.e., easiest) provides practice in the recognizing the proper name; Level 2 focuses on identifying the first name letter (e.g., *T* in *Tom*); and Level 3 (i.e., hardest) requires identifying pictures that start or end with the first name letter.

The game starts with an attractive animation to explain how to play (e.g., the main characters, Sim and Sanne, discuss their names and discover that they begin with the same sound). Errors are followed by increasingly supportive audio feedback in the following order: (1) repetition of the task (e.g., "Find the word that starts with the same sound as your name"); (2) a clue (e.g., "*Tom* starts with /t/"); and (3) demonstration of the correct solution (e.g., "You hear /t/ in *Tom* and *tent*"). Apart from increasingly supportive feedback, errors lead to one to three repetitions of the same assignment. Tasks, as well as oral feedback, are adapted to the child's name. Figure 8.1a shows a screenshot from Level 1: Sanne is the magician who finds words that start with the /s/ of Sanne. Figure 8.1b is from Level 2: Tom has to find the word that starts the same as his name. Figure 8.1c shows Bear, a personal tutor, providing a cue when the child has not succeeded twice to find his or her name among the three alternatives. Figure 8.1d is a screenshot from the scene at the end of a game level session.

Children, especially those showing early signs of delay in letter–sound knowledge, benefit from playing *Living Letters*, gaining ground in early literacy skills and building capacity to take advantage of beginning

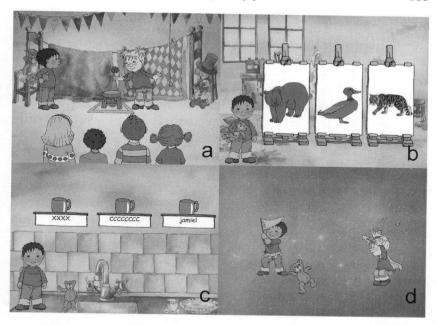

FIGURE 8.1. Screen shots from four different elements of the *Living Letters* game: (a) the animation at the game start, (b) a game task, (c) bear provides a cue after an error, and (d) game end after each level. From Kegel, van der Kooy-Hofland, and Bus (2009). Reprinted with permission.

reading instruction (Van der Kooy-Hofland, Bus, & Roskos, 2011). As a case example, *Living Letters* illustrates the thoughtful design of a "serious" digital game that combines specific educational goals with guided play. What to look for, then, in digital games that build learners' knowledge and capacity? Good concept–media match; educational content at the heart of game play; and feedback and hint structures that support and scaffold learners into challenging content (Fisch, 2005).

Outdoor Play

> *Several boys are huddling around a pile of sticks in the corner of the school garden. They are looking intently at one of the sticks using a magnifying glass. One of them says, "There's spiders in there." Another asks, "How do you know that, huh?" And the one with the magnifying glass says, " 'Cause I can see their eyes."*

Outdoor play is fun, exploratory, adventurous, invigorating—and rapidly disappearing from the lives of too many children. Excessive TV and computer use, unsafe neighborhoods, busy and tired parents, and elimination of school recess all take time away from outdoor play. Yet exploratory play outdoors is one of the best labs for learning about science, math, ecology, seasons, times of the day, and weather. Outdoor play can answer questions like: How does ice feel and sound? Can sticks stand up in sand? Why do we slide down instead of up? When are shadows long? When are they fuzzy? What does a chrysalis change into? Do butterflies have to learn to fly? (Johnson et al., 2007). Although these concepts can be taught in a variety of other ways (e.g., books, videos, or computer software), outdoor exploratory play provides direct, concrete experiences that can make it easier for learners to process and retain information (Ormrod, 1999).

Consider, for example, this play from Ms. Thompson's pre-K class where the children are studying water pipes and pumps. The children are busy building the Fix-It Plumbing Shop as the indoor locale for their studies. To get started they experimented with water pressure using plastic cups and pipettes. "We looked in the toilet [tank]," reported Tyrese, "and we were lookin' in there. We pushed the handle and the water went down, down, down. The yellow float thing went down, too, and the blue valve jumped up. Ms. Thompson told us." Then they went outside to investigate the water hose connected to a water pipe and tested different sprayer settings and decided that the little holes spray harder and mistier, noting again that water pipes create water pressure (i.e., force). Later they measured water pipes and they found that smaller pipes (like in a nozzle) create more water pressure than bigger pipes (like a hose without a sprayer).

A key feature of this example is the connection between indoor and outdoor play in the context of the children's Fix-It Plumbing Shop. The children, of course, are focused on their shop and their emerging expertise as plumbers, but going about it involves them in the scientific method: making guesses, testing them, and either proving or disproving them. To engage children in this kind of outdoor exploratory play requires planning on the part of the teacher—not to mention, in this instance, a good understanding of how water pipes and toilets work.

Here's another example of outdoor exploratory play. Although less structured and more imaginary in nature, it is not without its own lessons. Chris, Tyler, and Anubhav are three first graders who often play together during recess. In one corner of the playground they have "built" an imaginary fort, using a few loose pieces of concrete, small branches, and a stray bandana. Every day they race to the fort and prepare to defend it from imaginary enemies. On this particular day, they must go on a risky mission to retrieve the green energy crystals, stolen by the enemy, and return them to the fort. Their ensuing play is at once intensely physical, social, and conceptual. They coordinate their physical prowess with social interactions to create and maintain an imaginary world that they must negotiate and regulate to make the play work. This entails some rather sophisticated elements of thought: What is the purpose? What information is needed? How do I make sense of it? What's another point of view? As the imaginary play unfolds, each player must be self-disciplined, self-monitored and self-corrective, mindful of the problem, and willing to overcome egocentrism. Through joint participation around a shared mission, each player develops social, organizational, and linguistic skills related to real-world behaviors, as well as strategic thinking important for social success during childhood and, some would argue, adult life (e.g., Sluckin, 1981; Smith, 2010).

This is the important point from these two brief vignettes: outdoor play is not a recess from learning. Quite the opposite; it is a rigorous learning opportunity rich with potential for influencing growth and development, testing skills and knowledge, and exploring social relationships, not to mention forging lasting friendships. As educators, our goal should be more, not less, outdoor play. We should not be intimidated by fears that can be overcome if we put our minds to it. It may be cliché, but, to us, the Romans had the right goal: a sound mind in a sound body. We need to strive harder for that in childcare and at school.

Closing Remarks

Brian Sutton-Smith (1995), the eminent play theorist, commented that play is a "medium for propaganda for one propaedeutic sort or another" (p. 283), implying that "children learn something useful from their play" (p. 279). That they do learn something useful has not been scientifically proven, although considerable scholarship indicates that play provides opportunities for children to develop knowledge about the world in general and about academic content in literacy, mathematics, and science (see Van Reet, Chapter 2, this volume). Whether it has been proven useful or not, children play—and adults can tap the learning potential of this activity in ways that benefit children.

Our chapter describes several play pedagogies for tapping into play's learning potential toward the goal of increasing children's knowledge and skills, and cultivating their dispositions for learning. The pedagogies— story drama, topic-oriented play, board/digital games, and outdoor play—are instructional frameworks for organizing a wide range of play activities that may support and scaffold children's academic and social learning. They are adaptable, flexible, and manageable frameworks that can be used across educational settings and over time, from preschool to high school. Although there is no dearth of play activities in books and online and no lack of play advocacy in books, journals, and blogs, both are perhaps best served by pedagogic frameworks for instructional action applied faithfully and thoughtfully in educational practice.

Pedagogies, we argue, provide a means for putting play in the learning curriculum. This is not without a few caveats, however. First, educators need to ensure sufficient time and opportunity for play. In addition, they need ongoing professional development to fully engage all children in play and to help other adults and parents understand the role of play in human development, cognition, and health. They also need to respect, read, and pursue research that explains the role of play in academic learning from early childhood to adulthood. Above all, adults—educators, parents, policymakers, community members—must promise to preserve children's right to play. They need to interlock their little fingers and, as children say, "pinky swear."

REFERENCES

Anderson, J. R., Boyle, C. F., & Reiser, B. J. (1985). Intelligent tutoring systems. *Science, 228*(4698), 456–462.

Baines, E., & Blachford, P. (2011). Children's games and playground activities inh school and their role in development. In A. D. Pellegrini (Ed.), *The Oxford handbook of the development of play* (pp. 260–273). New York: Oxford University Press.

British Educational Communications and Technology Agency. (2001). *Computer games in education project: Report.* Retrieved July, 2011, from *http://partners.becta.org9.uk/index.php?section=rh&rid=13595.*

Christie, J. (2008). The SBRR approach to early literacy instruction. In L. Justice & C. Vukelich (Eds.), *Achieving excellence in preschool literacy instruction* (pp. 25–40). New York: Guilford Press.

Fisch, S. M. (2005, June). *Making educational computer games "educational."* Paper presented at the Instructional Design Conference, Boulder, CO.

Goldstein, J. (2011). Technology and play. In A. D. Pellegrini (Ed.), *The Oxford handbook of the development of play* (pp. 322–340). New York: Oxford University Press.

James, J. (1967). *Infant drama.* London: Nelson.

Johnson, J. E., Christie, J., & Wardle, F. (2007). *Play development and early education.* New York: Pearson.

Kegel, C. A. T., van der Kooy-Holfland, V. A. C., & Bus, A. G. (2009). Improving early phoneme skills with a computer program: Differential effects of regulatory skills. *Learning and Individual Differences, 19*(4), 549–554.

Kounin, J. S., & Doyle, P. H. (1975). Degree of continuity of a lesson signal system and the task involvement of children. *Journal of Educational Psychology, 67*(2), 159–164.

McFarlane, A., Sparrowhawk, A., & Heald, Y. (2002). *Report of the educational use of games.* Retrieved July, 2011, from *www.teem.org.uk/publications/teem_gamesined_full.pdf.*

McGee, L. (2007). *Transforming literacy practices in preschool.* New York: Scholastic.

Okita, S. (2004). Effects of age on associating virtual and embodied toys. *Cyberpsychology and Behavior, 9*(1), 1–4.

Ormrod, J. (1999). *Human learning* (3rd ed.). Columbus, OH: Merrill.

Owston, R., Wideman, H., Lotherington, H., Ronda, N. S., & Brown, C. (2007). *Computer game development as literacy activity* (Technical Report 2007-3). Toronto, ON: Institute for Research on Learning Technologies, York University.

Pellegrini, A. D. (1984). Identifying causal elements in the thematic–fantasy play paradigm. *American Educational Research Journal, 21*(3), 691–701.

Ramani, G. B., & Siegler, R. S. (2008). Promoting broad and stable improvements in low-income children's numerical knowledge through playing number board games. *Child Development, 79*(2), 375–394.

Rix, C., & McSorely, J. (1999). An investigation into the role that school-based interactive science centres may play in the education of primary-aged children. *International Journal of Science Education, 21*(6), 577–593.

Rogoff, B. (1990). *Apprenticeship in thinking: Cognitive development in social context.* New York: Oxford University Press.

Roskos, K. (1994, April). *Connecting academic work and play at school: Preliminary observations of young children's content-oriented interactions and talk under conditions of play in kindergarten.* Paper presented at the annual meeting of the American Educational Research Association, New Orleans, LA.

Roskos, K., & Christie, J. (2007). Play in the context of the new preschool basics. In K. Roskos & J. Christie (Eds.), *Play and literacy in early childhood: Research from multiple perspectives* (2nd ed., pp. 83–100). Mahwah, NJ: Erlbaum.

Saltz, E., Dixon, D., & Johnson, J. (1977). Training disadvantaged preschoolers on various fantasy activities: Effects on cognitive functioning and impulse control. *Child Development, 48*(2), 367–380.

Sarama, J., & Clements, D. (2009). Building blocks and cognitive building blocks: Playing to know the world mathematically. *American Journal of Play, 1*(3), 313–337.

Schuler, S., & Wittmann, G. (2009, January). *How can games contribute to early mathematics education?: A video-based study.* Paper presented at the Sixth Conference of European Research in Mathematics Education, Lyon, France.

Sluckin, A. (1981). *Growing up in the playground: The social development of children.* London: Routledge and Kegan Paul.

Smith, P. K. (2010). *Children and play.* Malden, MA: Wiley-Blackwell.

Speregen, D. (2005). *Snow day!* Philadelphia: Running Press.

Sutton-Smith, B. (1995). Conclusion: The persuasive rhetorics of play. In A. Pellegrini (Ed.), *The future of play theory: A multidisciplinary inquiry into the contributions of Brian Sutton-Smith* (pp. 275–305). Albany: State University of New York Press.

Van der Kooy-Hofland, V., Bus, A., & Roskos, K. (2011). Effects of a brief but intensive remedial early literacy computer intervention in a subsample of at-risk kindergartners with code-related skills delays. *Reading and Writing*. Available at *springerlink.com.*

Van Hourn, J., Scales, B., Nourot, P., & Alward, K. (1999). *Play at the center of the curriculum* (2nd ed.). Upper Saddle River, NJ: Merrill.

Wellington, M. (2005). *Zinnia's flower garden.* New York: Puffin Press.

Zigler, E., & Bishop-Josef, S. (2004). Play under siege: A historical overview. In E. Zigler, D. Singer, & S. Bishop-Josef (Eds.), *Children's play: The roots of reading* (pp. 1–14). Washington, DC: Zero to Three Press.

CHAPTER 9

■ ■ ■ ■ ■

The Research–Reality Divide in Early Vocabulary Instruction

Tanya S. Wright

I recently saw a prekindergartner drawing, and I asked her to tell me about her work. This was our conversation:

"What did you draw?" I asked.

"A tree."

"Can you tell me more about it?"

"That's the leaves, and that's the trunk," she said, pointing.

"Wow, what great work," I responded.

"Wait, but I forgot to make the *xylems*," she said while drawing vertical lines inside the trunk.

"*Xylem*, interesting. What are *xylem*?" I asked.

"Inside the tree to suck up the water," she responded

"How do you know about *xylem*?" I asked.

"With my teacher, we pretended we're plants and the straws are the *xylems* and we sucked them and got the water up in our mouth."

My first thought during this conversation was, *Wow, this kid has a great vocabulary!* Since this is my area of interest, it was exciting to see "real-world" evidence of a young child learning and spontaneously using words that are often considered "academic" and "sophisticated." My second thought, and the one that is more relevant to this chapter, was *Instruction matters!* Here was a case in which a preschool teacher purposefully structured an activity to build children's scientific knowledge

145

and taught the correct vocabulary to describe this content. The activity was clearly engaging and developmentally appropriate, and this child had retained this vocabulary and conceptual content.

Why should we be interested in vocabulary instruction (i.e., teaching word meanings) in the early childhood years? First, there is the well-established connection between vocabulary knowledge and long-term reading comprehension (Anderson & Freebody, 1981; Stahl & Fairbanks, 1986). Evidence from both correlational (e.g., Ricketts, Nation, & Bishop, 2007) and longitudinal (e.g., National Institute of Child Health and Human Development Early Child Care Research Network, 2005; Storch and Whitehurst, 2002) studies suggest that children's early vocabulary knowledge is highly predictive of their long-term reading comprehension. These findings have been replicated across countries (Muter, Hulme, Snowling, & Stevenson, 2004), language communities (Sénéchal, Ouellette, & Rodney, 2006), and in the reading disabilities literature (Catts, Adlof, & Weismer, 2006). But beyond the research evidence, it seems intuitively logical. If a student does not know or understand a vocabulary word when it is presented in oral language, it is unlikely that he or she could understand it when reading text. If a student brings strong vocabulary knowledge to the task of reading, by contrast, comprehension may be facilitated (Biemiller, 2003; Hirsch, 2003).

Second, gaps in vocabulary knowledge by socioeconomic status (SES) are evident even before the start of formal schooling (Hoff, 2003). Children growing up in poverty may be exposed to fewer words in their homes, resulting in more limited vocabulary knowledge than their middle-class peers by age 3 (Hart & Risley, 1995). These differences do not disappear as children move through school; they have been documented at the elementary school and middle school levels as well (Biemiller & Slonim, 2001; Chall, Jacobs, & Baldwin, 1990). Given that vocabulary knowledge is a key skill for reading comprehension, children from low SES homes might continue to struggle as readers if schools cannot provide vocabulary instruction to address these disparities.

Finally, there is evidence from intervention studies that vocabulary instruction can improve young children's vocabulary knowledge. In their meta-analysis, the National Early Literacy Panel (2009) analyzed 19 language intervention studies for children from birth through age 5 and found moderate effects for interventions specifically addressing oral language skills. In addition, the authors examined 16 shared book-reading interventions and again found moderate effects for children's vocabulary and more broad-based oral language measures. In a more recent meta-analysis of 67 vocabulary interventions targeting prekindergarten and kindergarten children, Marulis and Neuman (2010) found an overall effect size of .89—in other words, vocabulary instruction enabled young children to gain, on average, almost one standard deviation on vocabulary measures.

Taken together, there is clearly a compelling argument in favor of providing vocabulary instruction in school, beginning in the early childhood years. Over the past decade, consensus documents from the fields of literacy and early childhood have also acknowledged the importance of a focus on vocabulary and oral language in working with young children (e.g., National Association for the Education of Young Children [NAEYC], 2009; National Reading Panel [NRP], 2000; National Early Literacy Panel [NELP], 2009; Snow, Burns & Griffith, 1998).

Theories Connecting Comprehension and Vocabulary

Although studies consistently connect vocabulary and comprehension, there are several theories as to *why* vocabulary knowledge is so highly predictive of comprehension. These theories are not mutually exclusive (Bauman & Graves, 2010), but each one has distinct implications for designing instruction.

First, the *aptitude* hypothesis suggests that vocabulary is a proxy measure for general aptitude. This general aptitude enables the individual to both learn more words and comprehend text more easily. Proponents of this theory frequently cite the robust relationship between vocabulary and IQ. Anderson and Freebody (1981), for example, reviewed ten studies demonstrating that scores on the verbal component of intelligence tests are strongly correlated with overall scores ($r = .71$ to $.98$). They argued that verbal measures can thus be used as an estimate, or short measure, of overall aptitude. By this logic, classroom instruction may try to change children's aptitude by increasing, for example, reading time and decoding skills. More critically, the aptitude hypothesis might lead to the counterproductive assumption that vocabulary skill is a matter of innate ability that cannot be improved through instruction—despite contrary evidence reported by meta-analyses of vocabulary interventions (Marulis & Neuman, 2010; NRP, 2000; Stahl & Fairbanks, 1986).

Second, the *instrumentalist* hypothesis suggests that knowing more words enables better comprehension. Proponents of this theory cite the finding that increasing the difficulty of words in a text makes it more difficult to read. This leads to instruction focused on increasing children's knowledge of individual words. Beck and her colleagues (Beck & McKeown, 2007; Beck, McKeown, & Kucan, 2002), for instance, focus on teaching children "Tier Two" words. Rather than common, everyday words used regularly in oral language (e.g., *dog, house*) or words that are esoteric to a particular domain (e.g., *constructivism, psychometric*), Tier Two words are known by mature, literate language users and are found across a variety of domains (e.g., *coincidence, absurd, industrious*). This manner of selecting words subscribes to the theory that increasing knowledge of individual words is the key to increasing general vocabulary knowledge and thereby improving comprehension.

Third, the *knowledge* hypothesis suggests that a child who scores well on a vocabulary test has high general knowledge. For example, if a child knows the word *mast*, she probably also has knowledge about boats and sailing (Anderson & Freebody, 1981). Vocabulary knowledge thus represents conceptual knowledge, and knowing words means having developed schemas that enable comprehension. Proponents of this hypothesis argue that vocabulary learning should be embedded in content-rich instruction. Here, this strong background knowledge, along with the language to articulate this knowledge, enables an individual to have good listening and reading comprehension.

In recent years, many scholars have focused on the knowledge hypothesis to explain the connection between vocabulary and reading comprehension. Neuman and Celano (2006), for example, argued that vocabulary gaps by SES represent "knowledge gaps." In subsequent work, Neuman and colleagues proposed that early literacy skills should be integrated into content-rich instruction, thereby simultaneously advancing children's conceptual knowledge and vocabulary development in the early childhood years (e.g., Neuman & Dwyer, 2011; Neuman, Roskos, Wright, & Lenhart, 2007; Wright & Neuman, 2009). Indeed, the depth and breadth of children's background knowledge is positively related to both vocabulary and comprehension skills (Anderson & Freebody, 1981; Dochy, Segers, & Buehl, 1999; McKeown, Beck, Sinatra, & Loxterman, 1992; Shapiro, 2004). Taken together, this research suggests that children's vocabulary and background knowledge are two key predictors of long-term literacy development that should be explicitly addressed in school to help ameliorate both "vocabulary gaps" and "knowledge gaps."

Although the different theories may lead to different methodologies for instruction and word selection, the importance of vocabulary knowledge to children's academic trajectories is resoundingly clear. Vocabulary knowledge is not a finite skill that can be addressed and mastered at one age or stage of development. Instead, words are labels for objects and ideas, and understanding word meanings is intricately connected to reading and learning throughout schooling and beyond.

Features of Vocabulary Instruction

Recent research has generated an increasing consensus on the characteristics of vocabulary instruction that promotes children's vocabulary learning. This research emphasizes the development of instruction that includes rich and explicit explanations of words, in-depth discussions of words in multiple contexts, and review and practice of words on many occasions.

First, explicit explanations appear to enhance young children's word learning. Instruction is typically considered explicit when students are given definitions or other attributes of the words to be learned (NRP, 2000). In a recent meta-analysis, Marulis and Neuman (2010) reported significantly higher effects when interventions included explicit instruction. In comparison, smaller effects were reported for interventions with only implicit instruction, in which new vocabulary words were embedded in storybook reading without direct explanations of word meanings. Direct comparisons of these approaches have also reported that young children learn more words during storybook reading when teachers provide explicit explanations of target words (Coyne, McCoach, Loftus, Zipoli, & Kapp, 2009; Penno, Wilkinson, & Moore, 2002). These studies suggest that implicit instruction alone may be insufficient to significantly boost children's oral language development.

Exposure to words through implicit instruction likely promotes *breadth* of vocabulary knowledge, whereas more explicit instruction may promote greater *depth* of knowledge by providing children with opportunities to develop fuller understandings of carefully selected words. For example, applying a newly learned word to a variety of contexts may promote greater depth of vocabulary learning than using the word only in a single context. Beck et al.'s (2002) "rich vocabulary instruction" focuses on promoting depth of word learning through explanation of word meanings in child-friendly language, use of words in a variety of contexts, opportunities to explain appropriate and inappropriate uses of words, and review. In fact, children who received rich instruction on challenging words learned significantly more words than children in a control group (Beck & McKeown, 2007).

Silverman (2007) argued that the multidimensional features of vocabulary instruction may promote greater depth of vocabulary knowledge. She developed an intervention in which children actively engaged in more decontextualized analysis of word meanings (e.g., comparing and contrasting words, thinking of antonyms and synonyms) after the book was read. Consistent with Beck and McKeown (2007), Silverman found that children who received multidimensional teaching learned more words than children who had discussed word meanings only in the context of a specific book. Moreover, Coyne et al. (2009) found that extending instruction to include multiple opportunities to interact with target words outside the context of the story led to greater depth of word learning for kindergarteners.

When encountering new words in multiple contexts, children also experience repeated exposures to those words. Although children might establish some baseline information about a new word after a single exposure ("fast mapping"), word meaning is developed through repeated exposure in conjunction with information about the word's meaning (Booth, 2009; Carey, 1978). Biemiller and Boote (2006), for example, found that young children learned 22% of new words when exposed to a single explanation of the word. But when teachers provided two additional reviews of each word's meaning, children learned 41% of the target words, almost double what was learned with only a single exposure.

In comparison to the substantial literature on the characteristics of instruction, relatively little attention has been paid to the selection of words. There is a growing consensus, however, that instructed words should be selected from sophisticated or rare words, outside children's day-to-day lexicon, that are appropriately challenging, in order to support long-term comprehension (Nagy & Hiebert, 2010). Beck et al. (2002), for example, recommended teaching Tier Two words, whereas Biemiller (2006) suggested that words should be selected by age of acquisition, moving children toward more complex words as they become word conscious. Focusing on "sophisticated words" (i.e., words outside the 3,000 most common words on the Dale–Chall list; Chall & Dale, 1995), Weizman and Snow (2001) found that the density of mothers' use of sophisticated words, as well as instructive interactions around these words, positively predicted children's vocabulary knowledge in kindergarten and beyond. Others have recommended teaching content-specific words to ensure that young children develop both the vocabulary words and background knowledge necessary to comprehend text relevant to science, mathematics and social studies (e.g., Hirsch, 2003; Marzano, 2004a; Neuman & Celano, 2006; Wright & Neuman, 2009).

Bauman and Graves (2010) recently suggested a classification scheme that consolidates many of these ideas. They proposed that students need five types of academic vocabulary to successfully comprehend text: (1) *domain-specific academic vocabulary* composed of low-frequency, content-specific vocabulary that occurs in content-area texts or technical writing (e.g., *bisect, meteorology*); (2) *general academic vocabulary,* or words that appear relatively frequently within and across academic domains (e.g., *assume, document, minor*); (3) *literary vocabulary,* or words that authors of literature use to describe characters, settings, and characters' problems and actions (e.g., *awkward, chortled, stern*); (4) *metalanguage* terms used to describe the language of literacy and literacy instruction, as well as concepts commonly included in content-area texts (e.g., *genre, glossary, calculate*); and (5) *symbols* including icons, emoticons, graphics, mathematical notations, and electronic symbols that are not traditional words (e.g., $, :), %). Bauman and Graves's scheme encompasses many of the ideas and concepts suggested in the research literature, and speaks to the range and volume of words and concepts that children need to acquire as they progress through their schooling.

Although each approach may have its unique strengths and limitations, the renewed interest and focus on challenging words is designed to help promote overall verbal functioning, particularly for students who may come from lower socioeconomic backgrounds and may have less opportunity to acquire these words outside of school. It might also represent the most efficient use of instructional time.

Vocabulary Instruction and the Curriculum

Vocabulary instruction may be influenced by the curricula in a classroom—both the enacted curriculum as well as formal curriculum materials. In studies of vocabulary instruction for young children, researchers have typically used read-alouds as the context for word selection and teaching word meaning. In instruction built around this context, researchers use word explanations (Biemiller & Boote, 2006), dialogic reading (Hargrave & Sénéchal, 2000; Wasik & Bond, 2001; Wasik, Bond, & Hindman, 2006; Whitehurst et al., 1994) or extended discussion of vocabulary words (Beck & McKeown, 2007; Silverman, 2007) to promote children's vocabulary learning. Vocabulary teaching has therefore typically been examined as part of language arts instruction.

Recently, however, researchers have embedded vocabulary teaching in content-area instruction to ensure that children develop the vocabulary words and background knowledge to comprehend science, mathematics, and social studies content (French, 2004; Neuman & Dwyer, 2011; Neuman, Dwyer, Koh, & Wright, 2007). This strategy allows vocabulary instruction to occur across the curriculum during all content areas. Another way that teachers might provide content-area vocabulary is through informational text read-alouds and discussions. Yet informational texts are surprisingly underutilized for read-alouds in early elementary school classrooms (Duke, 2000; Duke, Halvorsen, & Knight, Chapter 12, this volume). Marzano (2004b), for example, suggested that opportunities for vocabulary instruction in school generally have been underestimated because the focus tends to be on general word learning during language arts instruction rather than the words in key content areas.

Whether or not the use of a comprehensive (i.e., core) reading program might improve the amount and quality of vocabulary instruction has been the subject of debate in recent years. Over the past decade, Reading First and Early Reading First legislation have emphasized the use of core reading curricula (Al Otaiba et al., 2008; Carlisle, Cortina, & Zeng, 2010; U.S. Department of Education, 2002). Studies of these curricula, however, have been critiqued as providing limited support for vocabulary instruction. Core reading programs designed for lower elementary school may miss opportunities to build word and background knowledge during read-alouds and thematic instruction (Walsh, 2003). In fact, Neuman and Dwyer (2009) found little evidence of a deliberate effort to teach vocabulary at the prekindergarten level. Specifically, they reported a mismatch between explicitly stated goals in the scope and sequence; a general pattern of "acknowledging" the importance of vocabulary but sporadic attention to addressing the skill intentionally; little attention to developing background knowledge; and limited to no opportunities to practice, review, and monitor children's progress. Yet to my knowledge, there is no research examining whether different content areas within the curriculum or core curricular materials might promote greater vocabulary instruction.

The Current State of Affairs

Recent observational studies of early childhood classrooms suggest significant variability exists in vocabulary instruction. Al Otaiba et al. (2008), for example, found that the time dedicated to vocabulary instruction ranged from 2 to 24 minutes daily in Reading First kindergarten classrooms. They reported that teachers on the high end used a basal curriculum that specifically focused on vocabulary instruction. In another recent study, Silverman and Crandell (2010) provided prekindergarten and kindergarten teachers with a professional development workshop on vocabulary instruction, as well as books to use for read-alouds and target vocabulary words to teach throughout the year in relation to children's learning of the target words. Children's initial levels of vocabulary knowledge affected how they responded to particular instructional strategies.

Although previous research provides a compelling argument that vocabulary *can* and *should* actively be taught to young children in school, 10 years after the National Reading Panel (2000) recommended this as a key instructional practice to support children's reading, we have little evidence of the type of vocabulary instruction that is implemented in typical classrooms or supported by commonly used vocabulary curricula, particularly in the early childhood years. Moreover, given that a year of prekindergarten or kindergarten has almost no impact on children's vocabulary size (Christian, Morrison, Frazier, & Massetti, 2000; Skibbe, Connor, Morrison, & Jewkes, 2011), early schooling may simply reify the vocabulary trajectories associated with students' home experiences. If intervention studies can produce improved vocabulary for young children, why does "business as usual" schooling not affect children's vocabulary development? Over the past few years, my own research has set out to answer this question through in-depth studies of the day-to-day instruction and curricular materials in kindergarten classrooms. In this chapter, I specifically focus on two recent studies. In the first study (Wright, 2011), I investigated the vocabulary instruction that typically occurs in naturalistic kindergarten settings. In the second study, my colleague Susan Neuman and I (Wright & Neuman, 2011) conducted a content analysis that examined vocabulary instruction in the four most commonly used kindergarten core reading curricula. Together, these studies provide valuable insight into the current state of vocabulary instruction in kindergarten classrooms.

Vocabulary Instruction in Kindergarten Classrooms

To investigate the current state of vocabulary instruction, I observed 55 teachers from a range of socioeconomic backgrounds in their kindergarten classrooms four times over the course of 8 weeks (Wright, 2011). Classrooms were observed for 3 hours in the morning, which constituted the entire kindergarten day for the majority of classrooms. I looked for evidence of stand-alone vocabulary lessons, as well as instances in which teachers discussed the meaning of words embedded in other content (i.e., science or a storybook reading). Altogether, 660 hours were spent observing these kindergarten classrooms.

I found no evidence at all of stand-alone vocabulary lessons. This was surprising, especially considering the general agreement that vocabulary is important to children's comprehension. Although other researchers have described rich (Beck & McKeown, 2007) or multidimensional (Silverman, 2007) vocabulary instruction that promotes vocabulary learning beyond the context where the word is encountered,

I saw no evidence of this type of instruction across the 55 classrooms that were visited.

Instead, I found that teachers discussed the meaning of words with children, on average, 8.14 times per day, all while embedded in the context of other content. During a reading lesson, for example, a teacher said, "*Rhyming* words have to sound alike. They have the same ending sound and sound alike." At first glance, I thought that these word explanations may indicate content-rich vocabulary instruction where teachers taught academic vocabulary while building content knowledge. However, the data did not support this hypothesis. The characteristics of instruction did not align with the research on vocabulary instruction. The majority of the words that were discussed were common words (i.e., on the revised Dale–Chall list), with only 3.5 sophisticated words addressed per day. Also, teachers rarely discussed the meaning of the same word more than once: 7.44 different words were explained through 8.14 explanations per day. This negligible repetition and inconsistent word selection suggests that teachers may capitalize on "teachable moments" throughout the day to explain word meanings to children. This is clearly distinct from the intensive and planful vocabulary instruction described in previous research studies.

Still, if teachers provided these word explanations in the context of rich content-area learning, perhaps they focused on content that develops children's conceptual knowledge as well as vocabulary knowledge. Unfortunately, the data did not support this hypothesis. Shared book-reading contexts were most dense for word explanations (i.e., words explained per minute) and discussion of word meanings, reflecting the well-described role of the read-aloud context for promoting vocabulary learning. Interestingly, science and social studies had the next highest densities, suggesting that these content areas are fertile contexts for new vocabulary. Although explanations were dense during shared reading, science, and social studies, very little time was dedicated to these contexts in kindergarten classrooms. During the average 3-hour observation, teachers spent only 10.71 minutes on shared book reading, 2.3 minutes on science, and 1.2 minutes on social studies. In fact, many of the classrooms had no science or social studies instruction at all. Although shared book-reading, science, and social studies may have best promoted word explanations, these subjects were given very limited time and attention during the typical kindergarten day. Instead, teachers spent much of their time on the subjects with the lowest density for word explanations, including reading instruction (28.17 minutes), writing (19.35 minutes), and morning meeting (18.45 minutes).

Finally, I compared instruction across classrooms serving children from a range of socioeconomic backgrounds. Teachers from schools with 50% or more students receiving free and reduced lunch provided significantly fewer words explanations per day than teachers in schools serving a more affluent population. They also addressed fewer sophisticated words in these explanations. Although planful vocabulary instruction was minimal across the board, children who were most in need of school-based vocabulary instruction seemed least likely to receive it.

In summary, this school study paints a disconcerting portrait of vocabulary instruction in kindergarten. Across a large range of classrooms, there were no dedicated vocabulary lessons. Although teachers explained words throughout the day, most of the words were basic, and the instructional strategies did not reflect research-based recommendations. The content areas most fertile for vocabulary were least likely to be addressed. And, most disturbing, I found differential instruction by SES, whereby the children who may need vocabulary instruction the most, in fact, may receive the least in their classroom environments.

Vocabulary Instruction in Kindergarten Curricula

Considering the findings from the school observations, I wanted to understand how using core reading curricula might affect the classroom instructional environment. Presumably, these curricula provide for a more intentional, sequenced program of instruction in oral vocabulary development. Although approximately half of the teachers purported to use these core curricula in Wright (2011), there were no significant differences in the frequency or quality of vocabulary teaching in their classrooms compared to those using other materials. Perhaps this was due to the limited treatment of vocabulary in core reading programs or to the limited enactment of suggested vocabulary instruction in these classrooms. I explored these possibilities in an analysis of curricular materials (see also Wright & Neuman, 2011).

The overarching goal for this study was to understand how commonly used core reading programs support vocabulary instruction at the kindergarten level. To address this, I analyzed 12 weeks of instruction in the teacher manuals of the four most commonly used core reading curricula. These curricula together represent more than 50% of the current market for this type of curriculum (Resnick, 2010). The detailed content analysis focused on three issues: (1) the extent of vocabulary instruction in kindergarten core reading curricula; (2) whether vocabulary words addressed by these curricula reflect current research on word selection; and (3) whether instructional strategies in the curricula reflect the research on vocabulary instruction.

I found remarkable variability in the extent of vocabulary instruction provided across the four curricula. Each curriculum addressed vastly different numbers of vocabulary words per week; for example, one curriculum listed 20.19 target vocabulary words per week, while another listed only 2.25. Consequently, a kindergartner in a classroom using one of these curricula would likely be exposed to a very different number of vocabulary words compared to a peer in a classroom where an alternative curriculum was implemented.

Across the board, most vocabulary words selected for instruction were considered too easy or common by researchers to warrant school-based instruction. This finding held regardless of which research-based method for vocabulary selection was used (i.e., Beck et al., 2002; Biemiller, 2009; Weizman & Snow, 2001). It might be reasonable for curricula to briefly review the meanings of common words to ensure that children understand a specific text. However, if the ultimate goal is to promote general oral language development and reading comprehension, children should be taught sophisticated words that they may not learn on their own (Beck & McKeown, 1987; Beck, McKeown, & Kucan, 2007; Biemiller, 2006, 2009). Focusing the vast amount of instructional attention on easy words fails to optimize instructional time for vocabulary.

These findings suggest that curricula are likely to provide definitions and opportunities for children to practice using target vocabulary words. However, replicating previous research on prekindergarten curricula (Neuman & Dwyer, 2009), the kindergarten curricula at times listed words as target vocabulary with no additional supports for teaching word meanings to children. Also, the curricula were far less likely to use strategies associated with rich or multidimensional instruction such as contextualizing word meanings, illustrating or acting out word meanings, or providing review of meaningful information. Finally, only one curriculum of the four addressed progress monitoring and differentiated instruction of taught vocabulary words.

This content analysis indicates that a considerable range exists in the quantity and quality of support for vocabulary instruction across commonly used kindergarten reading curricula. In the area of vocabulary instruction, these curricula cannot be considered interchangeable or equivalent entities. All four curricula address words that are probably too basic to warrant instructional time, a finding that echoes the instruction observed in my previous study (Wright, 2011). Also, most instruction supported by these curricula did not reflect the depth and intensity of research-based recommendations for vocabulary instruction, again aligning with my observations of kindergarten classrooms.

Conclusion

Early vocabulary instruction is clearly important for children's long-term literacy. Words represent knowledge, and children's vocabulary has a powerful influence on their ability to make meaning from text. Although it would be impossible to teach all vocabulary through direct instruction, there is compelling evidence that good instruction can increase children's vocabulary knowledge. Young children can and should build sophisticated and academic words into their oral vocabularies, providing a foundation for their long-term reading comprehension.

Yet my research suggests that vocabulary is neglected in daily practice in most kindergarten classrooms. Across many hours of observation of classroom instruction, I did not find evidence of vocabulary instruction that reflected research-based instructional strategies in this area, and teachers serving children from economically disadvantaged backgrounds gave the least attention to vocabulary. Likewise, curricular materials were hit or miss in their attempts to support vocabulary instruction in the kindergarten classroom. Although there is agreement that oral vocabulary is a key area for long-term literacy development, this does not seem to be reflected in curricula and instructional practice.

In the future, researchers and practitioners will need to work together toward bridging this gap between research and daily practice in vocabulary instruction. Numerous challenges may prevent vocabulary instruction from being implemented in early childhood classrooms. Neuman (2011), for example, identified several stumbling blocks, including the sheer number of words that need to be taught, the difficulty of word selection, a belief that storybook reading is enough to build children's vocabulary, a focus on building print rather than oral vocabulary, and the challenge of having limited tools to assess children's vocabulary learning. Yet the more important question is how to move past these hurdles to ensure that what we *do* know about oral vocabulary instruction is reflected in curriculum and instruction in early childhood classrooms. The current paucity of instruction and disparity in children's opportunities to learn vocabulary may have long-term consequences for their literacy development and success in school. A pressing goal is to move research-based instructional practices into the reality of children's daily classroom experiences.

REFERENCES

Al Otaiba, S., Connor, C., Lane, H., Kosanovich, M. L., Schatschneider, C., Dyrlund, A. K., et al. (2008). Reading First kindergarten classroom instruction and students' growth in phonological awareness and letter naming–decoding fluency. *Journal of School Psychology, 46*(3), 281–314.

Anderson, R. C., & Freebody, P. (1981). Vocabulary knowledge. In J. T. Guthrie (Ed.), *Comprehension and teaching: Research reviews* (pp. 77–117). Newark, DE: International Reading Association.

Baumann, J. F., & Graves, M. F. (2010). What is academic vocabulary? *Journal of Adolescent and Adult Literacy, 54*(1), 4–12.

Beck, I. L., & McKeown, M. G. (2007). Increasing young low-income children's oral vocabulary repertoires through rich and focused instruction. *Elementary School Journal, 107*(3), 251–273.

Beck, I. L., McKeown, M. G., & Kucan, L. (2002). *Bringing words to life: Robust vocabulary instruction.* New York: Guilford Press.

Biemiller, A. (2003). Oral comprehension sets the ceiling on reading comprehension. *American Educator, 27*(1), 23, 44.

Biemiller, A. (2006). Vocabulary development and instruction: A prerequisite for school learning. In D. K. Dickinson & S. B. Neuman (Eds.), *Handbook of early literacy research* (Vol. 2, pp. 41–51). New York: Guilford Press.

Biemiller, A. (2009). *Words worth teaching: Closing the vocabulary gap.* Columbus, OH: SRA/McGraw-Hill.

Biemiller, A., & Boote, C. (2006). An effective method for building meaning vocabulary in primary grades. *Journal of Educational Psychology, 98*(1), 44–62.

Biemiller, A., & Slonim, N. (2001). Estimating root vocabulary growth in normative and advantaged populations: Evidence for a common sequence of vocabulary acquisition. *Journal of Educational Psychology, 93*(3), 498–520.

Blanchowitz, C. (1987). Vocabulary instruction: What goes on in the classroom? *Reading Teacher, 41*(2), 132–137.

Booth, A. E. (2009). Causal supports for early word learning. *Child Development, 80*(4), 1243–1250.

Carlisle, J. F., Cortina, K. S., & Zeng, J. (2010). Reading achievement in Reading First schools in Michigan. *Journal of Literacy Research, 42*(1), 49–70.

Carey, S. (1978). The child as word learner. In M. Halle, J. Bresnan, & G. A. Miller (Eds.), *Linguistic theory and psychological reality* (pp. 264–293). Cambridge, MA: MIT Press.

Catts, H. W., Adlof, S. M., & Weismer, S. E. (2006). Language deficits in poor comprehenders: A case for the simple view of reading. *Journal of Speech, Language, and Hearing Research, 49*(2), 278–293.

Chall, J., & Dale, E. (1995). *Readability revisited and the new Dale–Chall readability formula.* Cambridge, MA: Brookline Books.

Chall, J. S., Jacobs, V. A., & Baldwin, L. E. (1990) *The reading crisis: Why poor children fall behind.* Cambridge, MA: Harvard University Press.

Christian, K., Morrison, F. J., Frazier, J. A., & Massetti, G. (2000). Specificity in the nature and timing of cognitive growth in kindergarten and first grade. *Journal of Cognition and Development, 1*(4), 429–448.

Coyne, M., McCoach, D. B., Loftus, S., Zipoli, R., & Kapp, S. (2009). Direct vocabulary instruction in kindergarten: Teaching for breadth versus depth. *The Elementary School Journal, 110*(1), 1–18.

Dochy, F., Segers, M., & Buehl, M. M. (1999). The relation between assessment practices and outcomes of studies: The case of research on prior knowledge. *Review of Educational Research, 69*(2), 145–186.

Duke, N. K. (2000). 3.6 minutes per day: The scarcity of informational texts in first grade. *Reading Research Quarterly, 35*(2), 202–224.

Durkin, D. (1978–1979). What classroom observations reveal about reading comprehension instruction. *Reading Research Quarterly, 14*(4), 481–533.

French, L. (2004). Science as the center of a coherent, integrated early childhood curriculum. *Early Childhood Research Quarterly, 19*(1), 138–149.

Gonzalez, J. E., Pollard-Durodola, S., Simmons, D. C., Taylor, A. B., Davis, M. J., Kim, M., et al. (2011). Developing low-income preschoolers' social studies and science vocabulary knowledge through content-focused shared book reading. *Journal of Research on Educational Effectiveness, 4*(1), 25–52.

Hargrave, A. C., & Sénéchal, M. (2000). A book reading intervention with preschool children who have limited vocabularies: The benefits of regular reading and dialogic reading. *Early Childhood Research Quarterly, 15*(1), 75–90.

Hart, B., & Risley, T. R. (1995). *Meaningful differences differences in the everyday experience of young American children.* Baltimore, MD: Brookes.

Hirsch, E. D. (2003). Reading comprehension requires knowledge—of words and the world. *American Educator, 27*(1), 10–13, 16–22, 28–29, 48.

Hoff, E. (2003). The specificity of environment influence: Socioeconomic status affects early vocabulary development via maternal speech. *Child Development, 74*(5), 1368–1378.

Leung, C. B. (2008). Preschoolers' acquisition of scientific vocabulary through repeated read-aloud events, retellings, and hands-on science activities. *Reading Psychology, 29*(2), 165–193.

Marulis, L., & Neuman, S. B. (2010). The effects of vocabulary intervention on young children's word learning: A meta-analysis. *Review of Educational Research, 80*(3), 300–335.

Marzano (2004a). *Building background knowledge for academic achievement: Research on what works in schools.* Alexandria, VA: ASCD.

Marzano (2004b). The developing vision of vocabulary instruction. In J. F. Baumann & E. J. Keme'enui (Eds.), *Vocabulary instruction: Research to practice* (pp. 100–117). New York: Guilford Press.

McKeown, M., Beck, I., Sinatra, G. M., & Loxterman, J. A. (1992). The contribution of prior knowledge and coherent text to comprehension. *Reading Research Quarterly, 27*(1), 78–93.

Muter, V., Hulme, C., Snowling, M. J., & Stevenson, J. (2004). Phonemes, rimes, vocabulary, and grammatical skills as foundations of early reading development: Evidence from a longitudinal study. *Developmental Psychology, 40*(5), 665–681.

Nagy, W. E., & Hiebert, E. H. (2010). Toward a theory of word selection. In M.

K. Kamil, P. D. Pearson, P. A. Afflerbach, & E. B. Moje (Eds.), *Handbook of reading research* (Vol. IV, pp. 388–404). New York: Routledge.

National Association for the Education of Young Children. (2009). *Position statement: Developmentally appropriate practice in early childhood programs serving children from birth through age 8.* Retrieved June 28, 2011, from *www.naeyc.org/DAP.*

National Early Literacy Panel. (2009). *Developing early literacy: Report of the National Early Literacy Panel.* Jessup, MD: National Institute for Literacy.

National Institute of Child Health and Development Early Child Care Research Network. (2005). Pathways to reading: The role of oral language in the transition to reading. *Developmental Psychology, 41,* 428–442.

National Reading Panel. (2000). *Teaching children to read: An evidence-based assessment of the scientific research literature on reading and its implications for reading instruction* (NIH Publication no. 00-4769). Washington, DC: U.S. Government Printing Office.

Neuman, S. B. (2011). The challenge of teaching vocabulary in early education. In S. B. Neuman & D. K. Dickinson (Eds.), *Handbook of early literacy research* (Vol. 3, pp. 360–374). New York: Guilford Press.

Neuman, S. B., & Celano, D. (2006). The knowledge gap: Implications of leveling the playing field for low-income and middle-income children. *Reading Research Quarterly, 41*(2), 176–201.

Neuman, S. B., & Dwyer, J. (2009). Missing in action: Vocabulary instruction in pre-K. *The Reading Teacher, 62*(5), 384–392.

Neuman, S. B., & Dwyer, J. (2011). Developing vocabulary and conceptual knowledge for low-income preschoolers: A design experiment. *Journal of Literacy Research, 43*(2), 103–129.

Neuman, S. B., Dwyer, J., Koh, S., & Wright, T. S. (2007). *The world of words: A vocabulary intervention for preschoolers.* Ann Arbor, MI: University of Michigan Press.

Neuman, S. B., Roskos, K., Wright, T. S., & Lenhart, L. (2007). *Nurturing knowledge: Building a foundation for school success by linking early literacy to math, science, art and social studies.* New York: Scholastic.

Penno, J. F., Wilkinson, A. G., & Moore, D. W. (2002). Vocabulary acquisition from teacher explanation and repeated listening to stories: Do they overcome the Matthew effect? *Journal of Educational Psychology, 94*(1), 23–33.

Resnick, R. (2010). *EMR research corner: Reading market: 2010.* Retrieved March 3, 2010, from *www.educationmarketresearch.com/index.php?p=201&pass=02.*

Ricketts, J., Nation, K., & Bishop, D. V. M. (2007). Vocabulary is important for some but not all reading skills. *Scientific Studies of Reading, 11*(3), 235–257.

Scott, J. A., Jamieson-Noel, D., & Asselin, M. (2003). Vocabulary instruction throughout the day in twenty-three Canadian upper elementary classrooms. *The Elementary School Journal, 103*(3), 269–286.

Sénéchal, M., Ouellette, G., & Rodney, D. (2006). The misunderstood giant: On the predictive role of early vocabulary to future reading. In D. K. Dickinson & S. B. Neuman, *Handbook of early literacy* (Vol. 2, pp.173–182). New York: Guilford Press.

Shapiro, A. M. (2004). How including prior knowledge as a subject variable may change outcomes of learning research. *American Educational Research Journal, 41*(1), 159–189.

Silverman, R. (2007). A comparison of three methods of vocabulary instruction during read-alouds in kindergarten. *Elementary School Journal, 108*(2), 97–113.

Silverman, R., & Crandell, J. D. (2010). Vocabulary practices in prekindergarten and kindergarten classrooms. *Reading Research Quarterly, 45*(3), 318–341.

Skibbe, L. E., Connor, C. M, Morrison, F. J., & Jewkes, A. M. (2011). Schooling effects on preschoolers' self-regulation, early literacy, and language growth. *Early Childhood Research Quarterly, 26*(1), 42–49.

Snow, C. E., Burns, M. S., & Griffith, P. (Eds.). (1998). *Preventing reading difficulties in young children.* Washington, DC: National Academy Press.

Stahl, S. A., & Fairbanks, M. M. (1986). The effects of vocabulary instruction: A model-based meta-analysis. *Review of Educational Research, 56*(1), 72–110.

Storch, S. A., & Whitehurst, G. J. (2002). Oral language and code-related precursors to reading: Evidence from a longitudinal structural model. *Developmental Psychology, 38*(6), 943–947.

U.S. Department of Education Office of Elementary and Secondary Education. (2002). *Final guidance for the Reading First Program.* Washington, DC: U.S. Department of Education. Retrieved July 21, 2010, from *www2. ed.gov/programs/readingfirst/legislation.html.*

Walsh, K. (2003). Basal readers: The lost opportunity to build the knowledge that propels comprehension. *American Educator, 27*(1), 24–27.

Wasik, B. A., & Bond, M. A. (2001). Beyond the pages of a book: Interactive book reading and language development in preschool classrooms. *Journal of Educational Psychology, 93*(2), 243–250.

Wasik, B. A., Bond, M. A., & Hindman, A. (2006). The effects of a language and literacy intervention on Head Start children and teachers. *Journal of Educational Psychology, 98*(1), 63–74.

Weizman, Z. O., & Snow, C. E. (2001). Lexical input as related to children's vocabulary acquisition: Effects of sophisticated exposure and support for its meaning. *Developmental Psychology, 37*(2), 265–279.

Whitehurst, G. J., Arnold, D. S., Epstein, J. N., Angell, A. L., Smith, M., & Fischel, J. E. (1994). Picture book reading intervention in day care and home for children from low-income families. *Developmental Psychology, 30*(5), 679–689

Wright, T. S. (2011). *What classroom observations reveal about oral vocabulary instruction in kindergarten* (Doctoral dissertation). Available from the ProQuest Dissertations & Theses database (AAT 3458922).

Wright, T. S., & Neuman, S. B. (2009). Purposeful, playful pre-K: Building on children's natural proclivity to learn language, literacy, mathematics and science. *American Educator, 33*(1), 33–39.

Wright, T. S., & Neuman, S. B. (2011, December). *Evidence for research-based instructional features in four most-commonly used core curricula in kindergarten*. Paper presented at the Annual Meeting of the National Reading Conference, Jacksonville, FL.

CHAPTER 10

■ ■ ■ ■ ■

The Contributions of Curriculum to Shifting Teachers' Practices

David K. Dickinson
Erica M. Barnes
Jin-Sil Mock

As we entered the 21st century, there was growing recognition of the need for effective, scalable methods of fostering early literacy-related skills among children from homes where families have traditionally had difficulty providing the kind of experiences that translate into strong literacy skills early in school. Evidence had mounted and continues to accumulate that early language abilities predict later language (Dickinson & Tabors, 2001; National Early Literacy Panel, 2009; National Institute of Child Health and Human Development Early Child Care Research Network [NICHD ECCRN], 2005; Snow, Burns, & Griffin, 1998; Spira, Bracken, & Fischel, 2005). As the continuity between early and late abilities became apparent, early childhood education moved from the shadows of policy and educational research toward center stage and hopes were raised that, because the early childhood years are a time of relative malleability, interventions could have substantial and sustained effects.

Unfortunately, a number of studies that examined seemingly solid preschool programs failed to find robust evidence of effects. One of the first major endeavors of the newly formed Institute of Educational Sciences was to launch Preschool Curriculum Effectiveness Research

Studies (PCERS), but the results were disappointing. A recent meta-analysis examining 13 major curriculum-based studies, including all literacy-based PCERS studies, found no evidence of intervention effects on language outcomes (Darrow, 2011). Similarly, evaluations of Head Start and the first wave of Early Reading First projects failed to find much evidence of impact on language outcomes (Jackson et al., 2007; U.S. Department of Health and Human Services, 2010). Bright spots do exist in evaluations of state pre-K programs (Frede, Jung, Barnett, Lamy, & Figueras, 2009; Gormley, Gayer, Phillips, & Dawson, 2005; Lipsey, Farran, Bilbrey, Hofer, & Dong, 2011) and the Chicago Parent–Child centers (Reynolds, Ou, & Topitzes, 2004). Furthermore, more narrowly focused interventions have met with greater success (Marulis & Neuman, 2010).

This chapter focuses on a curriculum-based approach to intervention. Although this intervention also met with mixed success, we have detailed information about the delivery of the intervention that helps us understand what impacts we did, and did not, have on classroom practices. Our intention is to shed light on the challenges we face as we strive to improve the quality of early education for children from low-income homes. But before we discuss that recent endeavor, we begin with a review of the work of the lead author that led to this recent intervention study.

A Personal Historical Review of Early Language and Literacy Research and Interventions

In the late 1970s, reading researchers were primarily focused on decoding and the emerging issue of phonemic awareness. Researchers were only beginning to recognize that massive numbers of children from low-income homes were struggling to learn to read and that the roots of these problems lay in the early years (Dickinson & Snow, 1987). As students of children's language development, however, Catherine Snow (Snow, 1983) and the first author (Dickinson, 1987) hypothesized that early language competencies may be associated with later literacy, and that limitations in the home and classroom supports during the preschool years may contribute to these children's reading problems (Snow, 1991; Snow & Dickinson, 1991).

A Longitudinal Study

To test our hypotheses, we mounted the Home–School Study of Language and Literacy Development (HSSLD), a longitudinal study that described 85 children's language experiences in their homes and classrooms, beginning at age 3. All children were from families who qualified for free or reduced-cost preschool and spoke English in the home (Dickinson & Tabors, 2001).

We made audio recordings of the conversations of our target children and their teachers during a single day in preschool; these tapes were transcribed and coded. Children's language and literacy abilities were also assessed at the end of kindergarten and fourth grade using measures of receptive vocabulary, print knowledge (i.e., phonological awareness, alphabet knowledge, decoding), and reading comprehension. Classroom data were augmented by information collected when we visited children's homes when they were 3 and 4 years old. These visits provided a measure of the mean length of the child's utterances at age 3 and information about supports for language and literacy available in the home.

We ended with complete data on 57 children. We examined the effects of preschool language experiences on children's later abilities using statistical methods that allowed us to examine mediation effects. That is, we determined how preschool language experiences affected kindergarten abilities which, in turn, influenced end-of-grade-4 reading comprehension, vocabulary, and decoding (Dickinson & Porche, 2011). These analyses yielded correlational evidence that the density of teachers' use of relatively sophisticated words during individualized conversations and analytic conversations during book reading (e.g., talk about the meaning of words) positively contributed to end-of-kindergarten vocabulary. These preschool-related vocabulary benefits, in turn, had positive effects on kindergarten print knowledge and, ultimately, fourth-grade comprehension, decoding, and vocabulary.

Professional Development

As the HSSLD data were beginning to be analyzed, it was evident that the level of support for language was lacking in many classrooms, and conversations with preschool teachers made clear that few teachers were aware of new research on emergent literacy. This led to a project with colleagues from the Education Development Center (EDC) that culminated in a professional development course, the Literacy Environment Enrichment Project (LEEP). LEEP was delivered to Head Start teachers around New England through a series of classes that carried university credit. A comparison group study revealed that participation in LEEP resulted in significant and educationally meaningful improvement in teachers' classroom practices (Dickinson & Caswell, 2007). This effort made apparent that, when teachers are given information, taught useful classroom-based strategies, and supported by their supervisors as they seek to adopt more effective practices, significant improvements can occur.

A Classroom Observation Tool

When attempting to foster change in how teachers support children's language and literacy learning, it is difficult to know whether one is successful in meeting children's needs. Test scores give some indication of a teacher's effectiveness, but it can take weeks or months to know whether children are learning, and even then test scores say nothing about what specific experiences are contributing to growth. Thus teachers are given little guidance regarding areas of practice that need improvement. To address this need a team of EDC researchers and early childhood educators developed the Early Childhood Language and Literacy Classroom Observation (ELLCO) (Smith, Dickinson, Sangeorge, & Anastasopoulos, 2002). This tool has been used by Early Reading First evaluation teams and, equally important, has helped teachers improve instruction by giving them an objective and concrete description of the quality of their classroom's support for language and literacy development.

Curriculum

Even after it became apparent that the professional development approach to enhancing the quality of classrooms held promise, it seemed that linking professional development to a curriculum that guides teachers toward using strong children's literature, building vocabulary and concepts within thematic units, and systematically fostering alphabet knowledge and phonological awareness would confer the greatest benefits. In an effort to create such a curriculum, Judy Schickedanz and Dickinson developed *Opening the World of Learning* (OWL; Schickedanz & Dickinson, 2005).[1] Drawing on Schickedanz's 20 years of experience directing a university-based laboratory preschool, we developed an approach designed to deliver conceptually and linguistically rich instruction to children from less socioeconomically advantaged homes.

A Curriculum-Based Intervention

Conversations between Dickinson and his new Vanderbilt colleague, Ann Kaiser, led to a joint intervention project mounted in a large, high-quality Head Start. This ambitious project included 52 classrooms that were randomly assigned to one of three conditions: (1) practice as usual; (2) use of OWL; and (3) use of OWL plus delivery of Enhanced Milieu

[1]Note that Dickinson is an author of this curriculum and, as such, has a financial interest in it. Also note that this research was conducted on the first version of the curriculum; a new version currently being marketed is different in many respects from the first edition.

Teaching (EMT), a play-based one-on-one tutorial method of stimulating language growth among children with limited language abilities (Kaiser, Roberts, & McCleod, 2011). Creative Curriculum (Dodge, Colker, & Heoman, 2001) was used in the control classrooms, and implementation was enhanced by providing materials, associated lessons, and instructional objectives for each unit of study.

The intervention curriculum, OWL, recommends activities for use throughout the day and includes lesson guides for four settings: book reading, group literacy instruction and group content instruction, small-group activity, and center time. The curriculum also supplies books, nearly all of which were new to the teachers and many of which were longer and more complex than the books they typically read. Instruction in full and small groups included science instruction and a greater focus on vocabulary and higher-level conceptual knowledge than was commonly found in the practice-as-usual classrooms.

Thus the curriculum put heavy demands on the entire teaching team as they introduced new topics, read unfamiliar books, and sought to adopt new instructional methods. This effort lacked the kind of robust professional development that characterized LEEP; rather, teachers were introduced to the curriculum in large-group professional development sessions and were helped to implement this ambitious curriculum by Head Start staff, each of whom worked with about 10 classrooms. Teachers in the EMT + OWL condition were helped to learn EMT strategies, which required adoption of well-specified novel interactional methods in addition to OWL. The teachers in both conditions followed the same daily schedule, and all received professional development. The training for OWL teachers covered all aspects of the curriculum, with an emphasis on strategies for book reading.

When we examined the effectiveness of the curriculum in improving children's fall-to-spring growth in language and literacy skills, we were dismayed not to find evidence of any clear pattern of beneficial effects (Dickinson, Kaiser, Roberts, Hofer, & Darrow, 2011). Because we were interested in the fine-grained details of preschool interactions, we also videotaped all of the classrooms on multiple occasions. When we coded these videos for the fidelity with which the curriculum was implemented and the nature of teacher–child conversations, our analyses showed great variability in how teachers worked with children and revealed that teachers often did not employ critical instructional strategies.

Potential Contributions of a Curriculum to Instruction

Curriculum may be viewed as a capacity builder due to its potential to influence what teachers say and do (Han, Roskos, Christie, Mandzuk, &

Vukelich, 2005). A supportive curriculum that provides models, scripting, definitions, and examples may therefore assist in the development of teachers' professional expertise. New curricula may require teachers to shift their practice, thus expanding professional expertise through the uptake of new strategies and practices. Matching the curriculum to teachers' beliefs and practices places it within their zone of professional development, thus allowing for the further development of professional expertise. Domitrovich et al. (2009) found that the quality of uptake of a new curriculum is higher when a curriculum's philosophy is congruent with the teachers' beliefs and practice. Moreover, teachers who already utilize some of the strategies presented within a curriculum are more likely to reach proficiency faster than those who have more to learn (Hsieh, Hemmeter, McCollum, & Ostrosky, 2009). As a result, curricula that are not consistent with teachers' beliefs and current practices may be more difficult to implement.

Influence of Curriculum Support on Quality of Language

Although we lack information about teachers' beliefs and do not have observations prior to the introduction of the new curriculum, our randomized assignment method does provide us classrooms in which we can examine teachers who only used the approach that all had implemented prior to our study. In the following pages, we investigate the impact of the new curriculum on instruction in two large-group settings, book reading and content instruction, and during small-group instruction. We seek to identify how curriculum support may influence the quality of language used by assessing the lexical richness and diversity of teachers' talk and the instructional strategies they employ.

Fifty-two teachers were included in the study, with 36 assigned to the OWL condition. Levels of education were similar, with all lead teachers holding an associate's degree or CDA, and few having more advanced schooling. Years of experience were similar across groups, averaging 15 years for OWL and 19 for Creative Curriculum teachers. Teachers were videotaped during group content instruction and book reading in the fall of the school year. The videos were transcribed using the Codes for the Human Analysis of Transcripts (CHAT) format for analysis in the Computerized Language Analysis (CLAN) program from the Child Language Data Exchange System (CHILDES; MacWhinney, 2000) and verified by a second research assistant. This system was utilized to develop multidimensional descriptions of classroom discussions. Transcripts ranged in length from 1.7 to 21.9 minutes, with book reading averaging 12.5 minutes and group content instruction averaging 8.75 minutes.

Teacher talk was evaluated with two measures of language: lexical richness and lexical diversity. Lexical richness was determined by counting the frequency with which selected sophisticated, conceptually rich words were used. Sophisticated word types and tokens were defined as words not found on the Chall and Dale (1995) list of words most commonly known by fourth graders. We modified the list to include varied word endings (e.g., -s, -ed), resulting in a total of nearly 8,000 common words. Utterances were also coded to indicate vocabulary-related content. Lexical diversity was measured by D, which gauges how new words are added into speech samples. D is similar to type–token ratio; however, it is not constrained by the length of the sample and may be used with transcripts of differing lengths. Higher D values indicate more diverse speech. We used these fine-grained measures of indicators of high-quality, content-specific talk that demonstrates professional expertise.

Book Reading

There was a marked difference between the two curricula in the book-reading setting. In control classrooms, teachers exposed children to vocabulary and the language of books during book reading, but the instructional focus was primarily on print and very basic vocabulary. The focus in OWL classrooms, by contrast, was on helping children acquire richer language structures, a broad range of words, and the ability to understand and enjoy relatively complex books.

The differences between conditions began with the nature of the books that were read. The Creative Curriculum teachers typically selected texts that were written for children learning to read: books were short, predictable, and repetitive. These teachers read books with an average of 297 words overall and an average of four sophisticated word types. Books read in OWL classrooms, by contrast, had nearly twice as many words: 556 words overall and 16 sophisticated vocabulary word types. As we discuss below, the overall approach to how books were used was also different in the two conditions and seemingly reflected fundamentally different pedagogical goals.

Control Group Classrooms

Control group teachers viewed book reading as a setting to teach preliteracy skills and an opportunity to engage children in book-related activities. Print-related instruction was prevalent, with teachers pointing out letters and sounds in the text. Discussion involved teachers asking test-like closed-response questions that required children to label pictures and identify colors. The repetitive questioning allowed multiple children to participate in reconstructing the story while also affording high levels of teacher control. The following transcript excerpt represents a typical conversation following a book read in the control condition. The children (CHI) retell the story, page by page, while the teacher (TCH) asks the children to label animals and colors.

TCH: Now what came first in this book?

CHI: The monkey was the first.

TCH: Okay, well what animal came next, after the monkey?

CHI: The bird!

TCH: The bird came next.

TCH: Can you tell me what color the bird was?

CHI: Blue!

Although the children appeared highly engaged in the reading, little sophisticated vocabulary talk emerged. Labeling the pictures provided concrete representations, but explanations were largely absent. Control teachers averaged 19 vocabulary-related utterances, notably fewer than the 32 utterances averaged by teachers in the OWL condition. Use of sophisticated vocabulary was also limited (see Figures 10.1 and 10.2).

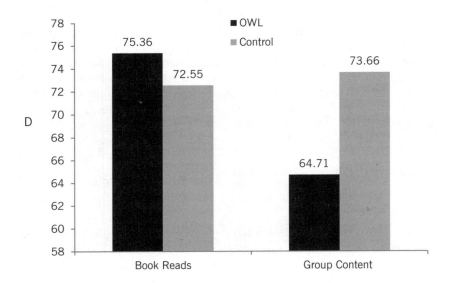

FIGURE 10.1. Lexical diversity as measured by D in intervention and control group classrooms.

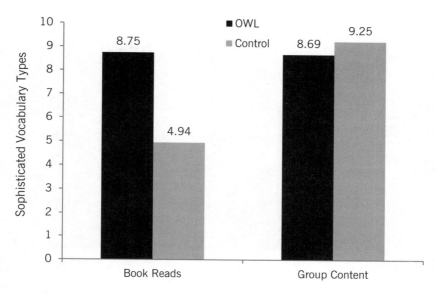

FIGURE 10.2. Sophisticated vocabulary types in intervention and control group classrooms.

In spite of the limited amount of vocabulary talk and use of sophisticated vocabulary, lexical diversity was relatively high and within the range of typical adult speech ($D = 72.6$; see Figure 10.3).

Opportunities to discuss vocabulary did occur; however, they were rarely capitalized on. In the following excerpt, the teacher polls the children following a reading of the *The Very Hungry Caterpillar*. She introduces the terms *sweet* and *sour,* but does not define the terms in spite of the students' obvious confusion:

TCH: Now are strawberries sweet or sour?
CHI: Sweet.
CHI: Sour.
TCH: Okay, raise your hand if you think they're sour.
CHI: It's sour.
TCH: Raise your hand if you think it's sweet.
CHI: It's sweet.
TCH: So about fifty–fifty on this one, good, good.

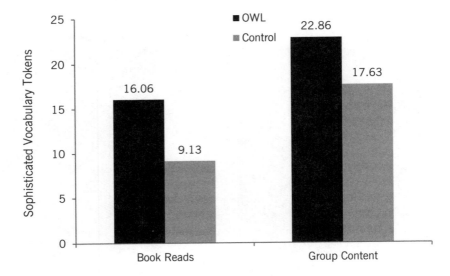

FIGURE 10.3. Sophisticated vocabulary tokens in intervention and control group classrooms.

The teacher may well have the knowledge to launch a conversation about sweet and sour, but she shifted to another topic, thus missing an opportunity to engage in conceptual discussion that could promote language development. Indeed, few examples of extended discourse were found. Even though the overt instructional focus of teachers was not on building language, these book-reading sessions did provide implicit support for language learning because the frequent rereading or reenactments in one sitting reinforced the words from the story while keeping children highly engaged.

OWL Classrooms

OWL is designed to use book reading as a setting to foster language development, introduce children to high-quality children's literature, develop enjoyment of books, and provide opportunities to comprehend stories with interesting characters and storylines. Books are read four times within 1 to 2 weeks, with each reading becoming progressively more interactive. The teachers' guide encourages use of language-stimulating techniques such as modeling predictions, defining key vocabulary terms, posing open- and closed-response questions, and clarifying the plot during the reading. Post-reading discussion include open-response questions that become increasingly more complex across the four readings. The guide provides definitions for target vocabulary terms and models of talk for each page of the storybook. The professional development and coaching reinforced use of the guide and adoption of these instructional strategies.

Several findings indicate that the curriculum did bring about a change in how teachers approached book reading. In many cases, the first and second reading of the stories followed the intended approach. Teachers gave a brief introduction followed by a reading that included definitions of target vocabulary, questions eliciting predictions, and comments to clarify the text. This style was intended to maintain student interest and comprehension. The question used to launch the following discussion was provided in the Teacher's Guide, along with prompts to elicit vocabulary terms:

TCH: Why do you think Jonathan's grandfather told him not to go outside?

TCH: It was dangerous but what else?

CHI: It's rainin(g) outside.

TCH: It was raining, okay.

CHI: And stormy.

TCH: It was stormy, which means there was thunder and what?

CHI: Lightning.

TCH: And lightning, that's right.

TCH: It was thunder and lightning.

Interactions such as this help account for the fact that, compared with teachers in the control condition, OWL teachers used both more sophisticated vocabulary types and tokens.

Group Content Instruction

In all classrooms, teachers had a group time during which they talked about topics related to the current thematic unit. In control group classrooms, teachers utilized materials and lesson plans prepared by the education specialist for group content instruction. The lessons and content were familiar and did not require changes in their practice (e.g., unit on animal traits and habitats). Materials, such as books, visual aids, and manipulatives, were often carefully woven into the lesson. For example:

TCH: Okay, these cats here have different feelings.

TCH: With their ears this way, he's peaceful.

TCH: His ears are straight up in the air.

TCH: Look what his ears are doing now (*points to another picture*).

TCH: That means he's angry.

TCH: Anybody knows what angry means?

CHI: Mad!

TCH: He's mad, yes.

The teachers in the classrooms using Creative Curriculum demonstrated nearly twice as much sophisticated vocabulary as during book reading. Lexical diversity also increased somewhat to 73.55. The amount of vocabulary-related talk was similar to book reads, averaging 16.50 utterances.

Unlike book reading, the OWL teachers' guide provides no scripting for content instruction. However, more support is given to OWL teachers than was provided to the control teachers. Suggestions for activities and related vocabulary terms are provided, although no definitions for words or explanations of concepts are supplied. Talk during the OWL lessons was similar to color commentary supplied during sports broadcasts; for example, the teacher described her actions while carrying out an experiment. But often teachers struggled to supply appropriate definitions for the scientific content:

TCH: And so I go down to y'all washer and she say while you in there, throw Love's shirt in there with you.

TCH: But Love's shirt is what color?

CHI: White.

TCH: White, her shirt is white and my shirt is black.

TCH: So if I was to put my black shirt in the water with Love's white shirt, Love's white shirt gonna do what?

TCH: What's the word?

CHI: Fade!

TCH: Fade, it's gonna fade.

Although the teacher uses the target vocabulary term, she does not provide a correct definition. It could be that she understood the processes, but failed to articulate them accurately. However, her struggle to define *fade* may be linked to a lack of content knowledge; it is illustrative of other lessons where teachers appeared to be hampered by lack of ready access to relevant terms and concepts.

OWL teachers did infuse sophisticated vocabulary types into the lessons at a rate comparable to book reads, but achieved no greater rate of use than their control counterparts (see Figure 10.1). The high number of sophisticated vocabulary tokens indicates that teachers were repeating words rather than introducing new vocabulary terms (see Figure 10.2). OWL teachers averaged half as many vocabulary-related utterances during group content instruction as during book reads, indicating they were less focused on teaching vocabulary (see Figure 10.4). The lexical diversity for OWL teachers was similar to that of a typical 5-year-old (*D* = 65; Duran, Malvern, Richards, & Chipere, 2004)—lower than that of the control teachers, and below their own level for book reads (see Figure 10.3). Thus provision of curriculum supports had a substantial impact on book reading: shifts in the books read, the nature of teachers' instruction, and the language children heard were quite different in the intervention classrooms. When group content instruction is viewed through a linguistic lens, however, instruction appeared similar in the

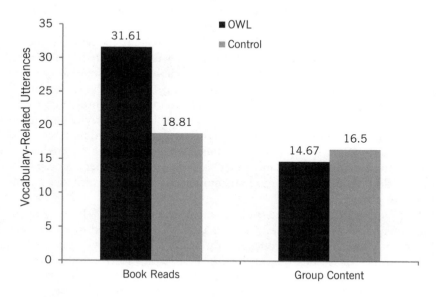

FIGURE 10.4. Vocabulary-related utterances in intervention and control group classrooms.

two conditions. Later, we discuss the potential impact of differential demands for content-based instruction associated with the two curricula.

Small-Group Instruction

In all the classrooms, children spent time each day in small teacher-led instructional groups. The OWL curriculum often recommends science-based instruction in small groups because engaging children in hands-on science activities creates a potent context for word and content learning that builds on their curiosity about the world (Duke, 2004). Furthermore, sophisticated words are most likely to be encountered in small-group settings (Dickinson, Cote, & Smith, 1993), and the time spent in small-group settings is positively associated with more engaged talk (Dickinson & Smith, 1991). The potential of small-group instruction for fostering growth of language and associated content knowledge is especially great if the instruction has a science focus (Hapgood & Palincsar, 2006). Peterson and French (2008), for example, examined the development of children's explanatory language in small-group science activities. By the end of a hands-on science unit, children produced more on-topic responses, used more standard science terms, and included more causal connectives in their responses to the assessment of explanatory language.

Given that the intervention curriculum sought to increase vocabulary and related content instruction, we were interested in knowing whether using OWL was associated with changes in instruction during small-group times. Each week, children engaged in three hands-on small-group activities tied to unit themes and designed to reinforce concepts and teach core literacy and mathematical skills. The activities required varied amounts of teacher support. Some were skill-based matching and game activities that required limited teacher support; others were hands-on activities that required more teacher support. For higher support level activities, the curriculum guide recommends words and provides examples of phrases to use.

We first compared the small-group lessons of the OWL and control groups to see whether use of the curriculum was related to changes in content instruction and conceptually based talk. We reviewed the first 10 minutes of lessons taught during small-group instructional time by all teachers at one time point to determine the content of instruction. Among the 36 OWL small-group lessons, 22% were hands-on science lessons such as "exploring mirrors and reflections." By contrast, only one of 16 (6%) control small-group lessons was science related. To determine the nature of support for conceptual and related vocabulary learning, we counted the number of teacher utterances related to science/world knowledge and vocabulary (e.g., "Does cardboard reflect light?"). We found dramatic differences by condition. Control teachers averaged 0.19 utterances per 10-minute segment, whereas teachers in the OWL condition averaged 13.81 utterances per 10-minute segment. In addition, OWL teachers talked about the meanings of words far more often (20.28 vocabulary-related utterances per 10-minute segment) than control teachers (7.33 utterances per 10-minute segment).

To more fully understand the impact of the curriculum on teaching practice, we asked whether close adherence to the curriculum guide enabled teachers to create a more linguistically rich learning environment. To address this question, we examined the words teachers used during 22 lessons (13 science-based and 11 focused on literacy). Teachers' adherence to the curriculum was measured by how closely the lesson matched the curriculum guide, as well as teachers' and children's use of curriculum-recommended vocabulary words. First, we rated how closely teachers' small-group lessons matched the curriculum guide using a 3-point scale (1 = the unit of the lesson is identifiable; 2 = matching lesson is found in the curriculum guide; 3 = teacher taught the matching lesson using all of the materials). We found that 32% of the lessons were Level 3: teachers followed the curriculum guide and used all the suggested materials. Forty-five percent of the lessons were Level 2; these lessons were similar to those in the curriculum guide, but did not use all the suggested materials. For instance, when teaching a lesson on exploring objects that reflect light, a teacher who did not use a flashlight as suggested was rated as Level 2. The remaining 23% of lessons were rated Level 1; although they were related to the unit, the teacher created lessons different from those suggested by the curriculum guide. Most Level 2 and 3 lessons were science-related lessons, whereas most Level 1 lessons were literacy related. This finding, combined with the almost total absence of science-related lessons in the control classrooms, strongly suggests that teachers are far more likely to deliver science-related instruction in small groups when following the curriculum guide.

Since Level 2 and 3 lessons had matching lessons in the curriculum guide, it was possible to examine use of the recommended words specific to the lesson. We calculated how many of the recommended words were used by teachers and children. On average, teachers in Levels 2 and 3 used about 45% of the recommended words for the particular lesson they taught. Children used 25% of the recommended words and were significantly more likely to use these words if the teacher also used them.

We also examined whether the level of adherence to the curriculum guide matched the use of recommended words by teachers and children.

Although there was no statistically significant relationship between the degree to which teachers' lessons matched the curriculum guide and the recommended words that were used by teachers, there was such a relationship for children. On average, Level 3 children used a greater percentage of recommended words (40%) than children in Level 2 (15%). Interestingly, recommended words used by children always came from the list of recommended words used by the teacher, and 94% of words were used by the teacher first. Level 3 teachers also tended to use a larger percentage of recommended words (59%) as compared to Level 2 teachers (41%). Although not statistically significant, this difference of 18% is nonetheless of practical significance for child language development, particularly given the significant correlation between teacher's use of recommended words and children's subsequent use.

Discussion

In this research, we examined the language used by teachers and children in classrooms in an effort to understand how curricula may foster improved instruction related to language and content knowledge, and to determine factors that make it difficult for teachers to deliver such instruction. Before discussing our findings, however, we want to make a methodological point. By examining the details of classroom instruction, we have sought to move beyond the limited lens of traditional randomized control trials research in which the only question of interest is whether the intervention resulted in greater learning by children. Certainly that is a worthy question, but increasingly we are finding that it is very hard to have an impact on children's learning, leaving us with a series of null effect studies (e.g., Dickinson & Darrow, in press; Dickinson, Freiberg, & Barnes, 2011) and only a limited sense of what to do next.

Typically, interventions draw on basic research that provides a roadmap of environmental factors that support the acquisition of valued knowledge and skills. This is certainly the case for language learning. Drawing on such foundational research, we suggest that, rather than simply admitting defeat and moving on to another intervention, the field will make more progress if we first understand what did and did not happen and why. We have found questions such as the following to be productive: Did teachers adopt recommended practices to the degree required to improve learning? What teaching practices changed and which were resistant to change? Did adoption of new strategies vary by settings? Did children display improved engagement and language during lessons that were delivered in the intended manner? An intervention that fails to result in improved learning by children may nonetheless have desired effects on necessary teaching practices. This was true in our case.

Fostering Language Growth and Story Understanding

In OWL, the primary focus during book reading is building language and fostering children's enjoyment and comprehension of stories. We found evidence that the nature of the book-reading event was altered as teachers adopted methods that were well delineated in the curriculum guide and reinforced by professional development and coaching. The curricular support provided by the intervention shifted the lessons from skills-based instruction to a greater focus on language and conceptual development. Evidence of this shift was the fact that the teachers moved beyond labeling to engaging children in more linguistically rich talk about language, characters, and plot. Many teachers were able to draw on their professional expertise reading books and used the suggested strategies in ways that shifted their practice as they read new, longer, and more complex books and engaged children in more conceptually based conversations. That teachers made such changes is likely due to a combination of factors: book reading is a familiar activity; the curriculum provided detailed guidance; and the practices were reinforced by professional development and coaching. But a cautionary note is important. Although we did note desired changes in the details of teaching practices, our coding during book reading revealed that, on average, teachers achieved less than 50% fidelity to desired practices. When teachers all have BA-level training and are provided far more coaching support, much higher levels of fidelity may be achieved (Wilson, 2010). These findings highlight the fact that even relatively detailed curriculum guidance may not lead to instruction that is sufficiently strong to improve children's learning.

An interesting picture also emerges when we link this qualitative examination of book reading with our evaluation of children's fall-to-spring gains. When we compared fall-to-spring growth in language abilities of the children with profiles typically seen in children from low-income homes (i.e., about one standard deviation below national norms) and those with extremely low initial language, the typical children responded better to the intervention than did those with low language skills. The book-reading event may partly account for these differential patterns. The high level of repetition of a relatively small number of new words during a single session seen in the control group classrooms may have been beneficial to children with limited initial language, whereas typically developing children may have benefitted more from the richer linguistic experiences afforded by the intervention curriculum.

Building Content Knowledge

In OWL, instruction related to building content knowledge occurs during group content instruction time and in small groups. Examination of group content instruction presented a different case from what we saw in book reading because instruction in the control classrooms was generally consistent with the type of instruction we sought to introduce. The intervention curriculum did not enable teachers to engage children in ways that were different from the practice-as-usual classrooms. In our analyses, we described the conceptual richness of instruction by examining teachers' language use. In particular, we reasoned that lexical diversity (D) provided an index of such instruction because it has previously been found to be related to content knowledge (Duran et al., 2004). Unfortunately, many features of classroom instruction can complicate the matter. For example, D may be influenced by the number of topics introduced. Although the labeling activities found in the book readings of the control condition teachers had high levels of lexical diversity, the conversations were not extended and did little to build content knowledge. Therefore, we found it prudent to use D in conjunction with our measure of sophisticated vocabulary, which may also indicate topical knowledge because a rich fund of specific vocabulary terms reflects strong content knowledge. When we examined the number of sophisticated vocabulary terms along with lexical diversity, the intervention OWL teachers outperformed the control teachers during book reading on all measures, despite no differences between the two conditions in the group content instruction setting.

We speculate that the lack of difference between the two conditions during group content instruction resulted from a combination of factors. First, the teachers in the control condition were teaching about content with which they were already familiar and within their frame of reference. They could adapt and enrich lessons drawing on experiences and information readily available to them. Also, the program supplied general guidance regarding concepts and associated terms, helping to provide an instructional focus for the activities. Intervention teachers, however, were presented with instructional topics that were new and, in some cases, included concepts and vocabulary with which they were not familiar.

Our review of instruction in small groups provides yet another way of understanding how a curriculum may support improved content instruction. It is striking that, when teachers were not guided by a curriculum that specified what should be taught in small groups, science-related instruction almost never occurred. By contrast, science instruction was relatively common in OWL classrooms. This kind of impact on what is happening in classrooms echoes the changes in the kinds of books that were read. Furthermore, effects of the curriculum on small-group instruction were also similar to what was seen in book reading: teachers who followed the guidance of the curriculum were able to create more conceptually and linguistically rich learning opportunities. In each case, teachers benefitted from having detailed guidance for their lessons.

Concluding Thoughts

Curricula have the potential to provide a platform that will enable teachers to expand children's language abilities and knowledge of the world. They can encourage the use of diverse and challenging books and ensure that instruction is not rigidly driven by concerns that children master basic literacy and numeracy skills. Detailed guidance for what teachers should say and do can enable some to use a broader range of instructional strategies, shift from a focus on skills to more conceptually based instruction, and use enriched language as they interact with children. However, we must always be on the alert for lurking problems. Teachers who lack strong content knowledge or have limited English proficiency can be overwhelmed by programs that ask more of them than they can deliver. No curriculum can make up for such limitations. Even teachers with strong knowledge and language are not likely to be able to engage children in conceptually oriented instruction without assistance because they may have rarely experienced or seen such instruction themselves. Professional development and coaching and mentoring will always be necessary to support teachers as they begin learning to deliver such instruction.

ACKNOWLEDGMENTS

We thank our Head Start partners for their collaboration with us on this project and acknowledge the work of the many research assistants who contributed to this effort. The research reported here was supported by the Institute of Education Sciences, U.S. Department of Education, through Grant No. R324E060088 to Vanderbilt University. The opinions expressed are those of the authors and do not represent views of the U.S. Department of Education.

REFERENCES

Chall, J. S., & Dale, E. (1995). *Readability revisited: The new Dale–Chall readability formula*. Cambridge, MA: Brookline Books.

Darrow, C. L. (2011, August). *Language and literacy effects of curriculum interventions for preschools serving economically disadvantaged children.* Paper presented at the Campbell Collaborative Joint Symposium on Evidence-Based Policy, Fairfax, VA.

Dickinson, D. K. (1987). Oral language, literacy skills, and response to literature. In J. Squire (Ed.), *The dynamics of language learning: Research in the language arts* (pp. 147–183). Urbana, IL: National Council of Teachers in English.

Dickinson, D. K., & Caswell, L. (2007). Building support for language and early literacy in preschool classrooms through in-service professional development: Effects of the Literacy Environment Enrichment Program (LEEP). *Early Childhood Research Quarterly, 22*(2), 243–260.

Dickinson, D. K., Cote, L., & Smith, M. W. (1993). Learning vocabulary in preschool: Social and discourse contexts affecting vocabulary growth. *New Directions for Child and Adolescent Development, 1993*(61), 67–78.

Dickinson, D. K., & Darrow, C. L. (in press). Methodological and practical challenges of broad-gauged language interventions. In T. Shanahan & C. J. Lonigan (Eds.), *Literacy in preschool and kindergarten children: The National Early Literacy Panel and beyond.* Baltimore, MD: Brookes.

Dickinson, D. K., Freiberg, J. B., & Barnes, E. M. (2011). Why are so few interventions really effective? A call for fine-grained research methodology. In S. B. Neuman & D. K. Dickinson (Eds.), *Handbook of early literacy research* (Vol. 3, pp. 337–357). New York: Guilford Press.

Dickinson, D. K., Kaiser, A. P., Roberts, M., Hofer, K. G., & Darrow, C. L. (2011, March). *The effects of two language-focused preschool curricula on children's achievement through first grade.* Paper presented at the semiannual meeting of the Society for Research on Educational Effectiveness, Washington, DC.

Dickinson, D. K., & Porche, M. V. (2011). The relationship between language experiences in preschool classrooms and children's kindergarten and fourth-grade language and reading abilities. *Child Development, 82*(3), 870–886.

Dickinson, D. K., & Smith, M. W. (1991). Preschool talk: Patterns of teacher–child interaction in early childhood classrooms. *Journal of Research in Childhood Education, 6*(1), 20–29.

Dickinson, D. K., & Snow, C. E. (1987). Interrelationships among prereading and oral language skills in kindergartners from two social classes. *Early Childhood Research Quarterly, 2*(1), 1–25.

Dickinson, D. K., & Tabors, P. O. (Eds.). (2001). *Beginning literacy with language: Young children learning at home and school.* Baltimore, MD: Brookes.

Dodge, D. T., Colker, L., & Heoman, C. (2001). *The creative curriculum® for preschool.* Washington, DC: Teaching Strategies, Inc.

Domitrovich, C. E., Gest, S. D., Gill, S., Bierman, K. L., Welsh, J. A., & Jones, D. (2009). Fostering high-quality teaching with an enriched curriculum and professional development support: The Head Start REDI program. *American Educational Research Journal, 46*(2), 567–597.

Duke, N. K. (2004). The case for informational text. *Educational Leadership, 61*(6), 40–44.

Duran, P., Malvern, R., Richards, B., & Chipere, N. (2004). Developmental trends in lexical diversity. *Applied Linguistics, 25*(2), 220–242.

Frede, E. C., Jung, K., Barnett, W. S., Lamy, C. E., & Figueras, A. (2009). *The APPLES blossom: Abbott Preschool Program Longitudinal Effects Study (APPLES): Preliminary results through second grade.* New Brunswick, NJ: National Institute for Early Education Research.

Gormley, W. T., Jr., Gayer, T., Phillips, D., & Dawson, B. (2005). The effects of universal pre-K on cognitive development. *Developmental Psychology, 41*(6), 872–884.

Han, M., Roskos, K., Christie, J., Mandzuk, S., & Vukelich, C. (2005). Learning words: Large group time as a vocabulary development opportunity. *Journal of Research in Childhood Education, 19*(4), 333–345.

Hapgood, S., & Palincsar, A. S. (2006). Where literacy and science intersect. *Educational Leadership, 64*(4), 56–60.

Hsieh, W. Y., Hemmeter, M. L., McCollum, J. A., & Ostrosky, M. M. (2009). Using coaching to increase preschool teachers' use of emergent literacy teaching strategies. *Early Childhood Research Quarterly, 24*(3), 229–247.

Jackson, R., McCoy, A., Pistorino, C., Wilkinson, A., Burghardt, J., Clark, M., et al. (2007). *National evaluation of early reading first: Final report.* Washington, DC: U.S. Government Printing Office, U.S. Department of Education, Institute of Educational Sciences.

Kaiser, A. P., Roberts, M. Y., & McCleod, R. H. (2011). Young children with language impairments: Challenges in transition to reading. In S. B. Neuman & D. K. Dickinson (Eds.), *Handbook of early literacy research* (Vol. 3, pp. 153–171). New York: Guilford Press.

Lipsey, M., Farran, D. C., Bilbrey, C., Hofer, K. G., & Dong, N. (2011). *Intitial results of the evaluation of the Tennessee voluntary pre-K program.* A report prepared for the Peabody Research Institute. Nashville, TN: Vanderbilt University.

MacWhinney, B. (2000). *The CHILDES project: Tools for analyzing talk* (3rd ed.). Mahwah, NJ: Erlbaum.

Marulis, L. M., & Neuman, S. B. (2010). The effects of vocabulary intervention on young children's word learning: A meta-analysis. *Review of Educational Research, 80*(3), 300–335.

National Early Literacy Panel. (2009). *Developing early literacy: Report of the National Early Literacy Panel.* Jessup, MD: National Institute for Literacy.

National Institute of Child Health and Human Development Early Child Care Research Network. (2005). Pathways to reading: The role of oral language in the transition to reading. *Developmental Psychology, 41*(2), 428–442.

Peterson, S. M., & French, L. (2008). Supporting young children's explanations through inquiry science in preschool. *Early Childhood Research Quarterly, 23*(3), 395–408.

Reynolds, A. J., Ou, S. R., & Topitzes, J. W. (2004). Paths of effects of early childhood intervention on educational attainment and delinquency: A confirmatory analysis of the chicago child–parent centers. *Child Development, 75*(5), 1299–1328.

Schickedanz, J., & Dickinson, D. K. (2005). *Opening the world of learning:A comprehensive literacy program.* Parsippany, NJ: Pearson Early Learning.

Smith, M. W., Dickinson, D. K., Sangeorge, A., & Anastasopoulos, L. (2002). *The Early Language and Literacy Classroom Observation toolkit (ELLCO).* Baltimore: Brookes.

Snow, C. E. (1983). Literacy and language: Relationships during the preschool years. *Harvard Educational Review, 53*(2), 165–189.

Snow, C. E. (1991). The theoretical basis for relationships between language and literacy in development. *Journal of Research in Childhood Education, 6*(1), 5–10.

Snow, C. E., Burns, M. S., & Griffin, P. (Eds.). (1998). *Preventing reading difficulties in young children.* Washington, DC: National Research Council, National Academy Press.

Snow, C. E., & Dickinson, D. K. (1991). Skills that aren't basic in a new conception of literacy. In A. C. Purves & E. Jennings (Eds.), *Literate systems and individual lives: Perspectives on literacy and school* (pp. 179–192). Albany: State University of New York Press.

Spira, E. G., Bracken, S. S., & Fischel, J. E. (2005). Predicting improvement after first-grade reading difficulties: The effects of oral language, emergent literacy, and behavior skills. *Developmental Psychology, 41*(1), 225–234.

U.S. Department of Health and Human Services. (2010). *Head start impact study: Final report.* Washington, DC: Administration for Children and Families.

Wilson, S. J. (2010). *Early Reading First annual evaluation report: Enhanced Language and Literacy Success Project Year 2: 2009–2010 school year* (technical report). Nashville, TN: Vanderbilt University.

CHAPTER 11

■ ■ ■ ■ ■

Scaffolding Preschoolers' Vocabulary Development through Purposeful Conversations

UNPACKING THE ExCELL MODEL OF LANGUAGE AND LITERACY PROFESSIONAL DEVELOPMENT

Barbara A. Wasik
Annemarie H. Hindman

Preschool children's language development, and specifically their vocabulary development, lays the foundation for reading success and academic achievement more broadly (Storch & Whitehurst, 2002). However, vocabulary is one of the more difficult skills for educators to develop in young children (Dickinson, Golinkoff, & Hirsh-Pasek, 2010; Marulis & Neuman, 2010). Research in early child language development points to the important role that conversations with linguistically competent adults play in young children's acquisition of words and concepts (Hart & Risley, 1995; Huttenlocher, Haight, Bryk, Seltzer, & Lyons, 1991). Our own research has examined how purposeful conversations with teachers and peers during book reading and related activities can promote preschool children's word knowledge (Wasik & Bond, 2001; Wasik, Bond, & Hindman, 2006; Wasik & Hindman, 2011b). This chapter first reviews the research on the experiences that best promote children's vocabulary skills and then explains how vocabulary knowledge supports school success. We then discuss specific educational interventions that have been shown to increase children's vocabulary knowledge, including our model of teacher professional development, ExCELL. Finally, we look across several recent studies of the ExCELL model in an effort to identify the key features of this multifaceted program that most directly foster children's vocabulary knowledge.

How Children Learn Words

Aside from occasions when fast mapping occurs (Carey & Bartlett, 1978), children need multiple, meaningful exposures to new words in order to develop a rich, conceptual understanding of their meaning(s) (Beck & McKeown, 2007; Biemiller & Boote, 2006; Hoff, 2003). However, simply hearing new words over and over is not likely to be sufficient, as only certain contexts for exposure are optimally effective. First, children need to have a clear understanding of a word's meaning in order for them to integrate that word into their vocabulary, understanding its meaning and pronunciation well enough to use it accurately. Explicit definitions of words can increase vocabulary learning (Biemiller & Boote, 2006; Wright, Chapter 9, this volume), especially for children with more limited language skills (Penno, Wilkinson, & Moore, 2002). However, the type of definition matters. Booth (2009) found that 3-year-old children learned labels for novel objects best when researchers provided definitions that focused on their functions, particularly what one could do with the objects. Pictures and props can also be useful. For example, Han, Moore, Vukelich, and Buell (2011) found that when children were given the opportunity to learn book-related vocabulary by playing with props, they learned more of the words than children who were taught the same vocabulary using only child-friendly definitions. Wasik and Bond (2001) found similar results when teachers accompanied definitions of book-related vocabulary with props. Finally, recalling the importance of conversations (as above), Weizman and Snow (2001) found that word learning improved when adults tailored hints or definitions to children's individual understanding of words.

Second, children learn vocabulary best from conversations with adults who encourage them to talk about and use new words, and then provide meaningful feedback on their remarks in a way that scaffolds linguistic and cognitive development (Hirsh-Pasek & Burchinal, 2006; Smith, Landry, & Swank, 2000). For example, one longitudinal study found that extensive conversations in which teachers explicitly invited and commented on child talk during free play and book reading were linked to gains in children's language production and comprehension

(Dickinson, Barnes, & Mock, Chapter 10, this volume; Dickinson & Porche, 2011; Dickinson & Tabors, 2001).

Finally, children are helped when words are presented on multiple, interconnected occasions in a meaningful and playful context, such as in the context of a thematic curriculum (Hirsch-Pasek, Golinkoff, Berk, & Singer, 2009; Neuman & Dwyer, 2009). This finding is consistent with memory research suggesting that information is best learned when integrated around a story or concept, as opposed to delivered as a set of isolated facts, because this context helps children graft new information onto an already formed schema (Barlett, 1967; Bransford & Johnson, 1972). For example, Christie and Roskos (2006) found that children better recalled and used vocabulary related to building materials (e.g., *hammer, hard hat, nails*) when they were presented in the context of a theme on building rather than when they were presented in isolation. Similarly, Wasik and Bond (2001) found that when preschool teachers presented vocabulary in the context of a theme, highlighting words in storybooks and then in a variety of theme-related learning activities, children were more likely to learn the vocabulary.

In summary, children learn vocabulary (1) through multiple, meaningful exposures to words that are (2) nested within meaningful and integrative contexts, (3) supported by high-quality definitions, and (4) embedded within rich linguistic interactions with adults. A key implication is that, while children may build vocabulary rapidly during the "word spurt" of the earliest years of life, opportunities to learn the particular kinds of words and concepts that children need for school is not automatic and may not be readily available, particularly for children in poverty.

Word Learning and Later School Outcomes

Critically, children's acquisition of new words is an outward manifestation of their acquisition of new knowledge; as children acquire words, they are simultaneously acquiring, developing, and refining the concepts that those words represent. As a consequence, there is a significant and meaningful correlation between rich, well-developed vocabularies and success in learning to read (Dickinson, McCabe, Anastasopoulos, Peisner-Feinberg, & Poe, 2003; Storch & Whitehurst, 2002). For example, one recent meta-analysis found educationally meaningful associations between children's language skills in preschool and their reading competence at the end of first and second grade (National Early Literacy Panel [NELP], 2009), while other studies have shown that language in the preschool years predicts reading in later elementary grades (e.g., fourth grade) and middle school (Dickinson & Porche, 2011; National Institute of Child Health and Human Development Early Child Care Research Network [NICHD ECCRN], 2005; Walker, Greenwood, Hart, & Carta, 1994).

Several interconnected mechanisms likely underlie these relations. First, as noted above, building vocabulary is, in a fundamental sense, acquiring knowledge about the world. A preschooler who can use the word *hibernation* to explain what bears do in the winter has demonstrated his knowledge of multiple concepts, including what hibernation means, what a bear is, and what winter is. When this child comes across *hibernation* in print, this child's understanding of this word and idea will help him make sense of the entire sentence and perhaps the entire text in which the word appears. Without accurate reading comprehension, the value of literacy for academic achievement is greatly attenuated. Furthermore, well-developed vocabulary knowledge helps children begin to "crack the code" of print by aiding them in recognizing a word using the context in which it appears and the first several letters and sounds (NELP, 2009). In contrast, children without this knowledge are less able to leverage these cues and instead need to intentionally work through each letter–sound connection, which can be a lengthy process. Thus vocabulary knowledge in preschool plays an important role in long-term achievement.

Vocabulary and Reading Skill among Children in Poverty

Unfortunately, children in poverty often have limited language and vocabulary development relative to middle-income peers (Lee & Burkam, 2002). Hart and Risley (1995) found that, by age 3, young children growing up in poverty knew about half as many words as peers in higher income homes. Similarly, as recently as 2006, the nationally representative Family and Child Experiences Survey (FACES) data suggested that the average vocabulary score among Head Start preschoolers fell nearly a full standard deviation below the national average (Hammer, Farkas, & Maczuga, 2010; Hindman, Skibbe, Miller, & Zimmerman, 2010; Zill & Resnick, 2006). Over time, as children are exposed to explicit and implicit instruction in language and vocabulary, those with more background knowledge are better able to take advantage of these experiences. Consequently, the early gap between those with more and less vocabulary knowledge widens, and without targeted instruction, disadvantaged children fall further behind (Connor, Morrison, & Slominski, 2006; Stanovich, 1986). As a result, by fourth grade, nearly half of all children in poverty cannot read with even basic proficiency

(National Assessment of Educational Progress [NAEP], 2010). In part because of this reading challenge, children in poverty are far more likely to perform poorly academically, to be retained in a grade, or even to drop out of school entirely (Alexander, Entwisle, & Horsey, 1997). This gap is rooted in the number and quality of opportunities that children from different socioeconomic strata have to learn words at home and school.

Home Factors

Hart and Risley's (1995) seminal work underscored that many children in poverty are exposed to a relatively limited number of vocabulary words at home and have fewer conversations that allow them to use the language that they hear. Specifically, whereas children in higher income homes heard, on average, more than 2,000 words per hour, children in low-income homes heard approximately 600 words per hour. Remarkably, some children in higher income homes actually used more words than some parents in lower income homes. Furthermore, qualitative research by Snow, Dickinson, Tabors, and colleagues in the Harvard Home–School program (e.g., Dickinson & Tabors, 2001; Snow & Tabors, 1993) showed differences in the number and the nature of the words used at home. Specifically, families in poverty used fewer rare (i.e., unusual or sophisticated) vocabulary words relative to higher income families. Thus the early vocabulary gap between more and less affluent children is at least partly entangled with disparities in how families talk to and with children at home (see also Callanan, Rigney, Nolan-Reyes, & Solis, Chapter 4, this volume).

School Factors

Teachers can also play a critical role in building preschoolers' vocabulary skills through language-focused activities such as book reading and conversation. Indeed, for children who have few opportunities to hear and use new words at home, school may represent the primary venue in which they learn new words. Yet optimal, evidence-based strategies, such as engaging in meaningful dialogue that allows children to use language and receive feedback on their comments, are not typically implemented in preschool classrooms, particularly those serving children in poverty who most need these experiences (Justice, Mashburn, Hamre, & Pianta, 2008; Mashburn, 2008). Observational data indicate that most preschool (and kindergarten) teachers engage in surprisingly little explicit instruction in vocabulary (i.e., 5 or fewer minutes per day) (Cunningham, Zibulsky, Stanovich, & Stanovich, 2009; Wright, Chapter

9, this volume). Interestingly, teachers often report far more frequent vocabulary instruction than they actually deliver, suggesting that they may misjudge their own classroom activities in this area.

Implicit instruction in vocabulary is also relatively rare. Recent work by Gest and colleagues has revealed that, in the course of the typical classroom day, many educators use more teacher-directed talk, especially of a managerial nature (e.g., "Clean up," "Put X over by Y," or "Keep your hands to yourself"), than open-ended questions that model and promote language development (Gest, Holland-Coviello, Welsh, Eicher-Catt, & Gill, 2006; Hayes & Matusov, 2005). Moreover, Dickinson (2001) found limited book readings and language opportunities in many Head Start classrooms. When preschool teachers do read books, most highlight vocabulary words only infrequently and provide few opportunities for children to talk about those words, or about anything at all (Hindman & Wasik, 2008). Furthermore, follow-up activities in business-as-usual preschool classrooms are not necessarily well coordinated with the book reading, or even available (Hindman, Wasik, & Erhart, in press).

Need for Interventions

The research documenting the link between early word knowledge and reading acquisition, coupled with evidence that children in poverty have limited access to experiences that promote vocabulary development, suggests that effective interventions are needed to improve vocabulary among children in low-income settings. Unfortunately, although many interventions have been designed, evaluations of these interventions suggest that it is *not* easy to increase low-income children's vocabulary. For example, the Preschool Curriculum Evaluation Research (PCER) study examined 11 curricula that focused on language development and found that only one of these programs yielded significant gains for language and reading readiness skills in randomized controlled trials (PCER, 2008). Similarly, reviews of other large-scale interventions funded by programs such as Early Reading First, Head Start, and NELP concluded that these interventions also have not had much success in improving children's vocabulary (Jackson et al., 2007; Moss, Jacob, Boulay, Horst, & Poulos, 2006; NELP, 2009).

One challenge that large-scale curricula and other interventions have faced in increasing early vocabulary knowledge is that most programs or initiatives provide teachers with little guidance on effective language and vocabulary knowledge instruction. For example, most curricula in the PCER study did not provide explicit instruction or guidance for teachers to develop children's language skills. Furthermore, in a recent review of popular commercial preschool curricula, Neuman and Dwyer (2009) found little explicit attention to vocabulary instruction in teachers' manuals and handbooks. Yet recent work on professional development interventions suggests that teachers and children can benefit when educators receive intensive training to promote language development.

Professional Development

One model of professional development (PD) that has been shown to be effective is coaching. Coaching, in which master educators provide teachers with individualized guidance—often repeatedly over a period of several weeks, months, or even years—began to receive widespread attention with the work of Joyce and Showers (e.g., Joyce & Showers, 1981) and has recently been the focus of special issues of several prominent journals (e.g., *Elementary School Journal, Early Education and Development*) and new, widely available handbooks (Blachowicz, Buhle, & Ogle, 2010; Casey, 2006; International Reading Association [IRA], 2004). Policymakers have also required literacy coaching for Reading First and Early Reading First projects (Gamse et al., 2008; Jackson et al., 2007; Moss et al., 2006).

Some well-designed coaching models of PD have shown that it is possible to raise the quality of teachers' language- and vocabulary-related instruction. For example, both a college course approach without direct classroom contact (Dickinson & Caswell, 2007) and in-classroom coaching (Neuman & Cunningham, 2009) allowed teachers to significantly modify the way they interact with children, better aligning their practices with language-promoting behaviors. It was beyond the scope of these projects, however, to collect child data to understand the impact of teacher PD on children's language skills.

Of the few studies that have investigated how coaching changes teachers' classroom behaviors as well as child outcomes, most have yielded effects on phonological sensitivity, letter knowledge, and writing, all of which are important preliteracy skills (DeBarshye & Gorecki, 2007; Jackson et al., 2007; Powell, Diamond, Burchinal, & Koehler, 2010). However, almost none (including Early Reading First projects) have produced effects on children's vocabulary, even when studies were well designed. As indicated above, children's vocabulary is difficult to change, in part because providing children with multiple, meaningful opportunities to hear and use new words often requires preschool teachers to change how they talk with children. To alter deeply embedded and often unconscious patterns of language, teachers need high-quality professional development content that is delivered in carefully scaffolded ways.

The ExCELL Model

Dickinson, Freiberg, and Barnes (2011) and Marulis and Neuman (2010) describe our PD intervention, ExCELL (Exceptional Coaching for Early Language and Literacy), as one of few that has shown positive results for increasing children's vocabulary. In fact, to our knowledge, ExCELL and Landry's Center for Improving the Readiness of Children for Learning and Education (CIRCLE) model are currently the only two PD models that have demonstrated effects on children's language and vocabulary skills in peer-reviewed empirical studies (see Landry, Anthony, Swank, & Monseque-Bailey, 2009; Landry, Swank, Smith, Assel, & Gunnewig, 2006, for descriptions of the CIRCLE program).

Description of Program

ExCELL is a coaching PD program for preschool teachers designed to increase language and literacy skills—including vocabulary knowledge—in young children, especially those in poverty. Using research-based strategies, ExCELL focuses on developing oral language, vocabulary, phonological sensitivity, alphabet knowledge, and emergent writing skills in preschool children. ExCELL includes (1) intensive training, including a monthly, 3-hour group training and weekly coaching sessions; (2) materials such as lesson plans and books for thematic units of study, including activities that support language and literacy development; and (3) ongoing assessments of both teachers and children to monitor learning and, when necessary, target areas of difficulty. ExCELL has been implemented and evaluated in more than 75 Head Start classrooms in Baltimore City, Maryland.

Group Training and Individualized Coaching

In the group training, a coach provides teachers with a rationale for focusing on a particular aspect of early language and literacy (e.g., asking open-ended questions during book reading) and explains how this practice supports children's learning. Then the coach describes and models a series of techniques for teachers to use when implementing this practice in the classroom. Finally, teachers plan how they will use these techniques in their own classrooms. During the 3 weeks after the training, a coach visits each teacher's classroom for 3 hours per week. During this time, the coach works individually with the lead teacher and follows a specified sequence of activities: (1) modeling specific strategies from the training, (2) videotaping the teacher using these strategies, (3) assessing the teacher's efforts using a fidelity of implementation measure, and (4) providing explicit feedback to the teacher on her classroom practices and particularly on her use of instructional language in the classroom. Thus teachers receive individualized guidance based on ongoing assessments of their classroom performance.

Materials

Teachers also receive high-quality materials to help them implement the target strategies in the classroom. Given that children benefit from multiple, meaningful exposures to new vocabulary words, teachers receive a variety of vocabulary-building tools organized around 3- to 4-week social or natural science themes (e.g., back to school, friends and family, visiting the zoo). For each theme, a set of approximately 35 vocabulary words—likely to be central to the ideas of the theme but unfamiliar to children—are selected, and a series of 10 to 12 age-appropriate books (including narrative, informational, and concept books) featuring several of the target vocabulary words are compiled. Props or pictures depicting the key vocabulary words are included as well. Finally, teachers receive brief lesson plans that, while less explicit than scripts, provide specific guidance on how to ask questions and foster conversation before, during, and after reading each book (including advice to read each book at least three times over the course of the theme) and ideas for follow-up small- and large-group activities that further reinforce the vocabulary. Teachers can select the themes they wish to study from a collection of approximately 15, and each theme can be customized to serve 3- and/ or 4-year-olds.

Assessment

The third component of the ExCELL model is ongoing assessment, which helps determine whether the program is having the desired effect on teachers and children. Three times per year, children receive a vocabulary (as well as sound awareness and alphabet) progress monitoring assessment, in which several target words from each theme the child has recently studied are randomly chosen. In a one-on-one setting, children are asked to identify a picture of each chosen word using an expressive vocabulary test protocol. Data are compiled so teachers can reflect on classroom trends and individual differences among their students and analyze the effectiveness of their instruction. In addition, coaches continually assess teachers using a fidelity measure at the time of the classroom visits.

Results of ExCELL

Several randomized control trials have been conducted on ExCELL (Wasik et al., 2006; Wasik & Hindman, 2011a, 2011b; Wasik, Hindman, & Jusczyk, 2009). Teachers in both ExCELL and comparison groups were pre- and posttested on the Early Language and Literacy Classroom Observation (ELLCO), Classroom Assessment Scoring System (CLASS), and measures of teacher knowledge. Children in both ExCELL and comparison classrooms were assessed on the Peabody Picture Vocabulary Test—Third Edition (PPVT-III), the Phonological Awareness Literacy Screening—PreK (PALS-PreK), an alphabet assessment, and curriculum-specific progress monitoring vocabulary measures. The results show that Head Start teachers who received ExCELL training improved the quality of their vocabulary instruction on standardized tools such as the ELLCO (measuring the presence and use of language and literacy materials) and the CLASS (measuring the quality of language modeling, feedback, and concept development) ($d = 1.00$, on average). Teachers also made significant gains on their conceptual knowledge of children's language and literacy development and procedural knowledge of best practices for the classroom, both of which were heavily emphasized in the trainings and individualized coaching (Hindman & Wasik, 2011).

Children in ExCELL learned, on average, 85%–90% of book-related words, which was assessed three times per year using progress monitoring (Wasik et al., 2009). In addition, children's standardized scores on the PPVT-III, a receptive vocabulary measure, increased substantially (average d of 1.50, as indicated by Marulis & Neuman, 2010). Therefore, children in ExCELL performed significantly better compared to the comparison group on both curriculum-specific and standardized measures of vocabulary. In addition, children in ExCELL performed significantly better than children in the comparison group on phonological sensitivity measures of the PALS-PreK. Children in both ExCELL and control classrooms made significant but equal gains in alphabet knowledge (Wasik & Hindman, 2011b).

Identifying Active Ingredients

Although ExCELL has been shown to have an impact both on teachers' classroom behaviors and on children's vocabulary knowledge, it is important to understand precisely how these effects are translated from coaches to children. In the second portion of this chapter, we look across and within the corpus of research on ExCELL to attempt to distill the precise mechanisms through which the program affects teachers and children. In general, ExCELL's unique effectiveness, or active ingredients, lies in its evidence-based group training content and its individualized coaching for teachers, which teachers translate into child vocabulary gains primarily through (1) interactive book readings, (2) book extension activities, and (3) opportunities for children to talk and receive meaningful feedback around the classroom. Below, we explain how each of these "active ingredients" or core experiences highlights vocabulary for children to a greater extent than other parts of the day such as Circle Time, Morning Message, mealtime, or outside play.

Interactive Book Reading

As has been extensively researched in early childhood, books are special tools for expanding children's vocabulary knowledge (see Duke, Halvorsen & Knight, Chapter 12, this volume; Pinkham, Chapter 6, this volume). Books present words that children may not experience in their daily lives, often with explicit definitions, rich narratives to provide context, and/or illustrations that highlight their meaning (Ganea, Pickard, & DeLoache, 2008; Jalongo, Dragich, Conrad, & Zhang, 2002). However, book readings most effectively foster vocabulary knowledge when adults highlight words and provide opportunities for children to use those words (Hindman & Wasik, 2008; Sénéchal & Cornell, 1993; Whitehurst et al., 1994). In ExCELL, considerable attention during training and coaching focuses on how the book reading experience can be optimized to support vocabulary learning. First, in ExCELL, teachers are trained to select books to support theme learning (thematically organized materials, including books, are provided during the intervention to serve as models, or implicit PD). Therefore, in a unit on transportation, books read during the unit will be related in some way to the concept of transportation, helping children build knowledge about a specific topic. In addition, teachers are guided to select a core set of key vocabulary words related to the theme and to identify books that focus on one or more of these vocabulary words. Books vary in genres and include storybooks and informational texts.

Beyond book choice, teachers are trained to implement a series of book-related activities and routines before, during, and after the reading that provide children with multiple, meaningful exposures to words, and especially those words identified as critical for the theme. Before reading the book, teachers introduce children to unfamiliar vocabulary in the text. Teachers provide a child-friendly definition of each word along with either a visual image (a picture) or a three-dimensional prop that represents the word. When a word can best be defined through a demonstration (e.g., *quiet, gallop*) the teacher will act out the word and invite children to join in.

During the reading, the teacher emphasizes points at which the identified, theme-related vocabulary is used in the context of the story and, whenever possible, poses open-ended questions (i.e., questions with no specific correct answers, generally requiring multiple-word responses) about those words. As children use and discuss these new ideas, teachers provide meaningful feedback on children's remarks to further support their learning. For example, when reading Donald Crews's *Freight Train* (1996) during a transportation theme, the teacher might pause after reading "A train runs across this track" to prompt, "Describe the track that we see here" or "How does a track help the train run?" Teachers then follow children's responses with praise, corrections if necessary, and one or more additional open-ended questions to keep the conversation flowing. In addition, when other novel words not featured in the theme are encountered, teachers read the word and then define or recast it. For example, teachers would read the term *caboose* (not featured in the transportation unit) and say "a special kind of train car that comes at the very end of the train."

Finally, after the reading, teachers employ conversation strategies such as asking open-ended questions and providing meaningful feedback to encourage children to discuss the content of the story. In many classrooms, postreading conversations about storybooks are limited to simple and superficial questions such as, "Did you like the book?" In contrast, ExCELL trains teachers to pose analytical questions (e.g., reviewing with children what happened in the beginning, middle, and end of the book, asking children to recall how various kinds of transportation that appeared in the story were similar to or different from one another, or prompting children to identify a favorite part of the book and to justify why this was so interesting for them). Altogether, ExCELL classrooms provided truly interactive book reading experiences that made vocabulary salient for and accessible to children.

Extension Activities and Rereadings

Research on word learning is clear, however, that children rarely learn words through single exposures. In ExCELL, teachers extend the word learning experience in two explicit ways. First, teachers design small-group activities in learning centers, as well as large-group activities for the entire class, that target and expand on the ideas and vocabulary from the book reading. For example, after reading *Freight Train,* teachers might transform the dramatic play area into the inside of a train using key props such as a conductor's hat and train tickets (along with children's imaginations); invite children to build and label an extensive set of train tracks using blocks in the construction center; guide children to write about trains and other forms of transportation in their journals in the writing center; ask children to draw or paint different train cars from the book and perhaps even invent their own; or help children work with adults to sort different kinds of train cars by shape, color, or other features at the manipulatives table. In this way, the stage is set for children to hear and use key vocabulary in interesting ways. In addition, as this work takes place, teachers circulate, asking questions and making comments that encourage children to use book vocabulary and concepts.

Second, and equally important, each book is read at least three times over a period of 10 days. Not only do repeated readings provide multiple opportunities for children to hear new words, but cognitive research indicates that reasonably spaced intervals between readings provide separate occasions for learning, or distributed practice with the target words (e.g., Bransford, Brown, & Cocking, 2000). These gaps allow time for children to process and integrate new information and increase the likelihood that they will learn and retain knowledge of new words.

Child Talk during Conversations

A final critical feature that merits additional focus as an avenue through which ExCELL contributed to children's increased vocabulary is the emphasis in ExCELL on formal and informal conversations among teachers and children. Although ExCELL focuses on all five key areas of literacy—oral language, print awareness, phonological sensitivity, alphabet knowledge, and writing—group training and individualized coaching continually emphasize that rich oral language exchanges in the classroom are necessary to build vocabulary as well as to communicate about all code-related content (e.g., letters, sounds, print conventions). In other words, clear and thoughtful oral language exchanges, especially but not only about the target vocabulary, are set forth as the fundamental characteristic of a high-quality classroom. These exchanges are designed to occur between teachers and children, or among children only, during book reading and extension activities (as explained above), as well as during all other segments of the day.

Training and coaching devote significant time to expanding teachers' conceptual and procedural knowledge around fostering conversations that allow children to talk at length about content and vocabulary. For example, in trainings coaches explain, model, and show videos focused on techniques to help teachers ask open-ended questions and provide meaningful feedback to scaffold language and vocabulary use. Furthermore, during individualized coaching, coaches shadow teachers as they work with children, videotaping their conversations and later visiting with teachers one-on-one to unpack strengths and areas for improvement in their classroom teacher–child and child–child discourse patterns. As above, results of quantitative data analyses show that ExCELL improved teachers' use of language in the classroom, as gauged by their stronger performance on the CLASS measure, including gains on all three subscales (i.e., language modeling, quality of feedback, and concept development).

However, more qualitative analyses of teachers' discourse with children around the classroom, and particularly their use of open-ended questions, revealed interesting and somewhat unexpected findings (see Wasik & Hindman, 2011b). Specifically during book reading, ExCELL teachers did not actually ask more open-ended questions overall than teachers in the control condition. However, differences emerged in children's responses. The data suggest that (1) more children in ExCELL classrooms answered each open-ended question, and (2) ExCELL children responded with more elaborated (i.e., multiple-word rather than one-word) answers. Upon closer examination, teachers in ExCELL were found to provide more children with the opportunity to answer each open-ended question (often calling on multiple children for different perspectives), and teachers allowed or even encouraged children to use more words and take more time in providing an answer. To facilitate these exchanges, ExCELL teachers had developed efficient management strategies to help children stay focused and on task even when they were listening to several of their peers' responses. Thus one of the reasons why ExCELL classrooms better fostered vocabulary knowledge, relative to control classrooms, was that children had greater opportunities to talk and use language, even though children in both classrooms were asked a similar number of open-ended questions.

Summary

Vocabulary knowledge is a valuable tool that helps young children learn to read and to succeed in school. In ExCELL, teachers are trained to use specific strategies during book reading, extension activities, and conversations throughout the classroom to help children develop vocabulary and related conceptual knowledge. As a result, Head Start teachers trained in ExCELL significantly increased the quality of their vocabulary (and literacy) instruction, and children significantly increased their vocabulary (and literacy) knowledge. Analyses of the corpus of data on

ExCELL suggest that book reading and related activities are important opportunities during which teachers can scaffold children's vocabulary, as are conversations (in book reading and other settings) that foster child talk. However, simply reading books without providing children with opportunities to engage in conversations using book-related vocabulary and discussing the book content may not affect children's language. In summary, the effectiveness of ExCELL for children's vocabulary learning appears to lie in making vocabulary meaningful, accessible, and interesting to children.

REFERENCES

Alexander, K. L., Entwisle, D. R., & Horsey, C. (1997). From first grade forward: Early foundations of high school dropout. *Sociology of Education, 70*(2), 87–107.

Bartlett, F. C. (1967). *Remembering: A study in experimental and social psychology.* Cambridge, England: Cambridge University Press.

Beck, I. L., & McKeown, M. G. (2007). Increasing young low-income children's oral vocabulary through rich and focused instruction. *Elementary School Journal, 107*(3), 251–271.

Biemiller, A., & Boote, C. (2006). An effective method for building meaning vocabulary in primary grades. *Journal of Educational Psychology, 98*(1), 44–62.

Blachowicz, C., Buhle, R., & Ogle, D. (2010). Hit the ground running: Ten ideas for preparing and supporting urban literacy coaches. *Reading Teacher, 63*(5), 348–359.

Booth, A. E. (2009). Causal supports for early word learning. *Child Development, 80*(4), 1243–1250.

Bransford, J. D., Brown, A. L., & Cocking, R. R. (2000). *How people learn: Brain, mind, experience, and school.* Washington, DC: National Academy Press.

Bransford, J. D., & Johnson, M. K. (1972). Contextual prerequisites for understanding. *Journal of Verbal Learning and Verbal Behavior, 11,* 717–726.

Carey, S., & Bartlett, E. (1978). Acquiring a single new word. *Papers and reports on child language development, 15,* 17–29.

Casey, K. (2006). *Literacy coaching: The essentials.* New York: Heinemann.

Christie, J. F., & Roskos, K. A. (2006). Standards, science, and the role of play in early literacy education. In D. G. Singer, R. M. Golinkoff, & K. Hirsh-Pasek (Eds.), *Play = learning: How play motivates and enhances children's cognitive and social-emotional growth* (pp. 57–73). New York: Oxford University Press.

Connor, C. M., Morrison, F. J., & Slominski, L. (2006). Preschool instruction and children's emergent literacy growth. *Journal of Educational Psychology, 98*(4), 665–689.

Crews, D. (1996). *Freight train.* New York: Greenwillow Books.

Cunningham, A. E., Zibulsky, J., Stanovich, K. E., & Stanovich, P. J. (2009). How teachers would spend their time teaching language arts: The mismatch between self-reported and best practices. *Journal of Learning Disabilities, 42*(5), 418–430.

DeBaryshe, B. D., & Gorecki, D. M. (2007). An experimental validation of a preschool emergent literacy curriculum. *Early Education and Development, 18*(1), 93–110.

Dickinson, D., & Caswell, L. (2007). Building support for language and early literacy in preschool classrooms through in-service professional development: Effects of the Literacy Environment Enrichment Program (LEEP). *Early Childhood Research Quarterly, 22*(2), 243–260.

Dickinson, D. K. (2001). Book reading in preschool classrooms: Is recommended practice common? In D. K. Dickinson & P. O. Tabors (Eds.), *Beginning literacy with language: Young children learning at home and school* (pp. 175–203). Baltimore: Brookes.

Dickinson, D. K., Flushman, T. R., & Freiberg, J. B. (2009). Language, reading, and classroom supports: Where we are and where we need to be going. In B. Richards, M. H. Dahler, D. D. Malvern, P. Meara, J. Milton, & J. Trefers-Dahler (Eds.), *Vocabulary studies in first and second language acquisition: The interface between theory and application* (pp. 23–38). Hampshire, UK: Palgrave-MacMillan.

Dickinson, D. K., Freiberg, T. R., & Barnes, E. M. (2011). Why are so few interventions really effective? A call for fine-grained research methodology. In S. B. Neuman & D. K. Dickinson (Eds.), *Handbook of early literacy* (Vol. 3, pp. 337–357). New York: Guilford Press.

Dickinson, D., Golinkoff, R. M., & Hirsh-Pasek, K. (2010). Speaking out for language: Why language is central for reading development. *Educational Researcher, 39,* 305–310.

Dickinson, D. K., McCabe, A., Anastasopoulos, L., Peisner-Feinberg, E. S., & Poe, M. D. (2003). The comprehensive approach to early literacy: The interrelationships among vocabulary, phonological sensitivity, and print knowledge among preschool-age children. *Journal of Educational Psychology, 25*(3), 465–481.

Dickinson, D. K., & Porche, M. V. (2011). Relation between language experiences in preschool classrooms and children's kindergarten and fourth-grade language and reading abilities. *Child Development, 82*(2), 870–886.

Dickinson, D. K., & Tabors, P. O. (Eds.). (2001). *Beginning literacy with language: Young children learning at home and school.* Baltimore: Brookes.

Dufva, M., Niemi, P., & Voeten, M. J. M. (2001). The role of phonological memory, word recognition, and comprehension skills in reading development: From preschool to grade 2. *Reading and Writing: An Interdisciplinary Journal, 14*(1–2), 91–117.

Gamse, B. C., Bloom, H. S., Kemple, J. J., Jacob, R. T., Boulay, B., Bozzi, L., et al. (2008). *Reading First impact study: Interim report.* Washington, DC: National Center for Education Statistics.

Ganea, P. A., Pickard, M. B., & DeLoache, J. S. (2008). Transfer between picture books and the real world by very young children. *Journal of Cognition and Development, 9*(1), 46–66.

Gest, S. D., Holland-Coviello, R., Welsh, J. A., Eicher-Catt, D. L., & Gill, S. (2006). Language development subcontexts in Head Start classrooms: Distinctive patterns of teacher talk during free play, mealtime, and book reading. *Early Education and Development, 17*(2), 293–315.

Hammer, C. S., Farkas, G., & Maczuga, S. (2010). The language and literacy development of Head Start children: A study using the Family and Child Experiences Survey database. *Language, Speech, and Hearing Services in Schools, 41*(1), 70–83.

Han, M., Moore, N., Vukelich, C., & Buell, M. (2010). Does play make a difference? How play intervention affects the vocabulary learning of at-risk preschoolers. *American Journal of Play, 3*(1), 82–105.

Hart, B., & Risley, T. R. (1995). *Meaningful differences in the everyday experience of young American children.* Baltimore: Brookes.

Hayes, R., & Matusov, E. (2005). Designing for dialogue in place of teacher talk and student silence. *Culture & Psychology, 11*(3), 339–357.

Hindman, A. H., Skibbe, L. E., Miller, A., & Zimmerman, M. (2010). Ecological contexts and early learning: Contributions of child, family, and classroom factors during Head Start to literacy and mathematics growth. *Early Childhood Research Quarterly, 25*(2), 235–250.

Hindman, A. H., & Wasik, B. A. (2008). Head Start teachers' beliefs about language and literacy instruction. *Early Childhood Research Quarterly, 23*(4), 479–492.

Hindman, A. H., & Wasik, B. A. (2011). Exploring Head Start teachers' early language and literacy knowledge: Lessons from the ExCELL professional development intervention. *NHSA Dialog, 14*(4), 293–315.

Hindman, A. H., Wasik, B. A., & Erhart, A. M. (in press). Shared book reading and Head Start preschoolers' vocabulary learning: The role of book-related discussion and curricular connections. *Early Education and Development.*

Hirsh-Pasek, K., & Burchinal, M. (2006). Mother and caregiver sensitivity over time: Predicting language and academic outcomes with variable- and person-centered approaches. *Merrill-Palmer Quarterly, 52*(3), 449–485.

Hirsh-Pasek, K., Golinkoff, R. M., Berk, L., & Singer, D. G. (2009). *A mandate for playful learning: Presenting the evidence.* New York: Oxford University Press.

Hoff, E. (2003). The specificity of environmental influence: Socioeconomic status affects early vocabulary development via maternal speech. *Child Development, 74*(5), 1368–1378.

Huttenlocher, J., Haight, W., Bryk, A., Seltzer, M., & Lyons, T. (1991). Early vocabulary growth: Relations to language input and gender. *Developmental Psychology, 27*(2), 236–248.

International Reading Association. (2004). *The role and qualifications of the reading coach in the United States.* Newark, DE: Author.

Jackson, R., McCoy, A., Pistorino, C., Wilkinson, A., Burghardt, J., Clark, M., et al. (2007). *National evaluation of Early Reading First: Final report.* Washington, DC: U.S. Government Printing Office.

Jalongo, M. R., Dragich, D., Conrad, N. K., & Zhang, A. (2002). Using wordless picture books to support emergent literacy. *Early Childhood Education Journal, 29*(3), 167–177.

Joyce, B. R., & Showers, B. (1981). Transfer of training: The contribution of "coaching." *Journal of Education, 163*(2), 163–172.

Justice, L. M., Mashburn, A. J., Hamre, B. K., & Pianta, R. C. (2008). Quality of language and literacy instruction in preschool classrooms serving at-risk pupils. *Early Childhood Research Quarterly, 23*(1), 51–68.

Landry, S. H., Anthony, J. L., Swank, P. R., & Monseque-Bailey, P. (2009). Effectiveness of comprehensive professional development for teachers of at-risk preschoolers. *Journal of Educational Psychology, 101*(2), 448–465.

Landry, S. H., Swank, P. R., Smith, K. E., Assel, M. A., & Gunnewig, S. B. (2006). Enhancing early literacy skills for preschool children: Bringing a professional development model to scale *Journal of Learning Disabilities, 39*(4), 306–325.

Lee, V. E., & Burkam, D. (2002). *Inequality at the starting gate: Social background differences in achievement as children begin school.* Washington, DC: Economic Policy Institute.

Marulis, L. M., & Neuman, S. B. (2010). The effects of vocabulary intervention on young children's word learning: A meta-analysis. *Review of Educational Research, 80*(3), 300–335.

Mashburn, A. J. (2008). Quality of social and physical environments in preschools and children's development of academic, language, and literacy skills. *Applied Developmental Science, 12*(3), 103–127.

Moss, M., Jacob, R., Boulay, B., Horst, M., & Poulos, J. (2006). *Reading First implementation evaluation: Interim report.* Washington, DC: National Center for Education Statistics.

National Assessment of Educational Progress. (2010). The nation's report card: Reading. Retrieved June 1, 2011, from *http://nces.ed.gov/nationsreportcard/reading.*

National Early Literacy Panel. (2009). *Developing early literacy: Report of the National Early Literacy Panel, executive summary.* Washington, DC: National Institute for Literacy.

National Institute of Child Health and Human Development Early Child Care Research Network. (2005). Duration and developmental timing of poverty and children's cognitive and social development from birth to third grade. *Child Development, 76*(4), 795–810.

Neuman, S. B., & Cunningham, A. E. (2009). The impact of professional development and coaching on early language and literacy instructional practices. *American Educational Research Journal, 46*(2), 532–566.

Neuman, S. B., & Dwyer, J. (2009). Missing in action: Vocabulary instruction in pre-K. *The Reading Teacher, 62*(5), 384–392.

Penno, J. F., Wilkinson, I. A. G., & Moore, D. W. (2002). Vocabulary acquisition from teacher explanation and repeated listening to stories: Overcome the Matthew effect? *Journal of Educational Psychology, 94*(1), 23–33.

Powell, D. R., Diamond, K. E., Burchinal, M. R., & Koehler, M. J. (2010). Effects of an early literacy professional development intervention on Head Start teachers and children. *Journal of Educational Psychology, 102*(2), 299–312.

Preschool Curriculum Evaluation Research. (2008). *Effects of preschool curriculum programs on school readiness (NCER 2008–2009)*. Washington, DC: National Center for Education Research, Institute of Education Sciences.

Sénéchal, M., & Cornell, E. H. (1993). Vocabulary acquisition through shared book reading experiences. *Reading Research Quarterly, 28*(4), 361–374.

Smith, K. E., Landry, S. H., & Swank, P. R. (2000). Does the content of mothers' verbal stimulation explain differences in children's development of verbal and nonverbal cognitive skills? *Journal of School Psychology, 38*(1), 27–49.

Snow, C. E., & Tabors, P. O. (1993). Language skills that relate to literacy development. In B. Spodek & O. Saracho (Eds.), *Yearbook in early childhood education* (Vol. 4, pp. 1–20). New York: Teachers College Press.

Stanovich, K. E. (1986). Matthew effects in reading: Some consequences of individual differences in the acquisition of literacy. *Reading Research Quarterly, 21*(4), 360–406.

Storch, S. A., & Whitehurst, G. J. (2002). Oral language and code-related precursors to reading: Evidence from a longitudinal structural model. *Developmental Psychology, 38*(6), 934–947.

Walker, D., Greenwood, C. R., Hart, B., & Carta, J. (1994). Prediction of school outcomes based on early language production and SES factors. *Child Development, 65*(2), 606–621.

Wasik, B. A., & Bond, M. A. (2001). Beyond the pages of a book: Interactive book reading and language development in preschool classrooms. *Journal of Educational Psychology, 93*(2), 243–250.

Wasik, B. A., Bond, M. A., & Hindman, A. H. (2006). The effects of a language and literacy intervention on Head Start children and teachers. *Journal of Educational Psychology, 98*(1), 63–74.

Wasik, B. A., & Hindman, A. H. (2011a). Factors contributing to high-quality, effective preschool interventions. In S. B. Neuman & D. K. Dickinson (Eds.), *Handbook of Early Literacy Research* (pp. 322–336). New York: Guilford Press.

Wasik, B. A., & Hindman, A. H. (2011b). Low-income children learning language and early literacy skills: The effects of a teacher professional development model on teacher and child outcomes. *Journal of Educational Psychology, 103*(2), 455–469.

Wasik, B. A., Hindman, A. H., & Jusczyk, A. M. (2009). Using curriculum specific progress monitoring to determine Head Start children's vocabulary development. *National Head Start Association: Dialog Journal, 12*(3), 257–275.

Weizman, Z. O., & Snow, C. E. (2001). Lexical input as related to children's vocabulary acquisition: effects of sophisticated exposure and support for meaning. *Developmental Psychology, 37*(2), 265–279.

Whitehurst, G. J., Arnold, D. H., Epstein, J. N., Angell, A. L., Smith, M. W., & Fischel, J. E. (1994). A picture book reading intervention in day care and home for children from low-income families. *Developmental Psychology, 30*(5), 679–689.

Zill, N., & Resnick, G. (2006). Low-income children in Head Start and beyond: Findings from FACES. In N. F. Watt, C. Ayoub, R. H. Bradley, J. E. Puma, & W. LeBoeuf (Eds.), *The crisis in youth mental health: Critical issues and effective programs: Early intervention programs and policies* (pp. 253–289). Westport, CT: Praeger.

CHAPTER 12

■　■　■　■　■

Building Knowledge
through Informational Text

Nell K. Duke
Anne-Lise Halvorsen
Jennifer A. Knight

Two-year-old Spencer announces that Jackie Robinson played
baseball a long time ago and that at that time "black people
had to sit in the back of the bus."
　　Five-year-old Cooper explains, "[Sharks] like the smell of
blood. To try to get away from a shark you should punch it in
the nose, eyes, gills, or maybe even fin. Hammerheads are less
likely to attack you than tigers, bulls, and great whites."

These children did not learn these things from personal experience (let's
hope!) or in conversation with their parents or teachers. They learned
these things from information books that were read aloud to them. The
focus of this chapter is informational text as a means of knowledge building in early childhood. We argue that reading informational text to children and, as they make their way toward conventional reading, engaging children in reading informational text themselves, can be a critical
strategy for knowledge building. In the first section, we discuss research
on the relationship between reading and knowledge. In the second, we
review research on informational text and its use with young children.
In the final section, we turn to specific resources and techniques for
building knowledge through informational text in early childhood.

The Relationship between Reading and Knowledge

In our view, the relationship between reading and knowledge is recipro-cal. The more a reader reads and is exposed to print, the more knowledge the reader builds; the more knowledge the reader has, the stronger the reader's comprehension will become (Cunningham & Stanovich, 1997) (see Figure 12.1).

The Importance of Knowledge for Reading

Many prominent theories of reading comprehension have posited a cen-tral role for knowledge (e.g., Kintsch, 2004; Rumelhart, 1981). Knowl-edge is viewed as necessary both for constructing a basic understanding of the text and for allowing readers to build their own unique mental model of the content. Consider the following excerpt on the American Revolution, readily understandable to most college-educated adults:

> Inaugurating an era of world revolutions, the American Revolution had points of similarity with the revolutions that followed. First of all, it was an anticolonial war waged by a colonial people for their inde-pendence; in that respect it was the seedbed for all later anticolonial movements in Latin America, Asia, or Africa. Second, it was a revolt against monarchy which supplanted the royal system by a republic. (Garrity & Gay, 1972, p. 753)

To comprehend this text, a reader of course needs concepts-of-print knowledge, such as the need to read left-to-right and top-to-bottom, as well as the considerable knowledge needed to decode and recognize individual words within the passage. But other, less obvious knowledge is needed as well. One needs syntactic knowledge, for example, to under-stand the meaning conveyed by the order in which the words are placed,

Knowledge   Reading

FIGURE 12.1. The knowledge–reading relationship: Knowledge is necessary for reading, and reading is an important tool for building knowledge.

to figure out that "it" in the second sentence refers to *the American Revolution* and "their" refers to *the colonial people*. One needs to know how to make use of specific informational text features in the passage, such as the title or an accompanying timeline. One also needs extensive content and conceptual knowledge, including the meaning of individual words (e.g., What is a *revolution*? What is a *seedbed*?) and terms (e.g., What is an *anticolonial movement*?). In summary, great breadth and depth of knowledge are needed to understand this passage.

Although some think of content and conceptual knowledge as important only to content area achievement, this kind of knowledge is central to reading achievement as well. As a case in point, consider an item from the National Assessment of Educational Progress fourth-grade reading test. Students were asked to complete this analogy after reading an informational article on blue crabs:

> The growth of a blue crab larva into a full-grown blue crab is most like the development of:
>
> A) a human baby into a teenager
> B) an egg into a chicken
> C) a tadpole into a frog
> D) a seed into a tree

The answer to this question was not explicitly stated in the text. So let's consider what readers would need to know in order to answer it correctly. Certainly readers would need to know how to decode the words in the question and the article, what these words mean, and how to make use of syntax to understand their relationships. But readers also need considerable content knowledge about both the correct and incorrect choices. For example, they need to know about the life cycles of four types of living things (humans, chickens, frogs, and trees), including key features of these cycles that compare or contrast with the life cycle of the blue crab. Tremendous content knowledge is thus needed to be successful on this item on a "reading" test.

Research confirms the importance of prior knowledge for reading comprehension. In one study, when two groups of readers had the same knowledge relative to a text, they comprehended equally well. But when one group had higher knowledge related to the text topic, they performed much better, particularly on generating inferences and summarizing (Yekovich, Walker, Ogle, & Thompson, 1990). Similarly, Moravcsik and Kintsch (1993) found that readers with high domain knowledge related to the topic of a text were better able to elaborate on the text's meaning. Recht and Leslie (1988) found that students with prior knowledge of a topic were better able to summarize and retell important details about a related text passage than their peers who had less prior knowledge, regardless of reading abilities. Pritchard (1990) determined that students who activated and utilized their background knowledge of a culturally familiar topic were better able to make strong connections, made more elaborations on the text, and had better understanding overall.

The Importance of Reading for Knowledge Building

It is not simply that knowledge aids comprehension, but also that comprehension facilitates knowledge building. Consider the aforementioned passage on the American Revolution. There is much one can learn from those three sentences. There is the content the text seems explicitly designed to teach: that the American Revolution was the first in a series of revolutions across the globe, it was similar to subsequent revolutions because they were also for independence from a colonial power, and so forth. But there is additional content that may not be as obvious. For example, the sentence, "Second, it was a revolt against monarchy which supplanted the royal system by a republic" (Garrity & Gay, 1972, p. 753), tells the reader that the political structure in place prior to the revolution was a monarchy and that the system of government established following the revolution was a republic. The latter point is notable because it may contradict many people's existing knowledge (i.e., the form of government in the United States is a democracy). Indeed, an important role of text is not only building knowledge but refining or replacing existing knowledge.

For young children, who may hold a number of conceptions different than those of adults, this is especially important. Although young children may typically not understand that plants are living things, for example, informational texts may help children correct this misconception earlier than if they had to solely rely on their direct experience. As the quotations that open this chapter demonstrate, young children can indeed build their content knowledge through informational text read aloud to them (see also Fingeret, 2008). As they become conventional readers, children may also begin to acquire content knowledge from informational texts they read themselves. In fact, having children read books in addition to engaging in hands-on experiences may result in greater learning than hands-on experiences alone (Anderson & Guthrie, 1999; Wang, 2005).

Of course, content knowledge is not the only type of knowledge that children may acquire through reading. Children also develop language and textual knowledge from being read to and reading independently. For example, Duke and Kays (1998) found that after being exposed to informational text during classroom read-alouds, children used more linguistic features characteristic of informational text language, such as technical vocabulary and "timeless verb constructions" (e.g., "Bees look for nectar" rather than "The bee looked for nectar"). Indeed, there appear to be myriad forms of knowledge that may be developed through reading informational text.

Summary

Knowledge is critical to children's comprehension, including their understanding of informational text. Text, especially informational text, is an important tool for building comprehension. As Duke, Pearson, Strachan, and Billman (2011) point out, this is a virtuous (rather than vicious) cycle:

> We bring knowledge to the comprehension process, and that knowledge shapes our comprehension. When we comprehend, we gain new information that changes our knowledge, which is then available for later comprehension. So, in that positive, virtuous cycle, knowledge begets comprehension, which begets knowledge, and so on. In a very real sense, we literally read and learn our way into greater knowledge about the world and greater comprehension capacity. (p. 53)

Informational Text and Young Children

Although children may develop knowledge from many types of text, informational text seems particularly well suited for the task. By definition, informational text is intended to convey information about the natural and social world (Duke, 2000). Evidence suggests that it generally succeeds in doing so better than other types of books, including fictional narratives (e.g., Cervetti, Bravo, Hiebert, Pearson, & Jaynes, 2009). Moreover, adults appear to attend more to knowledge building when reading informational texts with young children than when reading narrative texts (Pelligrini, Perlmutter, Galda, & Brody, 1990).

Yet despite its potential as a tool for knowledge building and literacy learning (Caswell & Duke, 1998; Duke, Martineau, Frank, Rowe, & Bennett-Armistead, 2011), informational text typically plays a relatively small role in preschool, primary grade, and intermediate grade curricula (Duke, 2000; Jeong, Gaffney, & Choi, 2010; Pentimonti, Zucker, Justice, & Kaderavek, 2010). This neglect, however, is not justified. In fact, there is considerable evidence that young children can respond to informational text in sophisticated ways if given the opportunity (Maduram, 2000; Oyler & Barry, 1996; Tower, 2002). Moreover, some children even prefer this type of text (Mohr, 2003; Monson & Sebesta, 1991).

Of course, informational text may present challenges for young readers. Such text may have many features with which young children have to contend: navigational features (e.g., index, page numbers); graphical devices (e.g., diagrams, maps); specific text structures (e.g., lists, problem–solution, cause–effect); and language features including those discussed earlier (Meyer & Rice, 1984; Purcell-Gates, Duke, & Martineau, 2007). Children must also learn new strategies (such as rereading and skimming) that may be used more commonly during informational reading. Despite these challenges, however, studies have shown that even young children can interact successfully with and learn from informational text. In the following section, we share specific resources and techniques for helping children successfully grapple with the challenges of informational text and build their knowledge through reading informational text.

Designing Instruction for Children to Gain Knowledge from Text

In this section, we offer practical applications for teaching children new knowledge through informational text. We describe ways to create natural situations in which children may want or need to use informational text, consider key criteria to use when selecting texts for knowledge building, suggest techniques to engage children and help build their knowledge, and suggest after-reading experiences to help children retain newly learned knowledge. Where appropriate, we provide particular teaching examples and suggested teacher talk. Although we constructed these activities for classroom settings, they could be readily modified for other settings in which informational texts are being used, such as home or extracurricular programs. Because many informational texts focus on content related to science or social studies, the examples are primarily related to these two subject areas.

Creating Situations in Which Children Want or Need to Use Text

Children must learn that there are reasons to both want and need to use text as a means of gaining new information (see also Pinkham, Chapter 6, this volume). One way to do this is to model natural situations in which people use text to obtain needed information. Another way is to design activities in which children directly experience how informational texts can provide useful knowledge.

Modeling

Although it is helpful for children to observe teachers and other adults engaged in reading texts such as a newspaper or information book, *explicit* modeling of how to use a text is especially critical for showing children how to use texts themselves. For example, a teacher may discuss a particular interest she has, such as the national parks. She could then model for her students how to locate and read informational texts, both on- and offline, related to our national parks. Teachers can also describe a particular question or problem they have encountered, explain that they need information to solve the problem, and demonstrate how that information was obtained. For example, a teacher may explain that a plant she received as a gift is not doing well (i.e., the problem) and then demonstrate how she looked in a book about plants to find out how to help her plant thrive (i.e., the solution). Throughout this process, she could engage in "thinking aloud" to help children better understand the steps followed in using informational texts, such as: (1) identify the need for an informational text, (2) locate the text, and (3) read and use the text to address the problem.

Designing Activities Requiring Informational Texts

In addition to observing adults using texts, children need opportunities to recognize a desire or need to use informational text themselves. This can occur spontaneously as well as in a planned manner. Children are naturally curious about the world around them. When they ask questions about why dinosaurs are no longer around or what happens to trash after the garbage truck picks it up, for example, teachers may suggest that children consult relevant texts to find answers. Children may also participate in projects that generate a want or need to know information, such as designing and producing a good or service to sell in the school community. When engaged in such an activity, children may need to consult informational texts to learn how to produce and market the particular good or service (see Duke, Caughlan, Juzwik, & Martin, 2012, for additional suggestions).

Selection of Texts

Informational texts may come in many forms, including information books, newspaper articles, magazine articles, and informational websites. Of course, not all informational texts are optimal for use with young children. This section describes criteria that may be used when selecting developmentally appropriate informational texts.

Content and Accuracy

Informational texts should be both content rich and accurate, and the content should be aligned with the questions or problems posed in the activities being implemented. If children are seeking to learn more about how rain is formed, for example, the text should specifically discuss the water cycle. Or if children need to know whom to contact if they want to initiate a neighborhood curbside recycling program, the text should explicitly describe the responsibilities of city government.

It is also critical that the content of the informational text is accurate. Authors often attempt to simplify the content with the intention of making it accessible, but this can lead to the unfortunate consequence of representing the information inaccurately. Inaccurate texts may have long-term consequences for children's knowledge development because the inaccurate content can remain ingrained in children's minds or perpetuate their preexisting misconceptions.

Culturally Sensitive Pedagogy

In addition to being accurate, informational texts should be culturally sensitive (Gay, 2000; Ladson-Billings, 1994). Culturally sensitive texts should emphasize both the unique qualities of people from different cultures as well as their similarities. Such texts should not perpetuate stereotypes about groups of people nor privilege one culture (or race, gender, socioeconomic level, religion) over another. They treat difference as a positive aspect of the world and often show how knowledge about other people can build tolerance, respect, and appreciation. However, they also do not downplay conflict among people or difficult events in history in which racial or other kinds of conflict occurred. Of course, some content of this kind may be inappropriate for young children; for example, we do not recommend dwelling on violent acts committed by or against historical figures. Nonetheless, even young children may be able to learn about concepts such as fairness and discrimination from informational texts.

Engagingness

Another important feature when considering informational texts is the quality of the writing and the illustrations or graphics. Writing should be clear, accessible to young children (e.g., less complex sentences that do not rely on too many unfamiliar words), and lively (e.g., questions posed directly to the reader; humor). Rhyming text can be engaging but should not come at the expense of accurate language. Graphics should be realistic illustrations or high-quality photographs that are tightly aligned with the text, clear, and not overly complex (see also Pinkham, Chapter 6, this volume).

Age Appropriateness

Informational texts are optimally used when they are appropriate for the audience. There are marked differences in the complexity of texts appropriate for infants relative to preschoolers, for instance, or young children relative to older children. An increasing number of high-quality informational texts aimed at infants and toddlers are available, and certainly many resources are available for preschool and school-age children. For example, *My First Animal Board Book* (DK Publishing, 2004) is appropriate for infants and toddlers, whereas *What Do We Buy: A Look at Goods and Services* (Nelson, 2010), which explains and gives examples of wants, needs, goods, services, and other economic concepts, works well with primary-grade children.

The revised Head Start Outcomes, developed specifically for children 3 to 5 years old, include two domains that are content oriented: science knowledge and skills, and social studies knowledge and skills (U.S. Department of Health and Human Services, 2010). In particular, the science domain includes conceptual knowledge of the natural and physical world, while the social studies domain includes self, family and community, people and the environment, and history and events. Informational texts may provide excellent opportunities to teach these domain elements to preschool-age children. Texts with clear, jargon-free language and high-quality images may help children understand aspects of the physical world such as animal life cycles, weather, solar energy, and earth materials. Even infants can be read informational texts with topics about the world around them, such as family members, food, and animals. Even if infants do not understand the language used (but often they do!), they can pick up on tone, facial expressions, and book handling skills that demonstrate how people can use informational text to gain knowledge.

Techniques to Use before, during, and after Reading to Engage Children in Building Knowledge through Informational Text

Often, simply reading a text from beginning to end may not be enough to ensure that children have gained important information or knowledge. In this section, we provide suggestions for techniques to use before, during, and after reading.

Before-Reading Strategies

When introducing an informational text, it is important to help children understand why this particular text is being read. Teachers may explain their rationale, or they can ask children to think about what valuable knowledge might be gained by reading the text. It may also be advisable to ask children do a quick preview of the text (although don't take too much time with this!). For example, a teacher could ask children to predict what they will learn from the text or to brainstorm what they already know about the topic of the text.

During-Reading Strategies

Make Content-Focused Questions and Comments

During the reading of the text, teachers may model their own thinking through their extratextual comments (e.g., "I didn't know whales are mammals"). Teachers may pose content-focused questions (e.g., "So what have we learned so far about whales?" or "Why do you think whales can survive in such cold waters?"). Such open-ended and higher-order questions may be particularly important. It may also be valuable to engage children in offering their opinion of the text or how the author has approached a particular aspect of the text (see also Bennett-Armistead, Duke, & Moses, 2005).

Employ Graphic Organizers

Graphic depictions of a text's content can frequently improve children's understanding. Flowcharts, t-charts, Venn diagrams, webs, and pictures may present the text's content in logical, organized, and meaningful ways. Depending on children's skill level, they may create these organizers independently, in pairs, or as a whole class. For example, after learning the stages in the life cycle of a frog, children could create a flowchart to present the stages. Later, when reading a compare–contrast text of frogs and toads, children could create a t-chart in which the left column features characteristics of the frog and the right column features unique characteristics of the toad. Venn diagrams could also be used, especially when there are overlapping characteristics between the items compared. Or, when reading about a particular geographic region, children could create a web in which the region is the main topic in the central circle. Web branches could then be attached to this circle, which also attach to smaller circles focusing on topics such as the climate, important natural resources, cultural groups, and so on. Children could also be asked to draw pictures of what they have learned from a text to demonstrate their understanding in a way that makes sense to them.

Engage Children in Short During-Reading Activities

Teachers can also embed short activities during read-aloud or small-group reading (e.g., "Let's all try to surface the way a whale does" or "I will demonstrate you how the baleen filters the water"). Informational reading is often selective (i.e., one does not read the entire text) and non-linear (e.g., one might first look in the index, then read a section in the middle of the book that addresses his question, then turn to the beginning of the book for an overview of the topic). Taking breaks for related activities, or even reading alongside an activity (e.g., reading to children about gerbils' diets while children are preparing foods for the class gerbil) may therefore be very appropriate for this type of reading.

After-Reading Experiences for Children to Demonstrate Understanding

All too often, after children finish reading a book, they immediately jump to the next topic or activity without taking time to really "own" the new knowledge gained. For information to truly "stick," children need to be provided with opportunities to apply their newly acquired knowledge in meaningful ways. It is important that children do not necessarily repeat exactly what was in the text, but to express the ideas and concepts in their own words. Three ways to do this are sharing their new knowledge with others, engaging with the content in firsthand experiences, and applying new knowledge in meaningful ways.

Sharing Knowledge Gained

After reading an informational text, children may participate in follow-up activities during which they share their new knowledge. For example, children could write letters to someone about something they have learned. They could also describe orally to others, such as children in a lower grade or other adults in the school community, what they have learned. Teachers could also create a bulletin board in which children "test their knowledge" about the content from a particular text.

Teachers may also arrange opportunities for children to share their knowledge with others outside of school. Children could wear stickers that say, "Ask me what I learned today about [topic of study]," to invite questions from family members and friends about the topic studied. We also suggest that teachers communicate with families about the content of the lessons so that families may ask specific, targeted questions (e.g., "What did you learn about volcanoes?") rather than broad questions (e.g., "What did you learn in school today?").

Firsthand Experiences

Another way to help children retain the knowledge learned through reading informational text is to engage them in firsthand experiences related to the topic. Many early childhood educators teach through thematic units, which, if done effectively, can provide multiple and varied opportunities for children to learn the content (Barton & Smith, 2000). When teaching a thematic unit on the local community, for example, the dramatic play area could be made into a store, library, post office, or police station. Or, for a thematic unit on seasons, the sensory table could be filled with season-related items, while a nearby bulletin board could identify the various objects and their definitions.

We also suggest creating a dedicated "science" or "social studies" space with topics that rotate periodically depending on the thematic unit. The space could feature items used in real life that apply to the topic. For example, photographs of families of different compositions and sizes could be used to illustrate a unit on families, while a unit on properties of matter could feature magnets and magnetic and nonmagnetic materials. When using firsthand experiences, however, it is critical to revisit the topic with children through discussion to ensure they have gained the appropriate knowledge and can successfully apply their understanding of the topic in accurate and meaningful ways (see also Kaefer, Chapter 1, this volume).

Opportunities to Use What Was Learned

Previously, we emphasized that informational text can help children address questions and solve problems in the real world. Children should have opportunities to use what they have learned to do just that. After reading a text on how to read maps, children could read and interpret a map of their own neighborhood, examine a map of the local zoo to help plan their upcoming field trip, or read a map of a museum in order to locate particular exhibits. Or, after reading about weather patterns, children could collect data on the temperature ranges and rainfall and represent the data in a series of simple graphs. They could then use their data to predict future weather patterns around their school, perhaps even sharing what they have learned with the school community.

Concluding Thoughts

Reading and listening to others read text can be critical activities for children's knowledge building. Informational text, in particular, can be an excellent source of content knowledge, as well as various kinds of linguistic knowledge. We hope the strategies we have suggested will enhance teachers' (and parents') use of informational texts as a tool for knowledge building. Although children sometimes want adults to "Just read the book!", weaving content-focused comments and activities throughout the text can help facilitate children's deeper understanding of the content. Importantly, beyond serving as sources of knowledge, informational texts can also be a great source of enjoyment to children, who love to learn new information and show off what they have learned (or correct others' misconceptions!). At the beginning of this chapter, we quoted young children conveying their new knowledge on topics that interested them. When 2-year-old Spencer was asked where he learned that information, he exclaimed proudly, "In my book!"

REFERENCES

Anderson, E., & Guthrie, J. T. (1999, April). *Motivating children to gain conceptual knowledge from text: The combination of science observation and interesting texts*. Paper presented at the annual meeting of the American Educational Research Association, Montreal, Canada.

Barton, K., & Smith, L. (2000). Themes or motifs?: Aiming for coherence through interdisciplinary outlines. *The Reading Teacher, 54*(1), 54–63.

Bennett-Armistead, V. S., Duke, N. K., & Moses, A. M. (2005). *Literacy and the youngest learner: Best practices for educators of children from birth to 5*. New York: Scholastic.

Caswell, L. J., & Duke, N. K. (1998). Non-narrative as a catalyst for literacy development. *Language Arts, 75*(2), 108–117.

Cervetti, G. N., Bravo, M. A., Hiebert, E. H., Pearson, P. D., & Jaynes, C. A. (2009). Text genre and science content: Ease of reading, comprehension, and reader preference. *Reading Psychology, 30*, 487–511.

Cunningham, A. E., & Stanovich, K. E. (1997). Early reading acquisition and its relation to reading experience and ability 10 years later. *Developmental Psychology, 33*(6), 934–945.

DK Publishing. (2004). *My first animal board book*. New York: Author.

Duke, N. K. (2000). 3.6 minutes per day: The scarcity of informational texts in first grade. *Reading Research Quarterly, 35*, 202–224.

Duke, N. K., Caughlan, S., Juzwik, M. M., & Martin, N. M. (2012). *Reading and writing genre with purpose in K–8 classrooms*. Portsmouth, NH: Heinemann.

Duke, N. K., & Kays, J. (1998). "Can I say 'once upon a time'?": Kindergarten children developing knowledge of information book language. *Early Childhood Research Quarterly, 13*(2), 295–318.

Duke, N. K., Martineau, J. A., Frank, K. A., Rowe, S. S., & Bennett-Armistead, S. V. (2011). *The impact of including more informational text in first-grade classrooms.* Unpublished manuscript, College of Education, Michigan State University, East Lansing, MI.

Duke, N. K., Pearson, P. D., Strachan, S. L., & Billman, A. K. (2011). Essential elements of fostering and teaching reading comprehension. In S. J. Samuels & A. E. Farstrup (Eds.), *What research has to say about reading instruction* (4th ed., pp. 51–93). Newark, DE: International Reading Association.

Fingeret, L. (2008). *March of the Penguins*: Building knowledge in a kindergarten classroom. *The Reading Teacher, 62,* 96–103.

Gay, G. (2000). *Culturally responsive teaching.* New York: Teachers College Press.

Garrity, J. A., & Gay, P. (Eds.). (1972). *The Columbia history of the world.* New York: Harper & Row.

Jeong, J. S., Gaffney, J. S., & Choi, J. O. (2010). Availability and use of informational text in second, third, and fourth grades. *Research in the Teaching of English. 44,* 435–456.

Kintsch, W. (2004). The construction–integration model of text comprehension and its implications for instruction. In R. B. Ruddell & N. J. Unrau (Eds.), *Theoretical models and processes of reading* (5th ed., pp. 1270–1328). Newark, DE: International Reading Association.

Ladson-Billings, G. (1994). *The dreamkeepers: Successful teachers of African American children.* San Francisco: Jossey-Bass.

Maduram, I. (2000). "Playing possum": A young child's responses to information books. *Language Arts, 77*(5), 391–397.

Meyer, B. J. F., & Rice, G. E. (1984). The structure of text. In P. D. Pearson (Ed.), *Handbook of reading research* (Vol. 1, pp. 319–352). New York: Longman.

Mohr, K. A. J. (2003). Children's choices: A comparison of book preferences between Hispanic and non-Hispanic first graders. *Reading Psychology, 24*(2), 163–176.

Monson, D. L., & Sebesta, S. (1991). Reading preferences. In J. Flood, J. Jensen, D. Lapp, & J. Squire (Eds.), *Handbook of research on teaching the English language arts* (pp. 664–673). New York: Macmillan.

Moravcsik, J. E., & Kintsch, W. (1993). Writing quality, reading skills, and domain knowledge as factors in text comprehension. *Canadian Journal of Experimental Psychology, 47,* 370–374.

Nelson, R. (2010). *What do we buy?: A look at goods and services.* Minneapolis: Lerner Publications.

Oyler, C., & Barry, A. (1996). Intertextual connections in read-alouds of information books. *Language Arts, 73*(5), 324–329.

Pelligrini, A. D., Perlmutter, J. C., Galda, L., & Brody, G. H. (1990). Joint reading between black Head Start children and their mothers. *Child Development, 61,* 443–453.

Pentimonti, J. M., Zucker, T. A., Justice, L. M., & Kaderavek, J. N. (2010). Informational text use in preschool classroom read-alouds. *The Reading Teacher, 63*(8), 656–665.

Pritchard, R. (1990). The effects of cultural schemata on reading processing strategies. *Reading Research Quarterly, 25*(4), 273–295.

Purcell-Gates, V., Duke, N. K., & Martineau, J. A. (2007). Learning to read and write genre-specific text: Roles of authentic experience and explicit teaching. *Reading Research Quarterly, 42,* 8–45.

Recht, D. R., & Leslie, L. (1988). Effect of prior knowledge on good and poor readers' memory of text. *Journal of Educational Psychology, 80*(1), 16–20.

Rumelhart, D. E. (1981). Schemata: The building blocks of cognition. In J. T. Guthrie (Ed.), *Comprehension in teaching* (pp. 3–26). Newark, DE: International Reading Association.

Tower, C. (2002). "It's a snake, you guys!": The power of text characteristics on children's responses to information books. *Research in the Teaching of English, 37*(1), 55–88.

U.S. Department of Health and Human Services. (2010). *The Head Start child development and early learning framework.* Retrieved from *http://eclkc. ohs.acf.hhs.gov/hslc/tta-system/teaching/eecd/Assessment/Child%20 Outcomes/HS__Revised__Child__Outcomes_Framework.pdf.*

Wang, J. (2005). *Evaluation of the Seeds of Science/Roots of Reading Project: Shorline science and terrarium investigations.* Los Angeles, CA: National Center for Research on Evaluation, Standards, and Testing (CRESST).

Yekovich, F. R., Walker, C. H., Ogle, L. T., & Thompson, M. A. (1990). The influence of domain knowledge on inferencing in low-aptitude individuals. *Psychology of Learning and Motivation, 25,* 159–178.

CHAPTER 13

■ ■ ■ ■ ■

Knowledge Acquisition in the Classroom
LITERACY AND CONTENT-AREA KNOWLEDGE

Carol McDonald Connor
Frederick J. Morrison

Children gain knowledge in the home, classroom, and larger community (Shonkoff & Phillips, 2000). Their influence on children's knowledge acquisition is reciprocal and interactive, building and supporting one another (Morrison, Bachman, & Connor, 2005). Among the most important environments is the classroom learning environment. First, schools have long been the traditional setting for knowledge acquisition. Second, they are an area of children's life that can be directly affected by policy and influences outside of the family. Hence, as a society, we have more opportunities to support children's learning in the classroom than, for example, in the home. Finally, there is increasingly rigorous research on classroom learning environments that can help us understand why and how children learn in some classrooms but not others.

In this chapter, we focus first on the skill of reading and then on the acquisition of academic knowledge. We argue that the skill of reading is critical to the acquisition of knowledge because children increasingly rely on text and other media as sources of knowledge as they progress through school (Shanahan & Shanahan, 2008). Classroom environments that support the acquisition of basic reading and comprehension skills are therefore important to consider. We then discuss some preliminary findings on the acquisition of content area knowledge, specifically science.

The Classroom Environment as an Important Source of Influence on Children's Knowledge Development

Studies that carefully examine the classroom learning environment have provided important insights into elements that are common among effective classroom learning environments but rare in ineffective classrooms (e.g., National Institute of Child Health and Human Development Early Child Care Research Network [NICHD ECCRN], 2002; Pressley et al., 2001; Taylor, Pearson, Clark, & Walpole, 2000; Wharton-McDonald, Pressley, & Hampston, 1998). When we consider classroom environment, we mean the impact of the teacher and instruction, peers, and the school context more generally. By examining what happens in classrooms and assessing students' learning, we have begun to understand how key elements of the classroom environment influence students' learning.

However, identifying elements of effective learning environments is neither as intuitive nor as straightforward as many policy experts and administrators claim. Indeed, in a recent paper (Strong, Gargani, & Hacifazlioğlu, in press), educational experts correctly identified effective versus ineffective teachers less than half of the time when they observed videotaped classroom instruction of fractions. This percentage is worse than had they just guessed (chance = 50%). In an additional study using a well-regarded metric, the Classroom Assessment Scoring System (CLASS; Pianta, La Paro, & Hamre, 2008), well-trained coders were no better than education professionals. They, too, identified effective teachers no better than chance. Yet identifying the characteristics of effective learning environments would seem to be crucial. A grasp of such characteristics would help to support teachers' efforts to provide effective instruction and to design classroom environments that promote student knowledge acquisition more generally (NICHD ECCRN, 2002).

The influence of peers in the classroom is important to consider as well. Recent studies have shown that classmates' aptitudes may influence students' achievement. Keeping in mind that language skills are the medium of learning (Locke, 1993) and a key predictor of later reading acquisition (Catts & Kamhi, 2004), Justice and colleagues (Justice, Petscher, Schatschneider, & Mashburn, 2011) discovered that preschoolers' language development is influenced by the language skills of their peers. Moreover, this effect was most evident for preschoolers with weaker language skills at the beginning of the preschool year. When they were in classrooms with peers who generally had stronger language skills, these children showed substantial gains in language. When they were in classrooms with peers who had less sophisticated language skills, by contrast, their language skills stagnated. Peer effects are also evident for executive function, a constellation of skills including attention, working memory, and inhibition that are considered key building blocks of learning in the classroom (Connor, Ponitz, et al., 2010; Skibbe, Phillips, Glasney, Brophy-Herb, & Connor, 2012).

Another important source of influence on children's knowledge acquisition in the classroom is socioeconomic status (SES), specifically whether students attend schools that serve a high proportion of students from lower-SES families (Brooks-Gunn, Duncan, Klebanov, & Sealand, 1993; McLoyd, 1998). Children living in higher-poverty families are less likely to arrive at school ready to learn (Morrison, et al., 2005), frequently have smaller vocabularies (Hart & Risley, 1995; Snow, 2001), and, with some notable exceptions, fail to catch up with their more affluent peers (Brooks-Gunn & Duncan, 1997). They also tend to attend lower-quality preschools and have less qualified teachers once they start formal schooling (Connor, Jakobsons, Crowe, & Meadows, 2009). Although there is some evidence that their rate of learning does not significantly differ from peers attending more affluent schools (Alexander & Entwisle, 1988), over the summer, children living in poverty learn substantially less than their more affluent peers (Entwisle, Alexander, & Olson, 1997), thus perpetuating the gap. Even children who begin school well above average in achievement are only 50% as likely to maintain this advantage if they attend a higher-poverty school (Neal & Schanzenbach, 2010).

Acquisition of Reading Skills and Reading to Learn

Reading is a key tool in the acquisition of knowledge. Children who fail to gain proficient reading skills are more likely to be retained a grade, to drop out of school, to be referred to special education, and to be underemployed throughout their lifetime (Reynolds, Temple, Robertson, & Mann, 2002). In general, children who fail to gain strong basic reading skills by the beginning of third grade are unlikely to catch up with their peers (Spira, Bracken, & Fischel, 2005).

An emerging concern about reading skills is the clear genetic influence on individual differences observed among children (Olson, 2008), with the companion hypothesis that classroom learning environment can have little influence on reading skill over and above heredity (Byrne et al., 2010). New twin research shows that effective teaching does matter, over and above genetic influences, and that there are gene × environment interactions. Taylor, Roehrig, Connor, and Schatschneider (2010) found that genetic influences were much stronger for students with effective teachers compared to students with ineffective teachers, suggesting that the latter failed to reach their genetic potential. As the authors conclude, "Putting high-quality teachers in the classroom will not eliminate variability among students nor guarantee equally high achievement from all children, but ignoring [effective teaching] as a salient contributor to the classroom environment represents a missed opportunity to promote children's potential in school and their success in life" (Taylor et al., 2010, p. 514).

Although research has identified instructional methods to improve students' decoding and word reading skills (NICHD, 2000), there is less evidence on ways to improve students' literacy when using a "reading to learn" definition of proficient reading (Chall, 1967) or when reading and content-area instruction are intertwined (Snow, 2001). Content-area literacy has been defined as students' ability to read, write, create, and interpret across various types of media (e.g., print, computer, spoken) in various content areas such as language arts, science, social studies, and mathematics (Readence, Bean, & Baldwin, 2004; Swafford & Kallus, 2002). It also includes reading and understanding expository or informational text (Duke & Bennett-Armistead, 2003; Moss, 2005). Content-area literacy implicitly assumes that students have attained the level of reading and writing skill required to understand and express themselves in particular subject areas (Readence et al., 2004). Particularly promising contexts for developing proficient reading skills are science and social studies (Guthrie et al., 2004; Morrow, Pressley, Smith, & Smith, 1997; Williams et al., 2005; Williams, Stafford, Lauer, Hall, & Pollini, 2009).

Although much of the content-area research has focused on upper elementary students (e.g., fourth and fifth grade), research suggests that beginning to encourage literacy development in the rich context of the content areas might also support beginning readers as early as second grade (Williams et al., 2005). Such focus is warranted, especially given the National Academy of Sciences's call for "vastly" increased efforts in K–12 science education to prevent the United States from falling behind in the global economy (National Academy of Sciences, 2006), as well as the adoption of the new Common Core Standards (*www.corestandards. org*). Moreover, academic knowledge (specifically) and background knowledge (more generally) contribute in important ways to students' reading for understanding (Cromley & Azevedo, 2007; Rapp, van den Broek, McMaster, Kendeou, & Espin, 2007). Emerging evidence suggests that the association is reciprocal: skilled reading allows learning from text, and this greater knowledge, in turn, supports more proficient reading.

Overview of Our Research

In our research, we have focused principally on literacy instruction and, more recently, on the content area of science. Understanding how teachers help students learn to read and gain content knowledge is important because fully 60% of U.S. students fail to read proficiently by fourth grade, and this percentage is even higher in schools serving children who live in poverty (National Assessment of Educational Progress [NAEP], 2007). This has serious implications for their emerging ability to learn from text.

Our model of the learning environment resembles a crystal (Connor, Morrison, et al., 2009). The model begins with the understanding that children bring many individual characteristics and skills with them. For example, children differ in the language and learning environment they experience at home (Connor, Son, Hindman, & Morrison, 2005; Hart & Risley, 1995; Huttenlocher, Vasilyeva, Cymerman, & Levine, 2002), which influences their language and literacy skill development. Children also differ in their self-regulation, including their ability to pay attention, change tasks, and follow rules, as well as their ability to interact with peers (Blair, 2002; Hamre & Pianta, 2005; McClelland et al., 2007). These differences appear to influence their interactions with their teacher and peers, as well as their learning in the classroom. The composition of the classroom also differs with regard to the academic and self-regulatory skills of students' classmates.

We consider the foundational dimensions of the classroom environment to be necessary but not sufficient to support knowledge acquisition (see also Cohen, Raudenbush, & Ball, 2003). Foundational dimensions include well-researched constructs such as teacher warmth and responsiveness to students, classroom management and organization, discipline, and the social and emotional climate of the classroom (Connor et al., 2005; Hamre & Pianta, 2005; NICHD ECCRN, 2002). There are also characteristics that teachers bring to the classroom; for example, teachers' knowledge of the subject area (Moats, 1994; Piasta, Connor, Fishman, & Morrison, 2009) and other qualifications, including credentials and experiences (Darling-Hammond, 1999; Goldhaber & Anthony, 2003). Teachers' facility with interpreting assessment results for each student to inform instruction also appears to be an important foundational teacher characteristic (Connor, Morrison, Fishman, & Schatschneider, 2011). All of these are considered foundational skills in this model because they appear to contribute to student outcomes, although indirectly. Teachers who more automatically use their knowledge of the content area, of the curriculum or instructional regime, and of their students' skills and instructional needs (i.e., strong foundational characteristics), for example, should be able to interact with students in learning activities more responsively and flexibly, which in turn contributes to stronger student learning.

Moving up the model, the dimensions of instruction include the *content* of the activity, including academic area (e.g., literacy, science, mathematics) and their components (e.g., for literacy, encoding, decoding, comprehension); *management,* or who is focusing the child's attention on the learning activity at hand, including teacher, teacher/child, peer, and child self-managed; the *context* of the instruction (e.g., whole class, larger group, small group, individual); and the *duration* of these activities. Operating simultaneously, these dimensions define specific instructional activities. Consider, for example, a teacher working with a small group of students reading and discussing a science text and helping children understand the concepts. This would be considered a teacher/child–managed small-group science-text reading activity that includes encoding and discussion—or, more simply, a meaning-focused science activity. Another dimension we consider is whether the activity is explicitly or implicitly focused on a particular target outcome. For example, the described activity is explicitly focused on helping children extract and construct meaning from the science text and implicitly or indirectly on decoding. Using these and other dimensions of instruction, we can describe the complexities and dynamic nature of instruction and yet still be able to use the variables in analytic models, such as hierarchical linear modeling.

According to our model, the multiple dimensions of the classroom environment may operate globally at the classroom level or more specifically at the individual child level. For example, a teacher might be generally warm and responsive to his or her students (a global classroom characteristic) but, at the same time, interact differently with certain students, such as students with special needs. Instruction can be conducted at the classroom level (e.g., whole-class instruction) or at the individual student level (e.g., small-group instruction). Understanding the multiple dimensions of instruction reveals important elements of effective teaching more successfully than focusing solely on the more foundational dimensions of instruction. At the same time, we have found that these levels influence each other. For example, third-grade reading comprehension instruction provided by teachers who were judged to be more warm and responsive led to stronger student reading achievement than did the same amount of instruction provided by teachers who were judged to be less warm and responsive (Connor, 2011a).

Child Characteristic × Instruction Interactions and the Classroom Environment

Increasingly, research is revealing that the effect of particular instructional strategies on students' literacy outcomes depends on the oral language and literacy skills they bring to the classroom. Although the idea of child characteristic × instruction interactions is not new (Cronbach & Snow, 1969), more recent empirical evidence has focused principally on literacy outcomes (Connor, 2011b). As we discuss in this section, child × instruction interactions have been identified reliably from kindergarten through third grade, across samples, and by many researchers (e.g., Foorman, Francis, Fletcher, Schatschneider, & Mehta, 1998; Juel & Minden-Cupp, 2000).

Literacy Skills

Understanding the classroom environment has been critical to identifying child × instruction interactions. Our research reveals that children who share the same classroom participate in very different learning activities that systematically predict their literacy skill gains (Connor, Morrison, & Slominski, 2006; Connor, Piasta, et al., 2009). For example, one child might be writing on a computer while another is reading a book in the library corner with a peer. Using third grade as an example, Figure 13.1 shows the amount of teacher/child–managed small-group meaning-focused (TCMMFSG) instruction for approximately 397 students. The mean amount provided was 9 minutes/day ($SD = 9$) and ranged from 0 to 42 minutes/day. Figure 13.1 reveals the substantial variability between students, even within classrooms. When we examine one particular classroom, we find that the amount of instruction varies for each child during the literacy block (Figure 13.2). In this figure, the solid black bars represent the amount of TCMMFSG observed for the target children in this classroom. Note how the number of minutes provided varies across children who share this classroom, from less than 10 minutes to more than 20 minutes.

The gray bars in Figure 13.2 represent the estimated amount of time each child would require per day to reach grade level (or attain a year's worth of reading skill growth) by the end of third grade. These estimates were computed using Assessment-to-Instruction (A2i) software (Connor, Morrison, & Petrella, 2004; Connor, Piasta, et al., 2009). Child J,

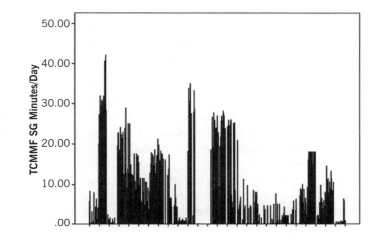

FIGURE 13.1. The mean amount of teacher/child–managed meaning-focused instruction provided in small-group contexts (TCMMFSG) in minutes/day during the 90-minute literacy block. Each bar represents the amount received by one student; students are clustered within classrooms.

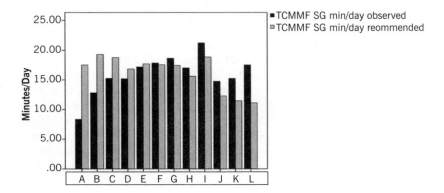

FIGURE 13.2. Comparing observed amounts (minutes/day) of teacher/child–managed meaning-focused instruction in small groups (TCMMFSG) actually observed (black bars) with amounts recommended by the assessment-to-instruction software (gray bars). The difference in the height of the bars is the distance from recommendation (DFR), which predicts third graders' reading comprehension gains.

for example, had strong reading comprehension skills at the beginning of third grade, so the software recommended relatively less time in TCM-MFSG activities. In contrast, Child B and Child I had skills well below grade expectations, so the software recommended substantial amounts of time in TCMMFSG instruction. By comparing the gray and black bars in Figure 13.2, we see that Child J and Child I received instruction that was fairly close to the recommended amount, whereas Child B received less than the recommended amount. The difference between the observed and recommended amounts is the *distance from recommendation* (DFR).

Across studies and grades, students' DFR strongly predicted their end-of-year literacy outcomes, whereas the total amount of instruction they received did not (Connor, Morrison, Fishman, & Schatschneider, 2011; Connor, Morrison, Fishman, Schatschneider, & Underwood, 2007; Connor, Morrison, Schatschneider, et al., in press). Students who received instruction closer to the recommended amounts made significantly greater gains in reading than did students who received instruction that was further from the recommended amounts. Importantly, children in Individualizing Student Instruction (ISI) intervention classrooms were significantly more likely to have smaller DFRs than were children in control classrooms (Connor, Morrison, Fishman, Giuliani, et al., 2011; Connor, Morrison, Schatschneider, et al., in press; Connor, Piasta, et al., 2009). This finding, coupled with significant treatment effects for ISI interventions in kindergarten, first, and third grade (Al Otaiba et al., in press; Connor, Morrison, Fishman, Giuliani, et al., 2011; Connor, et al., 2007; Connor, Morrison, Schatschneider, et al., in press), provide strong evidence that child × instruction interactions are causally implicated in the substantial variation in children's literacy learning observed both between and within classrooms.

Emerging evidence suggests that the effect of the ISI intervention is cumulative. Students who participated in individualized instruction in first, second, and third grade made significantly greater gains in reading comprehension than did students who participated in ISI in only first or first and second grade (Connor, Schatschneider, et al., 2011). These findings suggest that consistently effective instruction is required to truly support students' attainment of proficient literacy skills with implications for their knowledge acquisition.

Content-Area Knowledge

We have also begun to ask whether child × instruction interactions might also influence knowledge acquisition in specific content areas. A recently completed longitudinal study provides correlational evidence of child × instruction interactions that affect students' acquisition of academic knowledge as a result of science instruction (Connor, Rice, et al., in press). In this study, we followed second graders into third grade, assessing their vocabulary, reading, and academic knowledge in the fall and spring of each year. We also observed and characterized the science instruction they received in the fall, winter, and spring. In general, learning opportunities during science instruction appeared to support students' content-area knowledge (including science knowledge) acquisition, vocabulary growth, and reading comprehension—and may also support an instructional focus on developing proficient reading skills more generally. Moreover, there were child × instruction interactions: the effect of certain types of science instruction on students' literacy gains generally depended on students' initial reading, vocabulary, and content-area knowledge.

Hands-on and other science activities, including writing activities, in which students are involved in making sense of phenomena, are often considered an important part of high-quality science education (Duschl, Schweingruber, & Shouse, 2007). The assumption is that hands-on and exploration activities should be more strongly associated with greater science knowledge gains than with the other types of science instruction. However, previous research has not considered child × instruction interactions. When we did so, we found that the benefits of hands-on science activities depended on students' fall content-area knowledge in both second and third grade (Connor, Rice, et al., in press). Students with strong fall content knowledge who were in classrooms where they conducted their own experiments and worked with peers generally showed greater gains in content knowledge than did students in classroom where less time in such activities was observed. However, this was the case *only* for students with stronger fall content knowledge scores. Students with weaker fall content knowledge made weaker gains. But when such activities were teacher/child managed, students with weaker fall skills made important gains in content knowledge, vocabulary, and reading.

This observed child × instruction interaction has particularly important implications for students who attend schools in higher-poverty neighborhoods. Children with weaker fall vocabulary and content-area knowledge scores were more likely to have parents with less education (i.e., lower SES) and home literacy environments that were generally less supportive of literacy development (Griffin & Morrison, 1997). Thus providing students who have weaker vocabulary and content knowledge with relatively more time in student- and peer-managed science activities than in teacher-scaffolded science activities might limit their learning gains. This could then, potentially, contribute to well-documented achievement gaps (Jencks & Phillips, 1998).

Taken together, these results suggest that a "one-size-fits-all" approach to science instruction and content-area instruction more generally will not be effective for all students. Given the historical centrality of activity-based instructional approaches to science education, experimental research investigating the influence of these kinds of activities on students' science and literacy learning, and potential child × instruction interactions, would be informative (see also Marx & Harris, 2006). Moreover, our research suggests that designing effective content-area instruction may be more dynamic and less intuitive than current science education research indicates (e.g., National Science Board, 2007). At the same time, however, our results illustrate the promise of content-area instruction as a strategy to promote children's development of proficient literacy skills, including reading to learn (Chall, 1967) and reading for understanding (Snow, 2001), which in turn may promote further knowledge acquisition.

Based on these results, we have begun to develop and test content-area literacy instruction (CALI) designed to explicitly consider child × instruction interactions in science (Connor, Kaya, et al., 2010) and, more recently, in social studies. Using the well-regarded 5-E Learning Cycle (engage, explore, explain, elaborate, evaluate; Bybee, 1997) as the foundation, we individualized lessons in three ways. First, we used *strategic flexible grouping* of students at three levels (weaker readers, typical readers, and stronger readers) based on their reading comprehension and oral reading fluency. Children could thus work well together, yet the groups were heterogeneous with regard to science topic knowledge. The total number of groups was determined by the teacher, with a maximum of six groups, which teachers agreed helped them effectively facilitate and manage the groups. Leveling of groups by reading skills allowed teachers to provide extra support, scaffolding, and attention to children who were less independent. This helped foster greater independence while ensuring that children learned critical science knowledge and literacy skills.

Second, we individualized reading materials by using leveled texts, mostly from the *Seeds of Science/Roots of Reading* curriculum (Lawrence Hall of Science, 2007), which provides well-written and coherent texts. In some instances, however, we also wrote or adapted text so that children reading below a second-grade level could still read independently. Third, each student had a Scientist's Notebook (Palincsar & Magnusson, 2001). This was a loose-leaf binder in which students collected and organized observation records, lab worksheets, resource materials, and other handouts. The notebook became a reference to give students ready access to information they had accumulated from their observations, readings, and discussions. The lab worksheets were adapted for each of the three reading levels. For example, while a lab sheet for each group asked the same questions—"Why do you think earthworms help soil?" and "What have you observed or learned about your earthworms?"— the amount of scaffolding varied depending on the reading level of the group, with more scaffolding provided to groups that required it.

A key part of the intervention was to explicitly teach students how to read expository text, which can be difficult for many students (Williams et al., 2009). Strategies included attending to headings and highlighted words, using tables of contents, reading charts and graphs, and writing procedural text. We also used several well-established comprehension strategies (NICHD, 2000) to enhance discussion and to encourage greater student participation, including "think–pair–share" and brainstorming. During think–pair–share (Lyman, 1992), children were asked a probing question, asked to think about it, and then discussed it with a partner or small group. Once children had time for discussion, students were asked to share answers with the larger group. During brainstorming, children were encouraged to share and write down ideas (Rawlinson, 1981). In addition, teachers provided explicit decoding instruction, such as how to spell multisyllabic words. For example, if children asked how to spell a word such as *earthworm,* the teacher discussed that it was a compound word composed of two simpler words along with strategies about how to sound out and spell the word.

Lessons lasted 30 to 40 minutes for 3 to 4 consecutive days, and each unit was 3 to 4 weeks long. Based on feedback from our teachers, this was a reasonable amount of time to dedicate to science, given the other curricular demands on class time. The 5-E Learning Cycle lent itself well to integrating text and using peer instruction in small groups. Perhaps the most challenging aspect of developing the units was finding science expository texts that were appropriate for the wide range of literacy skills our second graders displayed. Unfortunately, many of the books provided by the science core curriculum were not well written, were not coherent (e.g., did not use *because* or other words that help children make connections), and did not cover content in sufficient depth. We successfully used the texts in the Seeds of Science/Roots of Reading curriculum (Lawrence Hall of Science, 2007), but had to adapt the text to meet the needs of some of the children with weaker reading skills.

Our results indicated that we were able to successfully develop and implement a second-grade science curriculum that supported students' literacy and science knowledge acquisition. Moreover, students who began the unit with weak science and literacy skills made gains in science content learning that were as great as students who began the unit with stronger skills. This was the case even though the school served many children living in poverty. Plus, teachers were able to implement the science curriculum effectively as designed and, indeed, contributed important ideas and extensions so that the intervention was more feasibly implemented in the classroom. Although encouraging, randomized controlled field trials are still needed to establish whether child × instruction interactions are causally implicated with regard to effective content-area knowledge acquisition.

Although some early elementary teachers may hesitate to teach science because they do not feel qualified or because they feel that reading and math take priority (Marx & Harris, 2006), teachers and schools are becoming increasingly accountable for their students' content-area learning. As our previous research on reading development shows, children, especially at higher-poverty schools, seem to be developing stronger decoding skills than comprehension skills. As children move from learning to read to reading to learn (Chall, 1967), explicitly integrating the use of text and comprehension strategies when learning science content offers a promising approach to support children's comprehension and science knowledge acquisition.

Implications and Future Directions

Over the past decade, our research has focused on how children learn. We have consistently found that the impact of instruction depends on the language, literacy, knowledge, self-regulation, and even genes children bring to the classroom. This has a number of important implications for knowledge acquisition, how we teach children, and how we define effective teachers and classroom learning environments. One size does not fit all when it comes to effective instruction. Effective reading or content-area instructional strategies for one student are possibly ineffective for his or her classmate with a different profile of skills and aptitudes. Hence, reliable and valid assessment of key skills is crucial to inform instruction. Most recently, we have identified children's academic knowledge as an important moderator of instructional efficacy. Thus, as we consider children's knowledge acquisition, we recognize that children bring varying amounts of academic and background knowledge to the classroom learning environment. This has direct implications for their own reading comprehension and future knowledge acquisition, their classmates' learning, and for the types of instruction that will be effective for them.

Perhaps one of the reasons many reading researchers do not include instruction in their models of reading is that considering the contexts in which children acquire literacy skills and knowledge is a complex undertaking. Important theories that do not consider instruction include the Simple View (Hoover & Gough, 1990), the Landscape Model (Rapp, et al., 2007), and others (e.g., Cromley & Azevedo, 2007; Perfetti, Landi, & Oakhill, 2005). These theories have been important in identifying component skills and how those components work together to support proficient reading. By considering only the "typical" child and not the learning environment in which children acquire these component skills, however, we fail to elucidate the mechanisms by which children learn new knowledge in general and learn to read more specifically. Hence, our work has focused on developing models that recognize multiple pathways to knowledge acquisition (NICHD ECCRN, 2004), which incorporate the dynamic and complex nature of the classroom learning environment, and that can be tested empirically.

Figure 13.3 provides a model of our most current thinking. Following Bronfenbrenner's bioecological model (Bronfenbrenner & Morris, 2006), we propose there are multiple sources of influence on children's

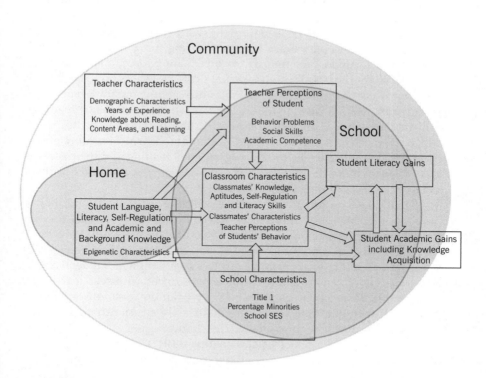

FIGURE 13.3. A model of reading and knowledge acquisition that includes instruction as well as home, school, and community contexts.

learning. In Figure 13.3, we focus on the most proximal: home, school, and community. Home includes the influence of parenting, SES, genetics, and other influences (e.g., nutrition, chronic illness) on children's development. We define community broadly to include the city or town and general attitudes toward education through policy and resource allocation. The school district and how it operates are also considered part of the community. Hence the teachers' qualifications, including teaching skill and knowledge are, at least in part, influenced by community and district hiring decisions, whereas teachers' perceptions of their students are influenced by both community and school beliefs and attitudes. School includes the more general school climate, quality of leadership, and resources, as well as the specific classroom environment.

Community, school, home, student, and classroom variables that can be observed and measured are in boxes. The arrows show hypothesized associations among them. Home, school, and community domains influence these associations, and, in turn, what happens in the boxes influences the oval spheres of influence. For example, a new principal might take over a school that systematically fails to teach its students to read proficiently. The principal might work with the superintendent of the district and community leaders to bring more resources to the school, to gain support for improving the teaching force, and to initiate critical building repairs. The more highly skilled teachers hired could, in turn, improve students' reading outcomes by reaching out to parents and providing more effective individualized instruction. As students' reading improves, the school, district, community, and parents might begin to change their attitudes about students' potential to learn. This more positive influence could then help improve students' reading and their access to knowledge. Note that although the classroom is at the heart of this model, all aspects of the model are important.

The model also portrays potential and tested mediators and moderators, suggesting reciprocal effects for the dynamics of the classroom. In addition to improving our understanding of the role of oral language skills in literacy and knowledge acquisition, emerging evidence suggests that children's self-regulation and executive functioning are crucial aptitudes that interact with the learning environment to affect learning. When and to what extent these executive regulatory functions are malleable is an open question. It may be that it will be easier to change the learning environment than to change the child.

Research on the impact of classmates' skills and aptitudes is also warranted but has gone largely uninvestigated. Peer effects may also have important policy and social implications. As Justice et al. (2011) observe, the segregation of preschoolers who live in low-SES families into programs designed to help them, such as Head Start, may actually undermine their ability to attain their maximum potential. Reciprocal effects are difficult to evaluate because they require longitudinal data, sophisticated analytic strategies, and strong theoretical foundations. Nevertheless, research on how moderators become mediators of learning is needed. Although there is accumulating evidence that children's academic and world knowledge directly influence their reading comprehension (Cromley & Azevedo, 2007; NICHD, 2000) and particular types of instructional strategies affect their learning (Connor, Rice, et al., in press), it is less clear how proficient reading for understanding improves academic knowledge, the level of reading proficiency required to learn from text, and what kinds of knowledge matter.

Finally, new methods and theories about gene × environment interactions are highly relevant for understanding children's knowledge acquisition in the home and classroom. For example, emerging evidence suggests that the rate at which infants process speech at the word, morpheme, and phoneme level predicts their oral language development and is affected by parent's language interactions (Hurtado, Marchman, & Fernald, 2008). However, there is compelling evidence that language is highly heritable (Stromswold, 2001) and that rate of language processing is at least in part an epigenetic phenomenon. Is it possible that gene × home environment interactions are at least partially responsible for the high variability among children's language skills? If so, this has implications for the classroom learning environment because children's language skills consistently interact with instructional strategies to affect their learning.

In this chapter, we have argued that the processes by which children acquire knowledge in the classroom are dynamic and complex, and are the result of multiple sources of influence. This means that there is no silver bullet or single way to ensure that children acquire the knowledge they will need in our global technology-based society. Home and community are important sources of influence on children's learning both directly and indirectly. Schools and classrooms are the traditional settings for knowledge acquisition and represent a central opportunity to make a difference in children's lives. By tailoring the classroom environment to optimize knowledge acquisition, taking into account child characteristics × environment interactions, we may be able to improve every child's opportunities to learn and allow them to reach their potential.

REFERENCES

Al Otaiba, S., Connor, C. M., Folsom, J. S., Greulich, L., Meadows, J., & Li, Z. (in press). Assessment data-informed guidance to individualize kindergarten reading instruction: Findings from a cluster-randomized control field trial. *The Elementary School Journal.*

Alexander, K. L., & Entwisle, D. R. (1988). Achievement in the first 2 years of school: Patterns and processes. *Monographs of the Society for Research in Child Development, 53*(2), 1–57.

Blair, C. (2002). School readiness: Integrating cognition and emotion in a neurobiological conceptualization of children's functioning at school entry. *American Psychologist, 57*(2), 111–127.

Bronfenbrenner, U., & Morris, P. A. (2006). The bioecological model of human development. In R. M. Lerner & W. Damon (Eds.), *Handbook of child psychology: Theoretical models of human development* (6th ed., Vol. 1, pp. 793–828). Hoboken, NJ: Wiley.

Brooks-Gunn, J., & Duncan, G. J. (1997). The effects of poverty on children. *The Future of Children: Children and Poverty, 7*(2), 55–71.

Brooks-Gunn, J., Duncan, G. J., Klebanov, P. K., & Sealand, N. (1993). Do neighborhoods influence child and adolescent development? *American Journal of Sociology, 99*(2), 353–395.

Bybee, R. W. (1997). *Achieving science literacy: From purposes to practice.* Portsmouth, NH: Heinemann.

Byrne, B., Coventry, W., Olson, R. K., Wadsworth, S., Samuelsson, S., & Petrill, S. A. (2010). "Teacher effects" in early literacy development: Evidence from a study of twins. *Journal of Educational Psychology, 102*(1), 32–42.

Catts, H., & Kamhi, A. G. (Eds.). (2004). *Language basis of reading disabilities* (2nd ed.). Needham Heights, MA: Allyn & Bacon.

Chall, J. S. (1967). *Learning to read: The great debate.* New York: McGraw-Hill.

Cohen, D. K., Raudenbush, S. W., & Ball, D. L. (2003). Resources, instruction, and research. *Educational Evaluation and Policy Analysis, 25*(2), 119–142.

Connor, C. M. (2011a, February). *Building third graders' reading comprehension and vocabulary: Considering the quality and amounts of third grade literacy instruction.* Paper presented at the 18th annual Pacific Coast Research Conference, San Diego, CA.

Connor, C. M. (2011b). Child by instruction interactions: Language and literacy connections. In S. B. Neuman & D. K. Dickinson (Eds.), *Handbook on early literacy* (3rd ed., pp. 256–275). New York: Guilford Press.

Connor, C. M., Jakobsons, L. J., Crowe, E., & Meadows, J. (2009). Instruction, differentiation, and student engagement in Reading First classrooms. *The Elementary School Journal, 109*(3), 221–250.

Connor, C. M., Kaya, S., Luck, M., Toste, J., Canto, A., Rice, D. C., et al. (2010). Content-area literacy: Individualizing student instruction in second grade science. *The Reading Teacher, 63*(6), 474–485.

Connor, C. M., Morrison, F. J., Fishman, B., Giuliani, S., Luck, M., Underwood, P., et al. (2011). Classroom instruction, child × instruction interactions and the impact of differentiating student instruction on third graders' reading comprehension. *Reading Research Quarterly, 46*(3), 189–221.

Connor, C. M., Morrison, F. J., Fishman, B., Ponitz, C. C., Glasney, S.,

Underwood, P., et al. (2009). The ISI classroom observation system: Examining the literacy instruction provided to individual students. *Educational Researcher, 38*(2), 85–99.

Connor, C. M., Morrison, F. J., Fishman, B., & Schatschneider, C. (2012). Assessment and instruction connections: The implications of child × instruction interactions effects on student learning. In J. Sabatini & E. R. Albro (Eds.), *Assessing reading in the 21st century: Aligning and applying advances in the reading and measurement sciences.* Lanham, MD: R& L Education.

Connor, C. M., Morrison, F. J., Fishman, B. J., Schatschneider, C., & Underwood, P. (2007). THE EARLY YEARS: Algorithm-guided individualized reading instruction. *Science, 315*(5811), 464–465.

Connor, C. M., Morrison, F. J., & Petrella, J. N. (2004). Effective reading comprehension instruction: Examining child by instruction interactions. *Journal of Educational Psychology, 96*(4), 682–698.

Connor, C. M., Morrison, F. J., Schatschneider, C., Toste, J., Lundblom, E. G., Crowe, E., et al. (2011). Effective classroom instruction: Implications of child characteristic by instruction interactions on first graders' word reading achievement. *Journal for Research on Educational Effectiveness, 4*(3), 173–207.

Connor, C. M., Morrison, F. J., & Slominski, L. (2006). Preschool instruction and children's literacy skill growth. *Journal of Educational Psychology, 98*(4), 665–689.

Connor, C. M., Piasta, S. B., Fishman, B., Glasney, S., Schatschneider, C., Crowe, E., et al. (2009). Individualizing student instruction precisely: Effects of child by instruction interactions on first graders' literacy development. *Child Development, 80*(1), 77–100.

Connor, C. M., Ponitz, C. E. C., Phillips, B., Travis, Q. M., Day, S. G., & Morrison, F. J. (2010). First graders' literacy and self-regulation gains: The effect of individualizing instruction. *Journal of School Psychology, 48*(5), 433–455.

Connor, C. M., Rice, D. C., Canto, A., Southerland, S. A., Underwood, P., Kaya, S., et al. (in press). Child characteristics by science instruction interactions in second and third grade and their relation to students' content-area knowledge, vocabulary, and reading skill gains. *The Elementary School Journal.*

Connor, C. M., Schatschneider, C., Underwood, P., Dombek, J., Crowe, E. C., Fishman, B., et al. (2011). *Cumulative effects of first, second, and third grade Individualized Student Instruction (ISI) in reading.* Manuscript submitted.

Connor, C. M., Son, S.-H., Hindman, A. H., & Morrison, F. J. (2005). Teacher qualifications, classroom practices, family characteristics, and preschool experience: Complex effects on first graders' vocabulary and early reading outcomes. *Journal of School Psychology, 43*(4), 343–375.

Cromley, J. G., & Azevedo, R. (2007). Testing and refining the direct and inferential mediation (DIME) model of reading comprehension. *Journal of Educational Psychology, 99*(2), 311–325.

Cronbach, L. J., & Snow, R. E. (1969). *Individual differences in learning ability as a function of instructional variables.* Stanford, CA: Stanford University Press.

Darling-Hammond, L. (1999). *Teacher quality and student achievement: A review of state policy evidence.* Seattle, WA: Center for Teaching and Policy, University of Washington.

Duke, N. K., & Bennett-Armistead, V. S. (2003). *Reading and writing informational text in the primary grades.* New York: Scholastic Teaching Resources.

Duschl, R. A., Schweingruber, H. A., & Shouse, A. W. (Eds.). (2007). *Taking science to school: Learning and teaching science in grades K–8.* Washington, DC: National Academies Press.

Entwisle, D. R., Alexander, K. L., & Olson, L. S. (1997). *Children, schools, and inequality.* Boulder, CO: Westview Press.

Foorman, B. R., Francis, D. J., Fletcher, J. M., Schatschneider, C., & Mehta, P. (1998). The role of instruction in learning to read: Preventing reading failure in at-risk children. *Journal of Educational Psychology, 90*(1), 37–55.

Goldhaber, D., & Anthony, E. (2003). *Teacher quality and student achievement* (Urban Diversity Series No. UDS-115). New York: Department of Education.

Griffin, E. A., & Morrison, F. J. (1997). The unique contribution of home literacy environment to differences in early literacy skills. *Early Child Development and Care, 127–128,* 233–243.

Guthrie, J. T., Wigfield, A., Barbosa, P., Perencevich, K. C., Taboada, A., Davis, M. H., et al. (2004). Increasing reading comprehension and engagement through concept-oriented reading instruction. *Journal of Educational Psychology, 94*(3), 403–423.

Hamre, B. K., & Pianta, R. C. (2005). Can instructional and emotional support in the first-grade classroom make a difference for children at risk of school failure? *Child Development, 76*(5), 949–967.

Hart, B., & Risley, T. R. (1995). *Meaningful differences in the everyday experience of young American children.* Baltimore: Brookes.

Hoover, W. A., & Gough, P. B. (1990). The simple view of reading. *Reading and Writing, 2*(2), 127–160.

Hurtado, N., Marchman, V. A., & Fernald, A. (2008). Does input influence uptake? Links between maternal talk, processing speed, and vocabulary size in Spanish-learning children. *Developmental Science, 11*(6), 31–39.

Huttenlocher, J., Vasilyeva, M., Cymerman, E., & Levine, S. (2002). Language input and syntax. *Cognitive Psychology, 45*(3), 337–374.

Jencks, C., & Phillips, M. (1998). *The Black–White test score gap.* Washington, DC: Brookings Institute.

Juel, C., & Minden-Cupp, C. (2000). Learning to read words: Linguistic units and instructional strategies. *Reading Research Quarterly, 35*(4), 458–492.

Justice, L. M., Petscher, Y., Schatschneider, C., & Mashburn, A. (2011). Peer effects in preschool classrooms: Is children's language growth associated with their classmates' skills? *Child Development, 82*(6), 1768–1777.

Lawrence Hall of Science. (2007). *Seeds of science/roots of reading.* Nashua, NH: Delta Education, LLC, and Regents of the University of California.

Locke, J. L. (1993). *The child's path to spoken language.* Cambridge, MA: Harvard University Press.

Lyman, F. (1992). Think–pair–share, thinktrix, thinklinks, and weird facts: An interactive system for cooperative thinking. In N. Davidson & T. Worsham (Eds.), *Enhancing thinking through cooperative learning* (pp. 169–181). New York: Teacher's College Press.

Marx, R. W., & Harris, C. J. (2006). No child left behind and science education: Opportunities, challenges, and risks. *The Elementary School Journal, 106*(5), 476–477.

McClelland, M. M., Cameron, C. E., Connor, C. M., Farris, C. L., Jewkes, A. M., & Morrison, F. J. (2007). Links between behavioral regulation and preschoolers' literacy, vocabulary, and math skills. *Developmental Psychology, 43*(4), 947–959.

McLoyd, V. C. (1998). Socioeconomic disadvantage and child development. *American Psychologist, 53*(2), 185–204.

Moats, L. C. (1994). The missing foundation in teacher education: Knowledge of the structure of spoken and written language. *Annals of Dyslexia, 44*(1), 81–102.

Morrison, F. J., Bachman, H. J., & Connor, C. M. (2005). *Improving literacy in America: Guidelines from research.* New Haven, CT: Yale University Press.

Morrow, L. M., Pressley, M., Smith, J. K., & Smith, M. (1997). The effect of a literacy-based program integrated into literacy and science instruction with children from diverse backgrounds. *Reading Research Quarterly, 32*(1), 54–76.

Moss, B. (2005). Making a case and a place for effective content-area literacy instruction in the elementary grades. *The Reading Teacher, 59*(1), 46–55.

National Academy of Sciences. (2006). *Rising above the gathering storm: Energizing and employing America for a brighter economic future.* Washington, DC: Author.

National Assessment of Educational Progress. (2011). *The nation's report card.* Retrieved January 31, 2012, from *http://nces.ed.gov/nationsreportcard/pubs/main2011/2012457.asp.*

National Institute of Child Health and Human Development. (2000). *Teaching children to read: An evidence-based assessment of the scientific research literature on reading and its implications for reading instruction.* Washington, DC: U.S. Department of Health and Human Services.

National Institute of Child Health and Human Development Early Child Care Research Network. (2002). The relation of global first grade classroom environment to structural classroom features and teacher and student behaviors. *The Elementary School Journal, 102*(5), 367–387.

National Institute of Child Health and Human Development Early Child Care Research Network. (2004). Multiple pathways to early academic achievement. *Harvard Educational Review, 74*(1), 1–29.

National Science Board. (2007). *A national action plan for addressing the critical needs of the U.S. science, technology, engineering, and mathematics education system* (NSB/EHR-07-9). Arlington, VA: National Science Foundation.

Neal, D., & Schanzenbach, D. W. (2010). Left behind by design: Proficiency counts and test-based accountability. *Review of Economics and Statistics, 92*(2), 263–283.

Olson, R. K. (2008). Genetic and environmental influences on word-reading skills. In E. L. Grigorenko & A. J. Naples (Eds.), *Single-word reading: Behavioral and biological perspectives. New directions in communication disorders research: Integrative approaches* (pp. 233–253). Mahwah, NJ: Erlbaum.

Palincsar, A. S., & Magnusson, S. J. (2001). The interplay of first-hand and text-based investigations to model and support the development of scientific knowledge and reasoning. In S. Carver & D. Klahr (Eds.), *Cognition and instruction: Twenty-five years of progress* (pp. 151–194). Mahwah, NJ: Erlbaum.

Perfetti, C. A., Landi, N., & Oakhill, J. V. (2005). The acquistion of reading comprehension skill. In M. Snowling & C. Hulme (Eds.), *The science of reading* (pp. 227–247). Oxford, UK: Blackwell.

Pianta, R. C., La Paro, K. M., & Hamre, B. K. (2008). *Classroom Assessment Scoring System (CLASS) manual, K–3.* Baltimore: Brookes.

Piasta, S. B., Connor, C. M., Fishman, B., & Morrison, F. J. (2009). Teachers' knowledge of literacy, classroom practices, and student reading growth. *Scientific Studies of Reading, 13*(3), 224–248.

Pressley, M., Wharton-McDonald, R., Allington, R., Block, C. C., Morrow, L., Tracey, D., et al. (2001). A study of effective first-grade literacy instruction. *Scientific Studies of Reading, 5*(1), 35–58.

Rapp, D. N., van den Broek, P., McMaster, K., Kendeou, P., & Espin, C. A. (2007). Higher-order comprehension processes in struggling readers: A perspective for research and intervention. *Scientific Studies of Reading, 11*(4), 289–312.

Rawlinson, J. G. (1981). *Creative thinking and brainstorming.* New York: Wiley.

Readence, J. E., Bean, T. W., & Baldwin, R. S. (2004). *Content-area literacy: An integrated approach* (8th ed.). Dubuque, IA: Kendall Hunt.

Reynolds, A. J., Temple, J. A., Robertson, D. L., & Mann, E. A. (2002). Age 21 cost–benefit analysis of the Title I Chicago child–parent centers. *Educational Evaluation and Policy Analysis, 24*(4), 267–303.

Shanahan, T., & Shanahan, C. (2008). Teaching disciplinary literacy to adolescents: Rethinking content-area literacy. *Harvard Educational Review, 78*(1), 40–59.

Shonkoff, J. P., & Phillips, D. A. (Eds.). (2000). *From neurons to neighborhoods: The science of early childhood development.* Washington, DC: National Academies Press.

Skibbe, L., Phillips, B. M., Glasney, S., Brophy-Herb, H. E., & Connor, C. M. (2012). Children's early literacy growth in relation to classmates' self-regulation. *Journal of Educational Psychology.*

Snow, C. E. (2001). *Reading for understanding.* Santa Monica, CA: RAND Education and the Science and Technology Policy Institute.

Spira, E. G., Bracken, S. S., & Fischel, J. E. (2005). Predicting improvement after first-grade reading difficulties: The effects of oral language, emergent literacy, and behavior skills. *Developmental Psychology, 41*(1), 225–234.

Stromswold, K. (2001). The heritability of language: A review and metaanalysis of twin, adoption, and linkage studies. *Language, 77*(4), 647–723.

Strong, M., Gargani, J., & Hacifazlioğlu, Ö. (in press). Do we know a successful teacher when we see one? Experiments in the identification of effective teachers. *Journal of Teacher Education.*

Swafford, J., & Kallus, M. (2002). Content literacy: A journey into the past, present, and future. *Journal of Content Area Reading, 1,* 7–18.

Taylor, B. M., Pearson, D. P., Clark, K., & Walpole, S. (2000). Effective schools and accomplished teachers: lessons about primary-grade reading instruction in low-income schools. *The Elementary School Journal, 101*(2), 121–165.

Taylor, J. E., Roehrig, A. D., Connor, C. M., & Schatschneider, C. (2010). Teacher quality moderates the genetic effects on early reading. *Science, 328*(5977), 512–514.

Wharton-McDonald, R., Pressley, M., & Hampston, J. M. (1998). Literacy instruction in nine first-grade classrooms: Teacher characteristics and student achievement. *The Elementary School Journal, 99*(2), 101–128.

Williams, J. P., Hall, K. M., Lauer, K. D., Stafford, B., DeSisto, L. A., & deCani, J. (2005). Expository text comprehension in the primary grade classroom. *Journal of Educational Psychology, 97*(4), 538–550.

Williams, J. P., Stafford, K. B., Lauer, K. D., Hall, K. M., & Pollini, S. (2009). Embedding reading comprehension training in content-area instruction. *Journal of Educational Psychology, 101*(1), 1–20.

CHAPTER 14

■ ■ ■ ■ ■

Building Literacy Skills
through Multimedia

Rebecca Silverman
Sara Hines

Children gain knowledge through a variety of sources, including parents and caregivers, first-hand experience, and books. One source of knowledge that is somewhat controversial is multimedia. Multimedia includes visuals, sounds, and animation delivered through such media as television and video, electronic books, and computer programs and websites. On one hand, opponents of the use of multimedia with young children suggest that "screen time" replaces other activities that are valuable for learning and cognitive development, such as outdoor play, book reading, and pretend play. On the other hand, advocates for the use of multimedia contend that visual, audio, and animation enhancements can support children's comprehension of content, and that interests generated through "screen time" can stimulate children's inquiry and knowledge acquisition in other activities such as playtime and book reading.

Although much more research is needed to fully understand the drawbacks and affordances of multimedia, there is no doubt that children are surrounded by multimedia in their daily lives. Therefore, it is worthwhile for educators to embrace the possibilities of multimedia and seek positive ways of using multimedia to their advantage in delivering content and supporting knowledge building. Accordingly, this chapter reviews research on the use of multimedia to encourage learning in early childhood. The chapter focuses on the areas of emergent literacy, vocabulary, and comprehension. These skills are essential to knowledge-building processes because they provide children with the foundation they need to acquire new information and integrate this new information with their background knowledge. The chapter closes by discussing implications for the use of multimedia in the classroom and suggesting new directions for research on how multimedia can also be used to develop content-area knowledge across the curriculum.

Theoretical Background

There are two primary theories that underlie the view that the use of multimedia can enhance the knowledge building of young children. First, the dual coding theory posed by Paivio (1986) asserts that the human brain processes information through two separate paths. One of these paths processes verbal information (e.g., the words a teacher says as she reads aloud). The other of these paths processes nonverbal information (e.g., the gestures a teacher uses as she reads and the pictures she shows from the book she is reading). In dual coding theory, information that is encoded both verbally and nonverbally is represented more fully in memory than information that has been encoded through one channel alone. The robust mental representation of information created through dual coding will result in greater comprehension and easier recall. The potential of multimedia for supporting learning through the simultaneous verbal and nonverbal presentation of content is, therefore, aligned with dual coding theory.

Second, the theory of synergy by Neuman (1997) supports the use of multimedia in developing children's knowledge base. According to this theory, as children encounter information about specific content through different types of media, they add to their schema (i.e., their organized mental representation) of that content. In other words, upon hearing a story and watching a video on the same content, children may extract slightly different kinds of information that can inform their understanding of that content. For example, when children hear facts from a book about sharks, they may learn that sharks have been on Earth for roughly 400 million years and even existed when dinosaurs roamed the Earth; when they see sharks on a video, they may learn that sharks are sleek and fast and have many rows of teeth with which to attack their prey. Experiencing the content through the two different media like this might support children's understanding more than just hearing the book or watching the video repeatedly. In this way, exposure to content through multiple media may have an additive effect on children's knowledge acquisition.

The commonality between the dual coding theory and the theory of synergy is that both theories suggest that the benefit of multimedia for knowledge acquisition stems from its offer of multiple sources and types of information on the same topic, which enables children to develop a more multidimensional and extensive understanding of the content. Other affordances of multimedia include its potential to focus on salient features of content, to engage students as active participants in knowledge acquisition, to scaffold student learning, and to encourage motivation. Close-up shots in video can call children's attention to a particular object or even a particular aspect of an object being discussed (Salomon, 1981). Computer games, interactive electronic books, and even video in which characters ask the audience to respond all invite children to become actively involved participants (Segers, 2009). Features embedded in electronic storybooks and computer games such as text-to-speech narration, computer assistants (i.e., avatar characters that provide help), and "hotspots" (i.e., areas where users get additional information) can help children acquire content that they might not be able to access on their own (McKenna & Zucker, 2009; Shamir & Korat, 2009). In addition, the use of multimedia can motivate children, particularly children who are at risk for difficulties in reading, to engage with text (Kamil, Intrator, & Kim, 2000; McKenna & Zucker, 2009).

Despite the potential benefits of multimedia to support knowledge building, there are several possible problems that educators should consider before adopting multimedia tools to support learning. For example, there is some evidence that irrelevant (often fun or funny) visual and auditory information may distract children from learning the essential content (de Jong & Bus, 2004; Labbo & Kuhn, 2000; Turbill, 2001). For another example, children may interact with multimedia with a game-playing rather than a meaning-making approach, which may result in little learning of the embedded content (Bolter, 1998; Greenfield et al., 1996). Thus educators must take a critical stance in evaluating multimedia to ensure the product fosters, rather than deters, comprehension and knowledge acquisition (Labbo & Kuhn, 2000). In other words, not all multimedia are created equal, and educators must choose carefully when selecting multimedia applications for the classroom. With this caution articulated, the following section presents research on the benefits of two forms of multimedia, educational television and video, and electronic books, for supporting specific skills that are key for children's knowledge building.

Educational Television and Video

Educational television and video holds promise as a source of knowledge building because television and video are easily available in homes and schools and have a long history of positive outcomes for children. Marsh, Brooks, Hughes, Ritchie, and Roberts (2005), Rideout and Hamel (2006), and Linebarger and Piotrowski (2009) report that televisions and video players are nearly universal in homes, even homes of low-income families, and, on a typical day, children spend nearly 2 hours watching television or video. Whether this viewing leads to positive or negative outcomes depends on the type and content of television and video that children are viewing (see also Lavigne & Anderson, Chapter 7, this volume).

Wright et al. (2001) conducted a study investigating the relationship between television viewing in the home and reading and number skills, school readiness, and vocabulary for children ages 2 through 5. They compared outcomes associated with children's viewing of educational children's programs, noneducational children's programs, and general audience programs. Results revealed a negative relationship between noneducational and general audience program viewing and the academic outcomes assessed. However, findings showed a positive relationship between children's viewing of educational programs and the assessed academic outcomes. The study showed that, at age 5, children with higher scores on the academic outcome measures tended to watch more educational programming and less noneducational programming than their peers who had lower scores on these measures.

A more recent study by Ennemoser and Schneider (2007) reported similar results. These researchers compared educational and entertainment programs and found that while educational programs were associated with positive results for fluency and comprehension, entertainment programs were related to negative outcomes in these domains. Interestingly, this study showed that children who watched moderate amounts of educational television outperformed students who watched relatively more or less educational programming, suggesting that too much of even a good thing might not be optimal. A series of additional studies over the past 20 years, discussed below, has shown positive effects specific to different programs and uses of educational television and video in the home and in the classroom that help clarify how educational television supports student learning.

The Effects of Educational Television and Video

In 1999, Fisch, Truglio, and Cole synthesized 30 years of research on *Sesame Street*. Perhaps one of the most researched educational programs for children, *Sesame Street* was created to help prepare young children, especially those from low-income backgrounds, for school by introducing early numeracy and literacy skills. Fisch et al. (1999) found that children who viewed *Sesame Street* outperformed their peers who did not watch the show on various academic, social, and school readiness domains, including attentiveness and positive peer interactions. These researchers also found that adult coviewing led to greater effects compared to when children watched on their own and did not discuss the show with an adult.

Between the Lions, an educational program designed to support children's literacy development, has also shown positive effects for children. Linebarger, Kosanic, Greenwood, and Doku (2004) compared children who viewed the show and children who did not. They found that children who viewed the show outperformed children who did not on measures of word recognition and overall reading ability. Children who viewed the show also experienced greater growth in phonemic awareness and letter–sound knowledge compared to their peers who did not view the show. However, children who were not at risk or only moderately at risk for experiencing reading difficulties benefited more than children who were at risk for reading problems, suggesting that children with lower ability may need foundational skills and support from adults to benefit from the content provided by educational programming.

Another television program that has shown promising results is *Arthur,* which aims to encourage interest in reading and writing and positive social skills through cartoons presented via a traditional narrative storytelling structure. Uchikoshi (2005) evaluated the effects of *Arthur* on English language learning (ELL) children's narrative storytelling ability by comparing outcomes for children who viewed *Arthur* with children who viewed *Between the Lions,* which does not follow a clear narrative arc throughout the program. Children who viewed *Arthur* showed faster growth in their ability to produce effective narratives than children who viewed *Between the Lions.* In a related study, however, Uchikoshi (2006) found that ELL children who viewed *Between the Lions* had steeper growth on phonological awareness skills than children who viewed *Arthur.* These results show that the form and content of the television program may have an effect on the outcomes of viewing.

Comparing the effects of different types of educational television programming on children's story knowledge and narrative skills, Linebarger and Piotrowski (2009) found that children who watched a traditional narrative program or an embedded narrative program, which presents stories within stories, scored higher on these skills than children who viewed an expository program or none of the above programs. Furthermore, children who viewed the traditional narrative program gleaned more implicit information, while children who viewed the embedded narrative program recalled more explicit information. Together, these findings suggest that different program elements can affect different discrete skills that are required for knowledge building. Therefore, in choosing educational programs to meet particular educational objectives, educators should consider not just whether to use educational television or video but also which educational television or video is most appropriate.

Although research has accumulated suggesting that educational television and video can have a positive effect on children's foundational skills, an open question is whether this effect is as robust as the effect of reading books on children's early knowledge acquisition. Of course, there is a wide range of research showing the benefits of reading books with children (e.g., DeTemple & Snow, 2003; Teale, 2003). How do the media of television and video compare with book reading? A recent study investigated this issue by analyzing children's vocabulary learning through read-alouds, video, or read-alouds plus video (Freeman, Meddaugh, Greenwald, Silverman, & Kucan, 2010). Two educational programs based on children's literature were chosen for the study: *Arthur* and *Martha Speaks. Arthur* is based on a series of books by Marc Brown; *Martha Speaks,* a similar narrative program about a talking dog named Martha, is based on a book series by Susan Meddaugh. The educational objective of *Martha Speaks* is to bolster vocabulary development, and, accordingly, target words are explicitly defined and repeated throughout episodes.

Videos were chosen and books were created based on the scripts from the videos so that the videos and books had the exact same content. Children experienced stories from *Arthur* and *Martha Speaks* either in video only, read-aloud only, or video plus read-aloud conditions. No additional teaching was included in any condition so that the effect of the medium rather than the effect of instruction could be evaluated. Children were tested before and after the instructional period on their knowledge of words from the stories and their general vocabulary knowledge. There was no difference in vocabulary among the three conditions, but children learned more vocabulary from experiencing *Martha Speaks* than from experiencing *Arthur*. A second study on *Martha Speaks* (Freeman et al., 2010) compared one viewing versus three viewings of the television program. This study found that, similar to repeated readings of books, repeated viewing of videos led to more positive results than a single viewing. These studies show that television and video media may be as powerful as books for supporting children's learning, but much more research is needed to understand how listening to books and watching television and video compare.

The Use of Educational Television and Video in Classroom Instruction

Integrating television and video with traditional instruction is one way that multimedia can enhance children's learning in the classroom. Two studies conducted by Chambers and colleagues (Chambers, Cheung, Madden, Slavin, & Gifford, 2006; Chambers et al., 2008) compared the effects of beginning reading instruction through the Success for All program with and without embedded multimedia to reinforce instructed material. Embedded multimedia included several animated, live-action, and puppet-driven skits of roughly 30 seconds to 3 minutes in length that demonstrated sound–symbol relationships, blending and segmenting sounds, and vocabulary concepts. Some of the video clips were from *Between the Lions,* while others were produced specifically for Success for All. The researchers found positive effects of the multimedia on decoding and fluency, although effects were less substantial for comprehension, and vocabulary was not assessed. Many of the participants in these research studies were ELL, but there was no difference between ELL and non-ELL children on the benefits of embedded multimedia.

In another recent study, Silverman and Hines (2009) investigated the effect of read-alouds plus multimedia compared to the effect of read-alouds alone on children's vocabulary learning and growth. Children in prekindergarten through second-grade classrooms participated in the study; the sample included both English-only and ELL children. The intervention was developed around the topic of habitats and included both fiction and nonfiction texts. In both the read-aloud and read-aloud plus multimedia conditions, teachers delivered explicit vocabulary instruction on target words and supported comprehension of the books and videos. In the read-aloud–only condition, teachers read three books about each habitat for 3 days each. Children in the read-aloud plus multimedia condition read three books about each habitat for 2 days each, and watched a video on the habitat across 3 days.

Results showed that there was no difference between the read-aloud only and the read-aloud plus multimedia condition for the English-only children, but ELL children in the read-aloud plus multimedia condition learned more target words and grew more in overall vocabulary than children in the read-aloud–only condition. Many ELL children have limited English vocabulary knowledge compared to their English-only peers; therefore, learning new words and content in English may be a challenge. Nonverbal support in the form of multimedia may provide a scaffold for ELLs so that they can more readily access new information presented in class. However, much more research is needed to validate this claim.

Other studies have been conducted that have included multimedia as part of the instructional curriculum, although the studies have not explicitly tested the effects of including the multimedia component. For example, video clips were embedded in daily lessons in the World of Words (WoW) program, a preschool program aimed at improving the vocabulary and conceptual knowledge of low-income preschoolers (Neuman, Newman, & Dwyer, 2011). Video clips of 40 to 90 seconds were taken from *Sesame Street*. The clips presented information about the topic of the lesson, and teachers reinforced this information through follow-up questioning and read-alouds of books aligned with the video clips. In a randomized control trial, children who participated in the WoW curriculum scored higher than peers who did not participate in the program on vocabulary, concept development, knowledge of categories and properties, and inductive reasoning skills.

Following research that shows the potential of multimedia for use in supporting children's knowledge acquisition and using curricula such as WoW as an example, educators should consider including educational television and video in classroom instruction to build and reinforce conceptual understanding. It is likely that providing information in multiple formats (e.g., read-alouds, direct instruction, and educational television and video) helps children develop a deeper understanding of a topic. The nonverbal information available in educational television and video (e.g., two letters crashing into each other to show blending, the misty precipitation in the rainforest habitat, the wiggling antennae of a katydid) may be conveyed more clearly and comprehensibly through animation, live action, and other multimedia enhancements than through traditional methods of classroom instruction. Therefore, educational television and video should be considered a helpful tool in every educator's toolkit.

Electronic Books

Another multimedia source that can be used to support knowledge building is the electronic storybook, or e-book. E-books can range from simple texts with static pictures and words presented on electronic readers or computer websites to more dynamic texts with text-to-speech narration, highlighted text, music, animation, and sometimes even interactive games (de Jong & Bus, 2002; Horney & Anderson-Inman, 1999; Korat, Segal-Drori, & Klein, 2009). Readily available through libraries, free websites, and commercial vendors, e-books can encourage engagement, support independent reading, and provide scaffolding for emergent readers (McKenna & Zucker, 2009; Moody, 2010). However, similar to educational television and video, not all e-books are created equal. Some e-books that include distracting information and ineffective design features may actually hinder children's learning (Zucker, Moody, & McKenna, 2009).

Following Labbo and Kuhn's (2000) attention to "considerate" versus "inconsiderate" features of e-books, McKenna and Zucker (2009) identified several features that are supportive and instructive, and several features that are distracting and obstructive for achieving the objective at hand (e.g., literacy development or content learning). For example, embedded definitions, pronunciations, and translations, as well as text-to-speech, comprehensive prompts, and relevant nontext and hypermedia links that children can access for support are considered helpful features offered by e-books. Other features such as unrelated nontext and hypermedia links and extraneous hotspots (i.e., user-activated areas that present additional information or lead to activities and games) detract from student learning. In their review of research on electronic books, Zucker et al. (2009) found that, overall, effects of e-books were evident on measures of comprehension, and these effects were moderate.

There were few studies that investigated effects of e-books on decoding related outcomes, which prohibits conclusions about the use of this technology for supporting decoding. However, despite the limited research on the effects of e-books on children's learning, there are a few studies that suggest the potential of electronic books for supporting students' literacy development and knowledge acquisition.

The Effects of Electronic Books

As with educational television and video, a major question is whether e-books as a medium offer the same educational benefits as traditional books. In a study conducted in the Netherlands, Segers, Takke, and Verhhoeven (2004) addressed this question by comparing the effects of a story read aloud by a teacher and a story read aloud by a computer on children in kindergarten. In the teacher read-aloud condition, teachers were allowed to ask questions and engage children as they normally would. In the computer read-aloud condition, children listened to the computer read the story while they looked at static pictures and occasional short animations on the computer screen. The computer paused during reading to ask questions, and children responded by clicking on pictures on screen. After the story was read, children in both conditions arranged pictures according to the story sequence. Overall, results showed no difference between the conditions on vocabulary or comprehension. However, immigrant children (i.e., non-native speakers) learned more words when the teacher read the book compared to when the computer read the book, suggesting that immigrant children may have needed additional scaffolding from the teacher to optimally learn from the experience.

Korat and Shamir (2007) conducted a similar study in Israel in which they compared learning in 5- and 6-year-old children who heard a story read by a teacher to learning in children who experienced a story through an e-book. Outcomes for children in these conditions were compared with outcomes for children in a control condition. Children were stratified by socioeconomic status (SES) level (i.e., low and middle SES). In the e-book condition, children experienced the book with definitions and activities to play. In the teacher read-aloud condition, children were asked questions and provided with definitions to support comprehension and word learning. Children were pre- and posttested on vocabulary, word recognition, and phonological awareness. Findings showed no difference between conditions on word recognition or phonological awareness, but children in both intervention conditions (i.e., teacher read-aloud and e-book experience) outperformed children in the control condition on vocabulary. There was no difference between the two intervention conditions, suggesting that the e-book was as effective as the teacher book reading for promoting children's vocabulary.

Comparing different types of electronic books such as the more traditional e-book with static pictures and the more dynamic e-book with animation is another line of inquiry that has been pursued in research. Verhallen and Bus (2010) investigated the effect of "video storybooks" on the receptive and expressive vocabularies of 5-year-old children in the Netherlands from immigrant and low-SES backgrounds. The digital storybooks were presented to children accompanied either by static or video images, which were synchronized with, and representative of, the narrative. Children were randomly assigned to conditions and pre- and posttested on receptive and expressive word knowledge of lower-frequency words in the electronic text. Children listened to the story four times in both conditions with minimal adult interaction. Results indicated that video books were more beneficial to young ELL learners than static storybooks in developing expressive vocabulary. There were no differences by condition for receptive vocabulary development. The authors suggested that video storybooks, which seem to support ELL expressive vocabulary, might be an important addition to classroom instruction.

In addition to examining traditional versus dynamic e-books, research has investigated different modes of engagement with e-books. Shamir (2009) assigned kindergarten students to experience one of three modes of engagement: (1) read only the story; (2) read the story with dictionary support; and (3) read the story and play related activities. In the read-only mode, children were provided with an oral reading of the text, which included automatically activated dynamic visuals dramatizing the story. The story reading plus dictionary support mode added explanations associated with pictures of difficult words. Children could activate the dictionary support (i.e., the pictures and explanations) by clicking on specific words, which appeared in clouds. The read and play mode included activities (i.e., hotspots) designed to enhance story understanding as well as phonological awareness. Children could click on hotspots after hearing the story. Hotspots were related to characters, objects in the story, and specific words from the story to develop phonological awareness at the syllable level. According to the authors, all activities were designed to enrich story comprehension.

Children participated in the intervention in pairs, and the investigator recorded and then analyzed children's collaborative talk during the intervention sessions. Shamir (2009) found that children discussed word meanings, pictures, and plot in all conditions, and activating the hotspots helped trigger collaborative knowledge construction. Results showed that improvement in vocabulary was significantly positively associated with greater use of the dictionary option, but significantly negatively correlated with activation of picture hotspots, consistent with de Jong and Bus's (2004) findings that certain attractive e-books features can have a detracting effect on literacy goals. Shamir emphasized that e-book options designed for amusement alone should be minimized, if not excluded, but other e-book features such as embedded dictionaries that facilitate rather than distract should be seen as a benefit offered by e-books to support student learning.

The Use of Electronic Books with Adult Support and Peer Collaboration

In addition to studies comparing traditional books to e-books and even traditional e-books to dynamic e-books, studies have also focused on the effect of e-books when they are used with and without adult support and when they are used in individual versus peer contexts. To study the impact of teacher mediation on the e-book experience, Korat et al. (2009) investigated the differential effect of e-books with and without adult supervision with kindergarten children in Israel who were from low-SES families. Children were randomly assigned to one of four conditions: independent reading of an e-book; adult-supported reading of an e-book; adult-supported reading of a paper book; or a control group. The e-books selected for the intervention were purposefully designed to promote literacy and avoid the drawbacks identified in other studies of e-books (e.g., de Jong & Bus, 2002). Selected e-books provided oral reading of the text, visuals that dramatized the complete story scene as well as story details, and music and film effects to "bring the story to life" (Korat et al., 2009, p. 459).

The results of the study indicated that reading the e-book with adult support was preferable to all other conditions for children with relatively weak as well as strong emergent literacy skills. The authors found specifically that children with lower emergent literacy skills progressed in both phonemic awareness as well as word-reading skills, whereas children with higher skills progressed in word reading. The researchers concluded that literacy activities that combine use of new computer programs such as e-books with effective adult support might help young children in general, and children from lower-SES families in particular. They suggested that teachers of young children be encouraged to use e-book technology to promote children's emergent literacy in their classrooms. The authors also suggested choosing e-books with supportive features such as highlighted text (for word recognition) and segmented speech (for phonological awareness) aligned with instructional objectives, and avoiding e-books with features that might detract from text comprehension.

In addition to adult support, children may also find support from peers and benefit from peer collaboration when using e-books. Working with kindergarten students from low-SES families, Shamir, Korat, and Barbi (2008) examined the effects of peer versus individual work with e-books. They specifically selected an e-book that they defined as "high quality" in that most of the hot spots were congruent with and integrated into the story's content. Children in the sample were randomly assigned to one of four groups: tutor, tutee, individual learner, and control group. Tutors and tutees were then randomly paired. Children's emergent literacy skills (i.e., phonological awareness, word recognition, and concepts about print) were pre- and posttested. Story comprehension skills were also measured at posttest for children who participated in the experimental groups.

The intervention consisted of two half-hour e-book sessions in two modes: read the book or read and play with the book. Findings indicated significant improvement in phonological awareness, word recognition, and print concepts for children in the peer tutoring and individual learning conditions compared to children in the control condition. Tutors showed more learning than tutees, but both tutors and tutees showed more learning than children in the individual learning condition on phonological awareness, emergent reading, and story comprehension. The authors concluded that working in pairs with educational e-books might be a practical solution as well as an educationally beneficial one, and they recommend using carefully planned e-book peer collaboration activities with highly rated e-books to improve outcomes for preschool- and kindergarten-age children from families with low SES.

In summary, evidence suggests that carefully chosen e-books can enhance outcomes for young children, including those from families of low SES. However, children's use of this form of multimedia should include adult supervision or peer collaboration to maximize the potential learning from e-books. Finally e-books should be purposefully selected to minimize distracting options that may be attractive to young children but do not enhance story understanding or vocabulary development. Specific features that enhance literacy development include synchronous highlighting and narration, an option providing animations and explanations of difficult vocabulary words, as well as phonemic awareness–related options such as breaking works into phonemic elements. Furthermore, other multimedia animations should be directly related to plot and character understanding to improve comprehension. Game options unrelated to the storyline should be minimized. Another possible option would be to restrict hotspot activation until the story has been read in entirety.

Implications

Across studies of educational television and video and electronic storybooks, a few main themes emerge. First, having multiple representations of content through different media seems to support student learning, whether it is books and educational video on the same topic or pictures and oral definitions of words in e-books. Returning to the theoretical framework, then, the value of multimedia in knowledge building is in the coding of information with both verbal and nonverbal supports and in the use of redundant, multiple forms of representation to convey content. Second, distracting multimedia features, while they may add to motivation and engagement, will deter student learning. This is true of irrelevant sounds and animation in educational television and video and of unrelated hotspot content and activities in e-books. Therefore, educators should consider using multimedia to support student learning, especially for children who may need extra support (e.g., ELLs), but educators should evaluate multimedia with a critical stance and choose only multimedia supports that align with their educational objectives. A third theme that emerges across research on educational television, video, and electronic storybooks is that adult mediation can add to the potential of multimedia to support learning. Research on electronic storybooks extends this finding to peer collaboration as well. Additional research is needed on whether peer coviewing of educational television and video is also more beneficial than individual viewing. However, it is clear that multimedia should not be seen as a replacement or substitute for effective instruction by teachers, but rather as a supplement or complement to enhance the effects of high-quality instruction. Although many of the studies discussed in this chapter separate the instruction from the multimedia in order to test the added effects of the use of multimedia, the real promise of multimedia is not its singular potential, but in how it can be integrated into interventions and curricula to support efforts to achieve instructional goals and objectives related to knowledge building.

Future Directions

The research presented in this chapter specifically focused on two types of multimedia: educational television and electronic storybooks. There are many other types of multimedia such as computer games and websites that can support classroom learning. However, the current research base on these forms of multimedia is limited. Research is therefore needed on how these other types of multimedia may be used in and out of classroom settings to support knowledge acquisition. In addition, this chapter reviewed research on literacy skills including emergent reading, vocabulary, and comprehension. Although these skills are essential for knowledge building, multimedia could be used to support learning across the curriculum. Again, there is little research on the use of multimedia in supporting learning of math, science, and social studies content in the preschool and early elementary years. Thus research should focus on how multimedia can be used to address not only literacy skills but other content-related skills as well. Furthermore, the interventions discussed in this chapter were all supplemental in that they were not part of the regular classroom curriculum. As technology becomes more and more prevalent in preschool and early elementary school classrooms, research is needed on how teachers can seamlessly integrate multimedia experiences into their daily classroom instruction. In fact, a valuable start would include observing how teachers who are technologically inclined use multimedia to help inform future intervention research and curriculum design.

Conclusion

The use of multimedia to support knowledge building is in its infancy, as is research on how multimedia can be used most effectively to support knowledge building. However, the research reviewed in this chapter suggests the potential for multimedia to enhance student learning and support important educational objectives. Much more research is needed, but the research base provides enough evidence to suggest that educators should view multimedia as a promising option for supplementing instruction, supporting students, and engaging learners in the classroom.

REFERENCES

Bolter, J. D. (1998). Hypertext and the question of visual literacy. In D. Reinking, M. C. McKenna, L. D. Labbo, & R. D. Kieffer (Eds.), *Handbook of literacy and technology: Transformations in a post-typographic world* (pp. 3–13). Mahwah, NJ: Erlbaum.

Chambers, B., Cheung, A. K., Madden, N. A., Slavin, R. E., & Gifford, R. (2006). Achievement effects of embedded multimedia in a Success for All reading program. *Journal of Educational Psychology, 98*(1), 232–237.

Chambers, B., Slavin, R. E., Madden, N. A., Abrami, P. C., Tucker, B. J., Cheung, A., et al. (2008). Technology infusion in Success for All: Reading outcomes for first graders. *Elementary School Journal, 109*(1), 1–15.

de Jong, M. T., & Bus, A. G. (2002). Quality of book-reading matters for emergent readers: An experiment with the same book in a regular or electronic format. *Journal of Educational Psychology, 94*(1), 145–155.

de Jong, M. T., & Bus, A. G. (2004). The efficacy of electronic books in fostering kindergarten children's emergent story understanding. *Reading Research Quarterly, 39*(4), 378–393.

De Temple, J., & Snow, C. E. (2003). Learning words from books. In A. van Kleeck, S. A. Stahl, & E. B. Bauer (Eds.), *On reading books to children: Parents and teachers* (pp. 16–36). Mahwah, NJ: Erlbaum.

Ennemoser, M., & Schneider, W. (2007). Relations of television viewing and reading: Findings from a 4-year longitudinal study. *Journal of Educational Psychology, 99*(2), 349–368.

Fisch, S. M., Truglio, R. T., & Cole, C. F. (1999). The impact of *Sesame Street* on preschool children: A review and synthesis of 30 years' research. *Media Psychology, 1*(2), 165–190.

Freeman, D., Meddaugh, S., Greenwald, C., Silverman, R., & Kucan, L. (2010, April). *Martha Speaks: How a dog, a book, and a television program can impact oral vocabulary development.* Paper presented at the International Reading Association Conference, Chicago, IL.

Greenfield, P. M., Camaioni, L., Ercolani, P., Weiss, L., Lauber, B. A., & Peruchini, P. (1996). Cognitive socialization by computer games in two cultures: Inductive discovery or mastery of an iconic code? In I. E. Sigel (Series Ed.), P. M. Greenfield, & R. R. Cocking (Vol. Eds.), *Advances in applied developmental psychology: Vol. II. Interacting with video* (pp. 141–167). Norwood, NJ: Ablex.

Horney, M. A., & Anderson-Inman, L. (1999). Supported text in electronic reading environments. *Reading and Writing Quarterly, 15*(2), 127–168.

Kamil, M. L., Intrator, S., & Kim, H. (2000). The effects of other technologies on literacy and literacy learning. In M. L. Kamil, P. B. Mosenthal, P. D. Pearson, & R. Barr (Eds.), *Handbook of reading research* (Vol. III, pp. 771–788). Mahwah, NJ: Erlbaum.

Korat, O., Segal-Drori, O., & Klein, P. (2009). Electronic and printed books with and without adult support as sustaining emergent literacy. *Educational Computing Research, 41*(4), 453–475.

Korat, O., & Shamir, A. (2007). Electronic books versus adult readers: Effects on children's emergent literacy as a function of social class. *Journal of Computer Assisted Learning, 23*(3), 248–259.

Labbo, L. D., & Kuhn, M. R. (2000). Weaving chains of affect and cognition: A young child's understanding of CD-ROM talking books. *Journal of Literacy Research, 32,* 187–210.

Linebarger, D. L., Kosanic, A. Z., Greenwood, C. R., & Doku, N. S. (2004). Effects of viewing the television program *Between the Lions* on the emergent literacy skills of young children. *Journal of Educational Psychology, 96*(2), 297–308.

Linebarger, D. L., & Piotrowski, J. T. (2009). TV as storyteller: How exposure to television narratives impacts at-risk preschoolers' story knowledge and narrative skills. *British Journal of Developmental Psychology, 27,* 47–69.

Marsh, J., Brooks, G., Hughes, J., Ritchie, L., & Roberts, S. (2005). *Digital beginnings: Young children's use of popular culture, media and new technologies.* Sheffield, UK: University of Sheffield. Retrieved June, 2006, from *www.digitalbeginnings.shef.ac.uk/.*

McKenna, M. C., & Zucker, T. A. (2009). Use of electronic storybooks in reading instruction: From theory to practice. In A. G. Bus & S. B. Neuman (Eds.), *Multimedia and literacy development* (pp. 254–272). New York: Routledge.

Moody, A. K. (2010). Using electronic books in the classroom to enhance emergent literacy skills in young children. *Journal of Literacy and Technology, 11*(4), 22–52.

Neuman, S. B. (1997). Television as a learning environment: A theory of synergy. In J. Flood, S. Brice Heat, & D. Lapp (Eds.), *Handbook of research on teaching literacy through the communicative and visual arts* (pp. 15–30). New York: Simon & Schuster.

Neuman, S. B., Newman, E., & Dwyer, J. (2011). Educational effects of a vocabulary intervention on preschoolers' word knowledge and conceptual development: A cluster randomized trial. *Reading Research Quarterly, 46*(3), 249–272.

Paivio, A. (1986). *Mental representations. A dual coding approach.* Oxford, UK: Oxford University Press.

Rideout, V. J., & Hammel, E. (2006). *The media family: Electronic media in the lives of infants, toddlers, preschoolers, and their parents.* Menlo Park, CA: The Henry J. Kaiser Family Foundation.

Salomon, G. (1981). *Communication and education.* Beverly Hills, CA: Sage.

Segers, E. (2009). Learning from interactive vocabulary books in kindergarten: Looking back, looking forward. In A. G. Bus & S. B. Neuman (Eds.), *Multimedia and literacy development* (pp. 112–123). New York: Routledge.

Segers, E., Takke, L., & Verhoeven, L. (2004). Teacher-mediated versus computer-mediated storybook reading to children in native and multicultural kindergarten classrooms. *School Effectiveness and School Improvement, 15*(2), 215–226.

Shamir, A. (2009). Processes and outcomes of joint activity with e-books for promoting kindergarteners' emergent literacy. *Educational Media International, 46*(1), 81–96.

Shamir, A., & Korat, O. (2009). The educational electronic book as a tool for supporting childrens' emergent literacy. In A. G. Bus & S. B. Neuman (Eds.), *Multimedia and literacy development* (pp. 168–181). New York: Routledge.

Shamir, A., Korat, O., & Barbi, N. (2008). The effects of CD-ROM storybook reading on low-SES kindergarteners' emergent literacy as a function of learning context. *Computers and Education, 51,* 354–367.

Silverman, R., & Hines, S. (2009). The effects of multimedia enhanced instruction on the vocabulary of English-language learners and non-English language learners in pre-kindergarten through second grade. *Journal of Educational Psychology, 101*(2), 305–314.

Teale, W. H. (2003). Reading aloud to young children as a classroom instructional activity: Insights from research and practice. In A. van Kleeck, S. A. Stahl, & E. B. Bauer (Eds.), *On reading books to children: Parents and teachers* (pp. 114–139). Mahwah, NJ: Erlbaum.

Turbill, J. (2001). A researcher goes to school: Using technology in the kindergarten literacy curriculum. *Journal of Early Childhood Literacy, 1*(3), 255–279.

Uchikoshi, Y. (2005). Narrative development in bilingual kindergarteners: Can Arthur help? *Developmental Psychology, 41*(3), 464–478.

Uchikoshi, Y. (2006). Early reading in bilingual kindergarteners: Can educational television help? *Scientific Studies of Reading, 10*(1), 89–120.

Verhallen, M. J. A., & Bus, A. G. (2010). Low-income immigrant pupils learning vocabulary through digital picture storybooks. *Journal of Educational Psychology, 102*(1), 54–61.

Wright, J. C., Huston, A. C., Murphy, K. C., St. Peters, M., Piaton, M., Scantlin, R., et al. (2001). The relations of early television viewing to school readiness and vocabulary of children from low-income families: The early window project. *Child Development, 72*(5), 1347–1366.

Zucker, T. A., Moody, A. K., & McKenna, M. C. (2009). The effects of electronic books on pre-kindergarten-to-grade-5 students' literacy and language outcomes: A research synthesis. *Journal of Educational Computing Research, 40*(1), 47–87.

Index

"*f*" indicates a figure

Knowledge development in
early childhood